STREET LIVES

An Oral History of Homeless Americans

STEVEN VANDERSTAAY

PHOTOGRAPHS BY JOSEPH SORRENTINO

NEW SOCIETY PUBLISHERS

Philadelphia, PA   Gabriola Island, BC

8-93

Inquiries regarding requests to reprint all or part of *Street Lives: An Oral History of Homeless Americans* should be addressed to:
New Society Publishers
4527 Springfield Avenue
Philadelphia, PA 19143

ISBN USA 0-86571-236-0 Hardcover
ISBN USA 0-86571-237-9 Paperback
ISBN CAN 1-55092-178-9 Hardcover
ISBN CAN 1-55092-179-7 Paperback

Printed in the United States of America on partially recycled paper by Capital City Press of Montpelier, Vermont.

All photographs, including the cover photograph, by Joseph Sorrentino.
Cover design by g.e. jarret.
Book design by Martin Kelley.

To order directly from the publisher, add $2.50 to the price for the first copy, 75¢ each additional. Send check or money order to:
New Society Publishers
4527 Springfield Avenue
Philadelphia, PA 19143
In Canada, contact:
New Society Publishers/New Catalyst
PO Box 189
Gabriola Island, BC VOR 1XO

New Society Publishers is a project of the New Society Educational Foundation, a nonprofit, tax-exempt, public foundation in the United States, and of the Catalyst Education Society, a non-profit society in Canada. Opinions expressed in this book do not necessarily represent positions of the New Society Educational Foundation, nor the Catalyst Education Society.

® GCIU 196-C

"If there is knowledge, it lies in the fusion of the book and the street."

—Studs Terkel

TABLE OF CONTENTS

PREFACE

One night in the fall of 1980 I heard a homeless gravedigger begin his life story. It was an odd moment for such a narrative. Ronald Reagan was about to be elected president; Iran was about to release U.S. hostages; and there were as yet no listings under "Homelessness" in the *Readers Guide to Periodical Literature*. I was a junior in college and worked one night a week as a volunteer at the Downtown Emergency Center, a Seattle shelter. It was my job to register people and hand out mattresses—a task that took perhaps an hour.

I do not meet people easily. That I managed to strike up conversations with the people in this book has surprised many people, including myself. I simply cannot say how it happened. Nor can I say how I managed to win the trust of the gravedigger. All I know is that one night I happened to linger at the Emergency Center long enough to find myself sitting in a tight ring of men who had marked off a corner of the shelter as their space.

"I buried everyone they sent me but one," he began, leaping into a story whose preface I had missed. "We were out there digging one morning—middle of January and the ground so froze you could hardly break it—when the man tells me it's for one of the Timbers.

'John Timber?' I ask him.

'That the tall one?'

'Yup.'

'Well then it's for him.'

'Then I ain't a'diggin'. John Timber's a friend of mine and I ain't a'diggin' 'grave for no man I know.' And I walked off. Worked hard 'that place. But I never dug 'grave for no man I knowed."

Comments and sundry affirmations of the logic of this view followed; then other stories began. Stories of work on Alaskan trawlers, of fingers lost or shortened in salmon canneries. Eventually,

I grew bold enough to ask about the stories I wanted to hear: What is your life like? How did you end up here? What do you see on the street? Where did you come from and how do you live?

The questions fell hard and flat; the conversation died. The men grew restless as if suddenly uncomfortable. The circle broke up and I left, knowing I was no longer welcome and wondering what had gone wrong.

I never saw the gravedigger again, but the evening remained in my mind. I kept it in mind as the eighties wore on and the Emergency Center grew overcrowded. Families, runaways, unemployed laborers, and the working poor began to line up for food and mattresses alongside the street alcoholics and hobos I had worked with. Other shelters opened and still people slept in alleys and parks, laundromats and boathouses.

Articles and books explained where and what, not who or how. Reading and watching, I wondered, recalling my own attempt to learn how the gravedigger had come to the shelter. Somehow, I saw that the men had accepted me and had spoken freely until my interruption—the point at which I once again became the outsider. I had wanted answers, not stories. But perhaps there were no answers, just stories. Or was it that the answers lay in the stories?

For the last six years I have attempted to find out. Visiting shelters and soup kitchens, parks and back alleys, I've met and spoken with homeless people in cities and towns across the country. It was hard going at first. The interviews were awkward, stilted. Then, striving to succeed where I had failed with the gravedigger, I learned to listen for the story, and not the answer. Gradually, homeless people I had spoken with began to refer me to their friends and to direct me to the stories they thought I should hear. Introduced by one homeless person to another, my tape recorder became less intrusive, my presence less disruptive.

At moments I was treated as a midwife of sorts, one who would bring these stories out to the larger community. On other occasions the testimonies became nearly confessional, as the narrators searched among their stories for the key to explain their situation. "Where did I go wrong?" they would ask. "What did I do to deserve this?" There were people who cried as they spoke, and people who shook with rage. Some told me they needed to talk. Others said that I needed to listen. But all of them wanted their stories to be heard.

Street Lives is the aggregate of these moments, an anthology of the stories homeless people need to tell and want to be heard. Its purpose is a simple one: to provide an opportunity for homeless people to tell their stories and address their situation from their own point of view.

Because of this perspective, the crisis that *Street Lives* describes is different than that which has appeared in print elsewhere. To begin with, it is personal—the story of specific people, their families and neighborhoods. Ted tells of losing his job as a diesel mechanic; Tanya describes her life in the subway and bus stops of Philadelphia. The larger crisis becomes encapsulated in the smaller as Ted's narrative subsumes our broader view of the "new" unemployment of skilled, working-class laborers. Similarly, Tanya's story captures the fatalism of a generation of homeless mothers. In turn, personal isolation and the sense of abandonment these narrators feel are central to this book. Reestablishing connections or "community" with other people is key to the solutions it prescribes.

Second—and following from its personal nature—the homelessness described in *Street Lives* is at once simple and complex: simple by virtue of the economic shifts and inequities which emerge as the root causes of the crisis, and complex because of the great diversity of personal situations these forces impact. Few of the narrators blame their homelessness on a single cause, and most cite a combination of personal and societal factors—not one or the other—to explain the destitution they share with so many.

Third, many of the narratives presented in *Street Lives* contradict current and accepted notions of homelessness. Occasionally these narratives are employed to debunk a popular assumption, as occurs in the chapter "The Homeless Mentally Ill." More frequently, however, the contrary view "from the street" is offered as an alternative perspective or (re)vision, another way of looking at the situation. This is particularly true in the second chapter, "Work and its Discontents," where homeless people describe their many forms of employment.

Finally, *Street Lives* proposes solutions that prove viable when viewed from the perspective of homeless people. These include both "top-down" or societal solutions, such as establishing a system of universal health care that would include long-term assistance for substance abusers and the mentally ill, and "bottom-up" solutions whereby homeless people seek to better help themselves and each other.

Street Lives is divided into nine chapters. In the opening chapter, "Life on the Street," homeless people speak of the daily exigencies of life as a homeless person. "Work and its Discontents," the second chapter, carries the theme of daily life into the arena of work. In the third chapter, "Falling from Grace," homeless people describe the events by which they became homeless. The following five chapters focus upon a particular subgroup of homeless people: "Runaway and Homeless Youth," "Veterans," "The Homeless Mentally Ill," "Dependencies," and "Families." In the final chapter, "Solutions," homeless people speak to the wide range of measures they see as necessary to halt and reverse the tide of forces that has worked to push them into the street. Societal, "top-down" measures are summarized in my introduction to the chapter; specific, "bottom-up" strategies homeless people advocate for themselves are described in the narratives.

Each chapter begins with an introduction. The introductions were written after the testimonies were arranged, and serve to establish a context for the narratives that follow. They are not essential to the book and should be seen as subsidiary to the narratives themselves. Similarly, a brief character description precedes each narrative. Readers who find these more distracting than useful should simply skip to the testimonies.

Numerous shelters, soup kitchens, and agencies have been of assistance in this project. I wish, particularly, to acknowledge the National Coalition for the Homeless for its logistical support and guidance. A full listing of other participating agencies and organizations concludes the book. Any royalties *Street Lives* generates will be shared with these organizations.

Many individuals were also essential to the success of this project. Mary Janell Metzger read each chapter in progress and gave sound advice regarding gender issues and families; Wally Zisette and Andrea Akita brought common sense and their backgrounds in urban planning and social work to bear on the shape and structure of the book; Dana Lyons, Bev Mabee, Bob McConnel, Barbara Hunstables, and my parents provided much-appreciated doses of support and encouragement. Thanks, too, to my mentors: Tony, Ted, and Roger; to my editor, Todd Peterson, and to the many folks who fed and housed me in the course of my travels.

Most important, of course, were the homeless people themselves. Literally hundreds of homeless people participated in this book by speaking with me, some for minutes, others for hours. In each case I strove to do what I had not done with the gravedigger—to listen without interruption. In so doing I learned that our present crisis of homelessness, while fueled by societal trends and forces, is most essentially a personal one: a crisis in the life of someone with hopes, dreams, and a name. Someone we can know.

To the homeless people whose stories grace my cassettes but not these pages, I can only say thanks. In a deeper sense your stories, too, are told here. To those whose narratives do appear, I dedicate this book: it is much more yours than mine.

For:

Mark in Central Park
Joe on the Bowery
Ted, Aaron and the Bridge Man in Atlanta
Karla and her boys in St. Louis
Jacob who sleeps at 17th and JFK
Tony on the Embarcadero and Jaime at St. Anthony's
Will and Frank, wherever they may be
Dana, Lana and Martin in Seattle
The Batman in Lexington
J.D., Carlo, Spain, Hell and Tanya in Philly
Elaine, Nancy, Chuck and Floyd in DC
Duane, Johnny, Joshua and Trae Casey at CCNV
Stacey at the Capital Building
Billy and friends in Minneapolis
Don, Terri and their children in Roanoke, VA
The Coal Miner's Daughter in rural Virginia
Albert at Justice House
Molly in Gary or Bremerton
John, who lives in his car
Jerry who lives in the timber outside Iowa City
The Smith family in Des Moines
Marsha and her daughters in Arlington
John and family in San Francisco
Mark, Linda and their six children in Seattle
Chuck, between Puerto Rico and Philadelphia
Doug Castle and company in Seattle
Carol Quarles at ACE
Niki at Youth Care
Anne in the South Bronx
Jeff Tedder and community in Des Moines
Tara in Cambridge
Sue of Birmingman PATH
David and family in Port Orchard, WA
Debra, now out of LA
Sherry in San Fran
And Tim and Cyrell, on the street and lending a hand [1]

CHAPTER 1

LIFE ON THE STREET

"What's it like? Well let me tell you about it. By the way, I'm Ted."
We shake hands.

"First of all, Atlanta is a deadly city. You walk these streets after six o'clock and if you ain't with a partner you are subject to have your head bust wide open and your throat cut."

An unemployed diesel mechanic and ex-Marine, he whittles a stick the size of a broom handle as he speaks, pausing to shave off a small knot with two swift strokes. He uses a large pocket knife, the kind sometimes worn in a leather pouch on the hip: a deer hunter's knife.

"I've seen shootin's, I've seen killin's right here in Atlanta that'll curl your hair," he tells me. "One I walked up on myself when I was out here on Tenth and Peach Street, on a Sunday morning."

It is Sunday now. We sit on a bench in a small downtown park one would expect to be empty on the weekend. Scores of people sleep on the grass, some with their backs against benches. A woman crosses the park carrying a child on her hip. Men mill about the sidewalks in loose ovals of activity. Others lean against the walls of restaurants and businesses, all closed.

Eventually, Ted will tell me two of the stories that appear in this book. First, however, he shows me around.

"Them are just waitin 'round," he explains, gesturing with the knife as he points to a group of men. "Them over there been drinkin'. See the people over there who look like they're drunk? They ain't got an ounce of alcohol in 'em. It's all narcotics. And some of 'em, ones you think are on the street, have actually got a house to go to and a refrigerator full of food."

The knife dances in his hand, flashing. People look, catch his eye, then drop their gaze. He begins to whittle again, carving now, and I see that he is not simply passing his time. The act is a defensive one, a statement of defiance in the subculture of the park and its violence. "Here I am," it says. "Leave me alone."

The scene would be remarkable if it were not so common: a skilled mechanic, homeless through unemployment; a veteran, forced to pass long days in city parks; a man, defending himself even by day with the threat of a knife. Unemployment, lack of housing, and violence—elements of homelessness[1] sadly consistent throughout our nation.

Nor does homelessness make distinctions among its myriad causes. Displaced single mothers, the mentally ill, and the unemployed make their way on our streets together with the dispossessed, the drug-addicted, and the working poor who cannot afford housing. Pushed and pulled toward our inner cities, homeless people become the victims and statistics of violent crime, much of it a product of the very forces that generate homelessness itself. By night, especially, no one is more exposed to this crime than the homeless.

"But what about the daytime suffering?" asks Will, a homeless man to whom I tell Ted's story. Will is a transient, one whose homelessness becomes an endless quest for the job that will put him back on his feet, the city he can make a home in. He taps a nail on the cement steps of a Roanoke, Virginia, shelter as he speaks, explaining that homeless people suffer the torments of boredom and exhaustion as well as violence, crime, and exposure. "See most places will put you up only for the night. Then they set you out at five in the morning."

It is the coming day, not the hour of expulsion, that brings the torment and exhaustion. By day, most cities and municipalities tolerate the homeless people who live on their streets only as long as they are in motion. Ushered out of department stores, bus stations, libraries, even churches and synagogues, asked to move along by local police after a moment's respite on a park bench, homeless people with nowhere to go are often forced to spend their day getting there. Walking, remaining upright, and endlessly waiting become all-consuming tasks, full-time work.

Where loitering is permitted, or where the vast number of homeless people makes enforcement of loitering laws impossible, sanitation and hygiene become the principal concerns. Many communities work hard to shelter the poor and feed the hungry, but few provide enough toilets. This forces many homeless people to plan their entire day around the availability of a restroom. Facilities for washing clothes and showering are even more difficult to find. Ironically, these very issues, sources of great degradation for homeless people, generate the greatest antipathy toward them among those of us with homes.

"I wrote a poem about how bathrooms are like precious gems," states Rich, who carries his poetry and essays together with a few belongings in a knapsack. "Only people who can afford their own have access to them."

For women and homeless people with children these struggles are complicated by innumerable others. In Boston city officials take Ann's children from her, citing as neglect her inability to properly house them. Cut off from her children, she loses both the sense of purpose that had helped her "maintain" amid the squalor and violence of her neighborhood and the government assistance she had come to depend on. Left to wander the streets, she prostitutes herself and is raped and shot in street violence.

"I was out of control," she explains, "erratic. There was no help, no one to turn to. People taking advantage of me everywhere. And without my children there was no reason to live. Suicide seemed the only answer and I think that's what I was really trying to do with the way I was living—kill myself."

In San Francisco a young couple passes long days in Panhandle Park, waiting each evening to return to a family shelter with their four children.

"Friday we had our first incident with the police," they explain. "They tell us they're going to start giving out citations to people who look like they're camping. We're not camping, we're just staying there with the kids until the shelter opens up. Where else can we go?"

Homeless families like these now comprise one of the fastest growing segments of homeless people.[2] Though many live in the parks and subways of our cities, more stay in emergency housing, group and halfway houses, or city-sponsored hotels. In rural areas they occupy abandoned busses, tool sheds, or their cars.[3] The vast majority stay with friends or relatives, sometimes filling a single apartment, even a trailer, with ten or more people.[4] In areas of high housing costs, rates of such "doubling up" may be twenty times that of official homelessness. Families doubled up in this manner constitute a significant portion of the poor and precariously housed people from which the street homeless are drawn.

Of course, the more fortunate of homeless families do receive public housing. The more fortunate of these spend their days as anyone might: working, caring for children, looking for work, going to school. But such situations vary remarkably, depending on the area and the type of housing received; the least fortunate eke out lives in places arguably as horrid as the streets themselves.[5]

But most poor families are not publicly housed. Most—single women with children included—receive no assistance at all.[6] In rural states like Alabama and Texas, over 80 percent of the people (most of whom are children) living beneath the poverty line do so without assistance. Nationwide the average is 70 percent.[7] And of the great many families waiting for public housing in our urban centers, few receive enough assistance to cover even the cost of renting an apartment.[8]

Single homeless people have yet fewer opportunities for public housing.[9] At best they double up, make short-term arrangements with emergency shelters, or build shanties. Some turn to crime and prostitution. In cities like Baltimore and Philadelphia large numbers of people—street youth and runaways in particular—occupy abandoned buildings as squatters. Others sleep in cars or live in parks, caves, and forests.

Those who cannot secure such arrangements live on the street. Dumpsters, phone booths, loading docks, and septic tunnels become their refuge. Many of these people sleep in shelters and missions when they can, but most must endure an occasional night outside.[10] Others shun the degrading conditions of many shelters, choosing the hazards of street life and harsh weather over the indignities of charity, forced crowding, and dependency. Many sleep days—or not at all—risking sleep deprivation and sanity to better ensure their belongings and safety.

Since the people who actually live on the street are the most visible of homeless people, they are the ones most often associated with homelessness: the bearded man passing his Sunday on a bench, the vagrant, the family in the park every day, the woman sleeping in the subway.

Homeless people on the street are also the most feared and least identified with: people who die ignominious deaths in trash compactors, who freeze outside the doors of hospitals, and who have been burned alive while sleeping on park benches. They are the most hated of homeless people: loathed for their destitution, their apparent inability to provide for themselves, and for the conflicting array of emotions they evoke in passersby.

It is for this reason that I have placed first the following stories and portraits of life on the street. The selections also make it clear that violence, "the daytime suffering," the lack of available facilities, and the particular challenges faced by women and families are but a few of the many difficulties of homeless street life. The subject of much enmity and debate, people who live such lives deserve the chance to describe them in their own terms.

It is also my hope that these introductory scenes will establish a context for the stories that follow. Most of this book explores the past—the events through which the narrators found themselves "with no bricks around them." The characters tell their own stories, and it is through their eyes that we view their lives. By narrating they work to make sense of what has happened to them, to answer why and how. None of these people expected to be homeless. And while many were born into poverty, most look back on periods of success and happiness when there was money, family, friends, and a home.

Understanding the road from then to now is a tremendous task for homeless people. The tendency is to emphasize one side of it—usually the past—so as to reduce the dissonance between the two extremes. Thus few of the speakers identify themselves as homeless. "I'm not really homeless," they say. Or, as one man put it, "I don't really believe in it, in being homeless."

Ultimately, however, the narrators have no choice but to ackowledge the present. Indeed, they tell these stories from parks, street corners, and shelters—settings for their lives as homeless people. A few hours of talk may enable them to relive the past, but tonight they must somehow try to eat, sleep, and protect themselves.

Jacob
Philadelphia, Pennsylvania

"I wouldn't have asked you for your change if I had anyway else to get it," explains Jacob, a homeless but reluctant panhandler. Bent with age and injury, he asks that we sit down before speaking. His face is clean, worn, gaunt, and lined; the face of a man who eats poorly and lives on the street with as much dignity as he can muster.

Jacob is white and perhaps 55 years old.

WELL, I LIVE out in the street. I broke my neck fourteen years ago, nine places. I couldn't work for two and a half years. Lost my wife and my four kids, the apartment I had. And I ended up out here.

I've been to a few shelters around the city, but after you're there a while they send you back. And to try to get welfare here is almost impossible. They can give you an emergency check, but it's not enough. The only way you can survive around here is a boy and his father come by every night to feed people.

It does get to be a hassle. I don't like to ask people for money. But they say, with my broken neck—and now they tell me my age is against me—can't no one hire me. But I'm still able to do something, I know I am.

And you know, it gets monotonous. Every day you do the same thing, walk the streets. Sometimes you get to sit in the park once in a while, or walk down by the river. But most days my back and legs get to bothering me so bad I don't feel like doing anything else.

At least now on the weekends the cops don't say much. During the weekdays they give you a hassle. But there's really not much the city can do about it, as far as taking people into jail. There just aren't enough jails.

Nights I stay up on Seventeenth and JFK. Get a couple of cardboard boxes and sleep in them. The only bad feature is if you want to get a glass of water you have to walk clean down to Independence Hall. It's the only place they got a water fountain. Places want thirty-five to forty cents for a glass of water around here.

I fell down a flight of stairs. I was paralyzed from my neck down for two and a half years. I was on SSI [Supplement Security Income] when I got out of the hospital. But as soon as they got the brace off and I was able to walk without it, they stopped that.

So actually there's not much of a choice. Either you stay out here on the streets or you do something like some of these young people been doing: take your own life. 'Cause it's not really worth it. I've seen ten or twelve take their own life around here. One guy, he walked out on the bridge down here, tied a rock around his neck and fell overboard. I've seen a couple walk out in front of cars. I've seen 'em, like from here to there [he points to a woman across the street], run right out in front of 'em.

I don't know if you can really blame the people for doing that. Like I say, after you're out here a while ... you see a bed once in a while but they're hard to sleep on, you get so used to sleepin' on concrete and what have you. Like I say, it's the same thing, you know, every day. It plays hell with me, especially in my legs.

While walking around here this morning I kept thinking about my oldest daughter. She's got three kids of her own; I haven't seen any of 'em. I figure maybe two or three weeks I might be able to come across some type of work, so I can get enough money to buy a car to go see em.... But I'm not sure that's even possible anymore.

There's some places that hire guards over forty. But it's just trying to find what agencies are close by that you can walk to. There's one I walked to last week, from here to Kensington. It should take no more than an hour up and an hour back. It took me almost three and a half hours, one way.

I can't really blame those people. I guess their insurance companies are really on them. When the insurance company isn't going to cover you, there's no reason why they should give you a job. They won't cover me on account of my age and my neck. I still have trouble with it, especially sleeping. I turn one way or the other and it stiffens up on me.

Batman
Roanoke, Virginia

> *Batman's face tells the story of his homelessness: deep scars from beatings; the rough, cracked skin of living outside; a mouth of broken, rotting teeth. Remarkably, he has earned these features in just eight years of homelessness.*
>
> *Another portion of Batman's narrative appears in the chapter "Falling from Grace." He is white and 30 years old.*

I'VE SPENT MORE TIME in Lexington, Kentucky, than anywhere, I guess. The homeless situation there is just like everywhere else: they overlook it. Like it's common to see someone sleepin' on the sidewalk.

I usually sleep outside. There's this bridge where a railroad crossing runs under a main road. We've dug it out so there's this ledge—'bout five people sleep there any given time. Usually in a small camp like that people watch out for each other, but you've still got your problems with alcohol and stealin' and that.

I try to stay away from soup lines and depend on myself as much as possible. I usually kill my own food: rabbits, squirrels, stuff of that nature. You build box traps, there's snares—a lot of different ways about it. Catch a lot of fish. In Lexington the hills are right there.

When that don't work you got to do what you have to to survive. I've got to the point where I don't care what the next man thinks about me, I'm going to survive ... soup lines, dig in dumpsters, eat food out of garbage cans, steal, rob a time or two—didn't want to, you know, but got so I had to.

Any fast food joints got good dumpsters usually. Right around closing time they throw out everything they've got stashed for the day. Say like a McDonald's closes at 10:00 at night. You be there at 9:00, sitting at the curb. When the guy comes out with that white sack you tackle it: "Yeah Buddy, I'll take that." Half of them understand and are cool. Then again half of 'em don't. Like I've had the guy throw it over me into the dumpster, make me scrounge. Then the police pull up while I'm in there, lookin' for it.

"What are you doing?"

"Uhh, I'm looking for food. What's it look like?"

"You can't do that."

"Why? They threw it away. I'm hungry. Why can't I eat it?"

Dana
Seattle, Washington

> *Like most homeless teenagers, Dana lives an on-again off-*
> *again life on the street, spending a year or a weekend away, then*
> *coming home for a short period. Tall, intelligent, and*
> *good-natured, Dana wears a dark jacket and running shoes.*
> *Dana is an African-American male, and a teenager.*

I PROSTITUTED and I drank a lot that first year. I did some drugs, but not that much. Later it was acid, and a lot of crystal—just to get me through some of the nights. We'd go dancing at this place, or just fall to sleep there. Sometimes I'd get into a car with a guy just so I'd have a place to stay, you know. Not even ask for money. Or me and my friends would like ride around on the busses all night. Just, I don't know, just ... that was the only place I knew besides sleeping under bridges and stuff. Not very glamorous.

And oh God, the bad things ... people freaking out on drugs. And people with disabilities that get worse and worse. I remember this girl who had some sort of a limp. And now when I see her, she can hardly walk.

Then there was Lela ... watching that, you know, watching a good person drink themself to death. She got stabbed eventually ... just watching people progress in their sickness.

And there are a lot of weirdos. Like I remember this one guy I met. I got in the car and I was like bopping away, trying to be nice. I was opening up just totally, telling him everything because I felt so comfortable. We got home—no, we discussed before we got to the house what he wanted. He just wanted a backrub. So that was fine. Thirty dollars for a backrub. I was set.

So I started doing his backrub, just blabbing on, opening up my whole life storybook, and he was just taking it all in, kind of going, "Yeah." And then he goes, "Have you ever heard of bondage, or S and M?" Now me, being this progressive kind of rocker type person, you know—I was into this band called "Adam and the Ants," and "Adam and the Ants" dabbled in bondage—attire, just the wear, you know. I don't know if they were really into it or not.

So I said, "Oh, well one of my favorite band members dresses that way!" And we talked about that a lot. And he said, "Well, would you like to see some of my stuff?" And I'm like, "Oh sure, that'd be really cool" [he laughs]. So he got this suitcase out and I'm like … I'm acting like I'm stupid or something, 'cause I don't know what this stuff is.

Then he said, "Would you like to try some on? I'll give you ten dollars more if I can put you in this stuff and take a picture of you, 'cause it would really be a turn-on to me."

I don't know why I did it but … well, so he got me in this weird thing and this position, and this really weird get-up with all these strings, right? And I cannot get out. And then, to top it off, he had this like, this mouthpiece with this ring in the middle of it and then these two leather straps and this strap in the back. I put it in my mouth.

So I couldn't talk, and I was like gagged, and freaking out because then he started acting really weird. He was playing with himself and saying all this shit about how, "Yeah, you're gonna be my slave and I'm gonna shave your head." And I couldn't move, I was restrained. And I was like freaking out.

Then it was like, "Please, let me out," and I was crying. This guy was totally getting off on my fear. I couldn't talk because of this metal ring in my mouth, but I could make some sounds … I must of really looked ridiculous. "Just let me go," I was saying. He told me he was gonna put me downstairs and I was gonna be his slave forever. I was freaking out.

And then I got one of my hands free and I started hitting him. But then he got me restrained again and started fooling around with me. After about fifteen minutes he said, "So, you want to go do you?" Then he said, "Well, if I let you go I'm gonna shave your head first. And then I'm gonna send you to Juvie." I said, "Please, I'll go to juvie, anything! Just let me go." Then he said, "Well, you want to go, you promise me one thing." I said, "What? Anything, anything, just tell me." He goes, "Don't you ever let anybody ever tie you up again!" And then he gave me sixty dollars and I left.

I don't know what it is that makes people like doing weird stuff like that, things that are sick. Maybe circumstances that happened in their life, especially in their childhood. Here they like talking. A lot of guys ask you to talk dirty to them, or to tell them about your first experience. It's really quite gross. And they like … you're sitting there explaining to them and they like ask you if you had hair then. It's really weird.

J.D.
Philadelphia, Pennsylvania

> *J.D. approaches as I sit with another man. He stands and listens, nodding his head in agreement with the statements he supports. Gradually, he begins to interject comments of his own. As the man finishes he begins his own narrative, gesturing wildly to emphasize his thoughts.*
>
> *J.D. is an African American, and in his early forties.*

PEOPLE ARE HOMELESS for many different reasons. Only person that knows is that individual, 'cause every situation is unique. Now me, I was injured. But everybody else that's out here on the street, you never know what their problems are until you talk to them.

We used to walk around two, three days without sleep, just because we didn't want to go through the big, bureaucratic process of getting in a shelter where they look at you like, "I'm not going to give you a sandwich, I don't like the way you look."

See, it takes a lot to go up with a plate and say, "Put something in it." You understand what I mean? This is any human being. If nothing else a man wants to feed himself. But if you in no position to feed yourself you gotta humble yourself and say, "Give me something to eat." But these people who run these shelters, they use that. Everybody does, but these people especially. They'll wave that sandwich in front of you, taunt you with it.

The thing is, they don't have the social workers out here to help you. They say that we have job guidance counselors and all of this shit. Where are they? There's no help at the shelters. Why do they keep tellin' me about all these people and I never see 'em?

So it takes a strong individual to deal with the streets. We used to sit here and talk to dudes and a week later they out there in space somewhere. You see people you ain't never seen on the set before. And like, they're cool—for about a week or two. And then all of a sudden they start deteriorating. These streets will do it to you. I mean I don't know what you wanted to hear, but this is the pits—you talkin' skid row. And on skid row everything's the worst of everything.

Today's Sunday—you know what a homeless person does this time of day? Just walks the street, lookin' for food. You know how hard it is to find food on Sunday? It's impossible. Nobody feeds nobody on Sunday, Saturday either. Unless you beg.

The worst things happen to women. They tell women.... One girl just got kicked outta this shelter I was at. A guy on staff told her, "Either you gonna give me some sex or you're gonna be put out." I've seen that a couple of times. You see, it's not pretty.

You can look at it this way: you living an existence that only an animal can live. You understand? Digging in the trash cans and dumpsters to try to get somethin' to eat. Not washin'. And all of a sudden you have head lice, crabs, all this good stuff. I mean it is a heck of an existence ... and I hate it , I just hate it 'cause all this starts workin' on your mind ... then you go into a deep-set state of depression and eventually ... the eventual outcome is suicide.

I know a couple myself personally. When I was on the job this one young lady used to come over. I used to give her five dollars so she could get herself something to eat. Right? So one day she came over and she just started talkin' and ramblin' about going home—said, "I'm going home to Mommy."

Now I knew her mother was dead, you understand. So I asked her to wait for me till I got off of work. Then I took her up to a ladies' clothes store, bought her a new outfit, took her to my place, let her clean up. Then I took her out to dinner. And I said, "Now what are you talkin' about? I know your mom's dead." She said she couldn't take it no more, you know. She went back to my house, slept in the living room. When I woke up she was gone.

I heard about it two days later ... they found her body in the river, wearin' the clothes I bought her. She had blown her brains out. Still had the pistol in her hand.

Hell
Philadelphia, Pennsylvania

Tough, pleasant, opinionated, Hell limps as she walks. She wears a sweatshirt and cut-off shorts that reveal a row of livid red scars encircling her thigh. Hell is Puerto Rican and 28 years old.

I WAS IN A COUPLE OF SHELTERS and any shelter I was in, it was dirty. We had cockroaches the size of mice. I'm not crazy, I'm serious. I wouldn't lie. And the food ... and violence. There's a whole lot of violence, a whole lot of it. It's like, if you don't like to fight I'd advise you don't go.

If the shelters were any better a lot of people would go to them. But they're not any good. You know, you don't get any respect. It's like you're here under martial law. And it's hard.

If you choose not to go to a shelter and you're just livin' on the street, then you have to worry about ... well, a woman if she's by herself has to worry about being raped and beat up, and having any change she might have panhandled or whatever taken from her—you know, along with her mentality and her brain. They're gone too. Because it's just too hard. Sleepin' on the sidewalk hard.

But you still have the problem of showering, trying to keep clean. And sleeping. Because downtown you're not allowed to sleep anywhere, men or women. The cops will chase you all over the city, and you just be trying to take a nap, trying to go to sleep. You be forced to sleep places like underground with the subway system. You get to know the route of the trains by heart 'cause you hear them all the time. And it's hard, it really is. It's real hard. You have to be strong if you're going to be homeless.

Like this girl Diane, she got busted in the head. She gets beat up by her boyfriend, her body gets taken advantage of. They call her Dirty Diane because, well, she really don't take care of her monthly thing, just lets it dribble down her leg. Maybe she do that 'cause then nobody'll bother her. I don't know. She been put in the hospital about three or four times for her mental problems. She just don't care anymore.

Trae Casey
Washington, D.C.

Trae leans against a table with a group of friends in a large D.C. shelter. He is handsome and muscular, an African American in blue jeans and a T-shirt. He waves me over and asks what I'm up to.

"You want to know how it is?" he asks. "I can tell you that. I can tell you how it is." Trae is in his late twenties.

I'VE BEEN HOMELESS two years and what drove me here was pressure. Didn't want to deal with the situation at home ... pressure. Then I had a friend that was usin' drugs, takin' my money and things for drugs. Bills and things, all that pressure.

Fact of it is, I was stayin' up on 16th Street. Had an apartment there, run $565 a month. Then you had to pay utilities, plus I had a car. It was the bills—I wasn't makin' enough money. Then this friend of mine, he was takin' it and shootin' it into his arm.

Then I went home and my mom wasn't makin' it. She was havin' a lot of pressure, bills and things of that nature. And I just said, "The hell with it!" and gave up.

I've come a long way since I've been here. I've climbed back up. I've pulled myself back up. That's what I'm doing. But it's still hard, man. I need somebody to listen to me, listen to my problems ... somebody just to take five minutes. 'Cause a lot of times when you have so many problems and so much pressure, you walk around with it all built up inside of you and it just feeds into other things.

It's society, and the person himself to blame for this situation. Like me, I'm the only one in my family that's in the situation I'm in. The rest of 'em have nice cars, nice houses, you know what I'm sayin'. That's why I can't let 'em know I'm in the shape I'm in. And it bothers me, it really does.

Things like that get on your nerves. It just makes you frustrated as hell. Like I used to have a good job. I did electrical sales, sold supplies and the wire to run the electricity through the building. That was a while back, back in Nixon's time. He was the best president we ever had, you know that? And you know why he was the best president we ever had? 'Cause all of us had jobs then [he sweeps his arm to indicate the group of men; they nod, agreeing]. We were all workin' then.

But now it's Tracy Labor, $25 a day to bust your butt out of the labor pool. Hell, that gives you even more to be frustrated about.

But with good friends and good help, you could make it out of here. Some of the dudes down here, they'd be okay with some help. Some help with their problems, or the pressure.

Ted
Atlanta, Georgia

His full white hair and beard give Ted a soft, gentle appearance distinctly at odds with his quick, watchful eyes and the old soldier instincts he claims have kept him alive.

Another portion of Ted's testimony appears in the chapter "Work and its Discontents." He is white and in his fifties.

YOU BECOME SALTY on how to survive if you've been in the military any. I was in the Marine Corps and there's no reason in the world for me not to survive as long as I can see, hear, taste, and smell and walk. But other people … in the wintertime the shelters down here take in three, four thousand people a night. And there's a lot of crime in those shelters.

Right over here at the church—it's a shelter in the winter—two winters ago I walked out of that church early one morning. I was loadin' papers over here at Atlanta Journal. I walked out with the assistant pastor of the church. We were talking and he had a bunch of bundles going down the stairs. I helped him carry 'em down and put 'em in his car. He had a little station wagon.

As we're putting 'em in the car my feet are sticky and his are too. I'm lookin' down there, it's icy and slick; and it was kinda dark, except for some of the lights that's around the church here. So I screwed my foot in it and it stuck again. I says, "That's not paint, Reverend." So we walk back up through the shrubbery, to the side of it: There was a human body that was hacked in four pieces. It had to happen somewhere's after ten o'clock at night—on the shelter's property, in the hedge around the church. Right there a man was killed.

Another time I was going out of here to the Sixteenth Street Presbyterian Church to get breakfast. They have breakfast there year 'round. And as I was walking by the parking lot I seen somebody laying over next to a bumpin' block, where they park with their front wheels. I walked over there plumb, where I could get a closer look to see if he was just passed out or what. He ain't got no head no more. They squashed his head plumb unrecognizable with a cinder block.

And you take, like on the first of the month and the fifteenth of the month, then these streets are strictly a hell-hole. 'Cause they know the welfare checks come in and the government checks come in. And these kids on drugs will roam in twos and threes, lookin' for women and drunks that they know might have a check. They call it Mother's Day, Father's Day: welfare checks and government checks.

The crime down here is due to money and dope. It's not so much alcohol. It's all narcotics.

Like I worked with one ol' boy last Saturday night. He drives an '83 Ford Thunderbird and he goes to these soup lines every day. And he'll demand from his wife part of that welfare check. They got two kids. But all he wants to do is work out of that labor pool, get enough gas and some drugs. He don't give a damn about nothin'. And he's a family man, still lives at home.

And I ride with these young guys in cars now and then on weekends, going out of these labor pools to work. There'll be three, four of them out of the five that's got needles in their pocket or something to smoke. And they'll use it before they get where they're going.

And they're the ones that work, they're the good ones! Others'll steal for it. The street people get blamed for it but it's the young ones on dope that do it. And most of them not homeless! Fact is they rob the street people too. They'll sit in these labor pools and see who got out and who got overtime or two or three checks—'cause some of these labor pools will let you store 'em up. They'll see who it is and where you cash it.

One night I was going out of here to this place where I was staying and this guy came up, like he had an overcoat on his shoulders. It was cold as hell and I had my parka up around my head to keep the weather off of me. Dude went to go by me and threw the coat over me, jumped right on top of me. Another beat my legs apart with a piece of iron bar. I was trying to get my head uncovered and my legs are being crushed and beaten. They took everything. Absolutely. About 7:30 at night; I'd just got outta the labor pool at 6:00.

So you gotta change directions, don't let 'em become familiar with a pattern of your traffic. Alternate as much as possible. Don't let 'em figure out what you're gonna do next. These young kids on drugs, you gotta look at 'em just like they're the fuckin' enemy, 'cause they'll rob ya in a heartbeat. They're a slur on all the street people. When you're homeless they are your enemy.

Tanya
Philadelphia, Pennsylvania

Tanya is a quiet, gentle woman with soft features and a languid, pensive expression that rarely changes. She speaks slowly, breaking up her narrative with long, motionless pauses. Tanya spends large portions of her day thinking and staring, and remains puzzled and confused about all that has happened to her.

Another portion of Tanya's testimony appears in the chapter "The Homeless Mentally Ill." She is an African American and perhaps 30 years old.

THIS IS NOT REALLY THE FIRST TIME I've been homeless, but this is the first time I've been homeless since I've had a child. Lots of times they tell me, "You should sell your body. Go over there in that hotel, get fifty dollars overnight." I don't do it, but when people get down and out, see, their mind is like ... well it's open. Anything somebody got to offer, if you're homeless you're gonna hop on it most of the time.

Jobs is it, I guess, 'cause, the prices these days ... a one-bedroom apartment is at least $320, and you have to pay your own utilities, such as your gas and electric. And a lot of people out here that are working are not even getting enough to keep up with those bills. You try anyway, you know. You put a little bit on this and a little bit on that, but that's how people end up being homeless. All of a sudden they'll cut the electric off. You'll say, "Oh well, I'm not gonna let that bother me." They cut the gas off: "I won't let that bother me, I'm gettin' in enough income to pay my rent so I'm just gonna pay that."

Then the landlord gonna come out: "I don't want you livin' here, I'm gonna find somebody that's gonna take care of the place." Which they can. And you're out there again, trying to find a place to live.

And then you lose your kids. 'Cause you ain't got a place, or they don't think the way you live is fittin'. Most of the girls here in this shelter, their children have been taken away from them that way. And it leaves them homeless. It leaves you homeless if you have been a mother for so many years and you don't have a work history. Just like the situation I had. When they took my children away from me, that's when it all started.

I was like ... left alone. I spent the first nights in University City, under an awning. It's part of the University of Pennsylvania, across the street from a big bank. It's a big area; most of the time I was there. Or I would wrap up in a blanket and just, you know, go right off to sleep on a vent. I was hoping someone would see me and tell me how to get back on my feet, but it didn't happen.

Then I found a little shelter where you could go during the day. It was for women. Nights you would have to find some place to go. Just by going to the shelter I'd meet people who had an apartment and they would say, "Well, you can stay the night" or "You can stay a couple of days, but I can't let you stay forever." And it just kept going and going and going.

There were a couple of McDonald's and Burger King's and Roy Rogers that would stay open all night and they noticed me. You know, "Oh I seen that girl around a lot this year." And they'd say, "Hey, do you want something to eat?" And I'd say yes and they'd say, "Well here, you can't eat it in here, and don't hang around, don't let people notice that you're, you know, that you're ... outdoors."

I stayed in subways too. Most of the people stay around 30th Street Station. Or sleep on the street. I mean these days you can just lie down on the sidewalk. As long as you don't look like you fell off somethin' or you're sick nobody'll say anything to ya.

Joe
Philadelphia, Pennsylvania

Joe is a large, broad-shouldered man with round, brown eyes and thick, salt-and-pepper hair he keeps closely trimmed. He studies me as we get acquainted, watching and observing. His voice is deep and melodic, very comforting to listen to. I wish to myself that he would decide to trust me. Joe relaxes in a long pause, leans back and begins a narrative that lasts for hours: the story and history of all he has witnessed and endured in his many years on the street.

Joe is African American and middle-aged. Another section of his narrative appears in the chapter "Dependencies."

ME, I'M A LONER. After being out on the streets so long I enjoy being alone. The less people that you have around out on the street the better. Because you can see someone go from a mild, meek-minded person to a murderer in just a few minutes. And if you a street person that still have some type of moral fiber, you gonna be ticked away. You watch a man that's twenty maybe rob another man that's eighty years old. You really want to do somethin' 'bout it but you can't, 'cause you can't survive that way.

Today a lot of the street people are veterans, like myself. They see the corruption in society. A lot of people accept it but they don't. And they find themselves separate from their families. Or their pride won't allow them to go back when they don't have anything.

But the vast majority of the street people today are not old people, they all young. A lot of 'em are cocaine addicts, white and black.

And now there's other folks, families, mens that had good jobs. They in the street too. They're not street people yet but a lot of them do become street people. This happen because of the way you treated.

You see, you a human being, but you not treated like one. You go in the train station and the cops chase you out. It's rainin', it's cold, you gotta go someplace. You can't stay in the street. That changes the rules. 'Cause the streets are survival, total survival. And only a few actually survive and get out of 'em.

People don't know this. The mayors, the governors, people in power, most of the time they come from middle-class, upper middle-class, and wealthy families. They can't relate to a person who never had no money. Most of 'em can't. They've been taught, "Anything you want to be in America you can be." But that's not necessarily the case, not for everyone.

This especially true of the single male. People have no sympathy for the male, he the one society really hate and reject. 'Cause they've always had a stigma in this country that any man that's not out liftin' 200 pounds per load is a bum. So they treat you that way. And if you treated that way for long enough you start to act like one.

I put it to you this way: once you don't work for a while, you get to the point where you lose touch with what's happenin' beyond you, beyond your environment. Then when you fall far enough to hit the street, you actually start livin' in a different world, a different country. Maybe it's the Bowery, or L.A.'s skid row ... people sleepin' on pieces of cardboard in parking lots ... that's the new world.

In the new world you in society but you not really a part of it no more. And the society you live in, it really don't try to help. They make it as tough as they can on you.

They keep you alive, that's the name of the game, they keep you alive and say, "If you wasn't so lazy everything would be all right." You know what I mean? The society we live in treat you like dogs. "I gave you somethin', even if it was nothin' really to help ya, I gave you somethin'."

Sure, they give you a social worker who despise you, who can do nothing on his own 'cause the system say, "Well, we only allow this person to do this." And see, after they interview maybe two, three hundred people, they resent the street people. Because social workers take a lot of abuse too. And remember, you're talkin' about a person that maybe came from a middle-class family, that have no knowledge of what they doing except the things they have taught them in college. And when they should have gained experience they have a bad attitude due to the bad experiences they have had with street people. Same thing with the police. It's in their mind that you a bum.

Like every winter so many people freeze to death in the city. And the way they look at it, they say, "Well, we only lost this many this winter. You know, we try to keep it around this many every year. We maybe could reduce it, but who cares?" And then around election time they gonna get the newspaper come down, pen a story about how the mayor or someone was out on the street, helpin' the homeless at night or somethin'. This all politics.

So you find yourself dealing with a system that actually doesn't try to help ya. It's not even attempting to help ya. It may open shelters and different things, but shelters only breed more dissension in a person mind. He more rebellious towards society, towards other human beings, because of the horrible conditions they put him in.

Like I say, they may put a hundred people in one large room. First, they have no privacy. And the average street person cannot be trusted, not for one second. You can be kind to a person that's on the street and he will steal from you. As I said before, the moral fiber is very low. On the street most people see kindness as weakness. This is a slogan on the street. This is because you're no longer thinkin' like a normal person. When you on the street the rules change.

Like all the California hotels that should be cheap are not, 'cause of the slum lords. They got people livin' in those hotels that's on welfare, mostly women and children. And they're payin' an enormous amount of money for 'em.

In San Francisco they have a thing called a "Hot Line." All that you have to do is say that you want a room. You go to a place at night and stand out in the street. Sometimes you stand as much as six hours, then they give you a room from three to seven days.

These particular hotels fill up with people and charge the city incredible money. The city's sayin', "This is the only way we can give all these people a room, so we'll let the slum lords run things."

Several of the hotels are so rat-infested, so filled with lice and things—not all of them, just a large percentage. You might order a room and shit might be in the bed, human waste. Believe me, I been there.

In New York it's worse. They pay up to a hundred dollars a day for a woman and child to live in a ... a rat-infested place, with lice, broken toilets, cold water. 'Call 'em "welfare hotels." See, I been there, too. And remember, people make a fortune off of these places, off of the homeless. It's simply a money-making venture.

If these cities know what the conditions are in these places they don't care. If they care then they're not aware. They couldn't be aware 'cause no decent person would allow the homeless situation to get where it is in these hotels. But they're aware. They have to know. Everybody that's ever been in one knows.

But once you see all this, once you see through the system that we live in, you become an outlaw. Once a man become an outlaw the normal things that people get involved with or adjust to don't appeal to him much. Then everybody against you.

Lots of this comes from the police. You have sadism in most police departments. This is a well-known fact. Society tries to screen them out but a few of 'em still get on the force, it's a way they can get their pleasure. 'Cause the average policeman, he has license to beat a bum. He always did. Now I maybe could see the point if someone just committed a crime. But a bum? What he do? And I've seen so much of it; I still see quite a bit. I mean I've seen it in New York, I've seen it down South, I've seen it on the West Coast.

Once it was 2:00 in the morning. There was about five white guys out on the street. They be between 25 and 45 years old. One of them had took something from one of the other ones, they were wino-type guys. And a police car came by. There was a disturbance, see, 'cause all of 'em mad at the one guy.

The police actually subdued the situation, and they was just talkin' to the guy. Then another police car came—I think it was from the traffic department. Dead of the night. Two cops got out of the car, they asked the other policemen no questions, they just started beatin' these guys, beatin' 'em for fun. They made no arrests. I was watchin' the whole thing. They got their laughs, then they got back in the car.

Another time I saw a particular incident in Norfolk, Virginia, where there was a woman. See the woman was out in the street acting crazy and about seven or eight policemen responded to the scene. They was tryin' to get this woman in a patrol car and they were having a tough time gettin' her in. This one policeman got out to the side of the car and opened the door. Another policeman was trying to push her head, get it down and get her inside the car. This other guy, he went around, got in the other side of the car and was trying to bang her on the head with a night stick. And I said, "Now this guy's a total animal. They're trying to get her head in the car and he's bangin' her on the head like to keep her out."

What he did wasn't the point that was so bad. It's that the rest of 'em—and I was noticing two of 'em standin' there didn't particularly like what he did—they just looked, didn't do nothin'. As I see it, every one of their badges should be snatched off their chest. Because to wear a badge and do that, or to stand and watch ...

'Cause remember, you out on the street, you get a good understanding of things the average citizen never hears about. And I can tell you there's an unwritten rule there: murder's okay, it's okay for a thief, it's okay for a drug addict, it's okay for a policeman—if they do it to a bum.

This goes right back to the way society as a whole think, that's why you have it with the police. The system was already set up before he ever got to it, before he ever got to the precinct.

And most time people are homeless they from different cities. No one is actually pushin', checkin' what actually happened when a homeless person is found dead. They everyone victim. As they used to say in the tombs of New York, when a person die of an injury on the street they say he "fell down the steps." If it's a homeless person it really didn't matter anyhow. Lots of times you find a guy who think he doing society a favor if he gets rid of a couple.... That something straight out of Adolf Hitler world.

Our society considers the policeman a hero. Well, I know his job is tough—it ain't no easy street out there. But that don't give him the right to abuse his authority. I was a point man in Vietnam. As far as I'm concerned I look up to no policeman, not after the things I've seen them do. The things society would consider him a hero for, I had more of that in five minutes of my life than he have in a lifetime.

See once you hit the streets you realize that America is a great country, but there's a lot of ugliness about it, too. There's a lot of wrong.

CHAPTER 2

WORK AND ITS DISCONTENTS

One of the more noted paradoxes of homelessness is that the crisis worsened as unemployment dropped. This was particularly true in the Northeast, where clothing and retail stores once bid entry level wages over $8 an hour during Christmas seasons when shelters and soup kitchens were overrun with requests for food and shelter.

No situation could be more misleading—and few have so effectively maligned the public image of homeless people. Actually, employment rose among homeless people at a much faster rate than the rest of the population: up 13 percent in 1987, for example.[1] However, the upshot was not that there were less people homeless, but more homeless people who worked.

How many? For 1989 and 1990 the National Conference of Mayors estimated that 24 percent of all homeless adults were working, with averages ranging from 10 to 40 percent in various cities. Government experts in New Jersey estimated that up to 25 percent of that state's homeless population work, while the Washington, D.C., Department of Human Services reported that 60 to 65 percent of the homeless men in its shelters hold jobs.[2] And of the five hundred homeless families mentioned in the D.C. DHS report, fully 15 percent received their income solely from employment.[3] More importantly, a study of Chicago SRO residents found that no more than 3 percent were "neither working nor looking for work."[4]

In fact, while rates of employment among homeless people have begun to drop in response to the current recession, the sheer number of homeless people who work continues to rise due to the expanding nature of the crisis. More people may now be out of work than at any time since the 1930s, but more people living on the street are actually working.

Such percentages are remarkable given the many "hidden" or "at risk" homeless, living with friends or relatives, not included in the figures, and the large number of homeless people who can't work due to mental illness, physical disability, age, disease, addiction, or other health concerns. Others prove too antisocial, apathetic, or disillusioned to hold a job, while age discrimination and other biases work against many who want work and can't find it. Poor job skills and changing employment patterns also contribute to unemployment among homeless people, particularly in the inner city. And, of course, much of the "work" homeless people do, including prostitution, caring for children, panhandling, and "canning," is excluded from these figures.

Homeless people themselves claim the percentage of the officially working would be even higher if there were more opportunities for employment.

"If a man could work and live by it, I believe 73 percent of the people would come off the street in a flash," explained a homeless man I met in Atlanta. "People on the street—those that aren't on drugs and stealin' anyway—want to work."

The conditional statement "work and live by it" is an important one, since working, even working full-time, is frequently not enough to keep a person or family out of homelessness. Darlene, a woman who fell into homelessness after more than ten years of distinguished service in the military, explains:

> Okay, I got a little calculator here. There's a law here that if you work 40 hours they have to give you benefits ... so they'll give you 30, 35 hours. Okay, you make $3.35, minimum wage ... that times 35—we're pushing it to the max—you're making $117.25 per week.

> Each place differs on how much taxes they take out, but it's usually 28, 25 percent ... let's cut it down and just say 10. That brings you to $207 a paycheck, $414 a month. The average studio apartment runs you $295, but you've got deposit, you've got first and last month's rent ... so you need $1,000 to move in. Then you've got electrical, gas, transportation, clothes, and you gotta eat.

> So you're lookin' at the fact that you need to make at least five or six dollars an hour. The new minimum wage, what's it gonna be? $4.25? That's still not enough. You'll have to get two minimum wage jobs and work 60 hours a week. And you'll maybe have to do that for two months before you've saved enough to move in. Now where are you gonna stay while you're doing that? How will you stay clean? And if, say, you're in the predicament where you have two children, not even all that will begin to close the gap.

There are also those who will not work when the work they can find is not enough to feed and house them. Others say they would work for the minimum wage if they had housing, received benefits, childcare, or, in the case of families on assistance, could continue to receive aid until they were firmly established on their own. Most who come to these conclusions do so after trying, and failing, sometimes over the course of various jobs and several years, to provide for themselves. And all do so at a great disadvantage.

"Because by the time all this happens to you all your credit's ruined," explains Ted, whose second narrative appears in this chapter. "All your morale and ego is undermined because you can't get started again. There's no place to get a decent job, no place to stay, to stay even while you look for one. And to get a job without a residence is just about impossible."

Impossible, that is, if the job one wants is "decent." Few of the jobs homeless people hold would warrant such a description. Instead, they fall into an altogether different category: "Not even working-class," as Darlene puts it—work for the desperate and destitute; work that is relatively unmentioned in the debate over homelessness; work that makes even the lowest grades of prostitution seem a viable alternative.

It is hardly surprising that this has occurred. Emergency food programs are inadequate in almost half of our cities, and for every ten people who approach a shelter, two are turned away.[5] That hustlers, pimps, and drug dealers regularly exploit such people is common knowledge. However, it is not commonly known that the larger, "legitimate" economy also plays a role in this "underground" exploitation. Two principal venues for this exploitation are "labor pools" and migrant work.

Labor pools provide temporary, day labor in cities across the country. Ostensibly, and like all temporary services, labor pools contract employees to companies that find themselves short-handed. The company pays the labor pool an hourly fee and the pool gives the employee some percentage of that figure. While part of the larger trend toward temporary employment, most labor pools can be distinguished from other agencies by their skid-row locations.

Companies accrue a number of advantages from this arrangement. For one, all payroll, taxation, and workers' compensation responsibilities are handled by the labor pool. In this way, too, companies free themselves of the benefits they provide full-time employees and create an important buffer between themselves and any liability claim made on behalf of a worker. Consequently, the work that labor pools provide homeless people is often dangerous. Few states have passed laws or regulations that specifically apply to labor pools, however, and few cities adequately monitor their operations. The U.S. Department of Labor keeps no data on them.

And labor pools are big business. In fact, the growth of the industry parallels the rise in homelessness, and the profitability of many firms is a direct consequence of the great supply of laborers they readily have on hand. A report by the Atlanta-based Southern Regional Council, for example, listed 3 temporary agencies among the 19 fastest-growing companies in Georgia for the years 1982 to 1986—a period that saw rates of homelessness soar for Georgia's largest cities.[6]

The abuse of homeless workers by labor pools has not gone unnoticed. After a four-month investigation of temporary agencies in 1983, the Wall Street Journal concluded that day laborers "face some of the same abuses as powerless workers of the 19th century did during the Industrial Revolution."[7] Five years later an independent study of labor pools in 37 cities warned that the situation appeared to have worsened and would continue to "worsen with time"—a prediction that has come true.

But today little is said of labor pools. One of the most significant facts of life for homeless people, labor pools are rarely mentioned in discussions of homelessness and receive scant attention in the media. Sadly, the testimony by Ted, which opens this chapter, is probably the most extensive discussion of the use of homeless workers by labor pools to have ever appeared in a book.

The exploitation of homeless people in migrant labor is similarly unacknowledged despite the fact that, again, it is a common occurrence in the lives of thousands of homeless people—particularly those in the Southeast.[8]

Homeless people find themselves working as migrant laborers by virtue of the "camp vans" that stop at shelters or pull up alongside bread lines. While large Southeastern cities like Atlanta and Fort Lauderdale see the most vans, they regularly travel as far North as Washington, D.C., to find their clientele. The drivers, who may be paid "by the head" they bring in, promise shelter, food, and a wage—a good spiel for the audience at hand. Inevitably a few men accept the offer and climb in.

What happens next depends on the camp they are sent to. With luck they will find hard work at minimum wage and the shelter they were promised. More commonly, however, they fall into a literal slave trade of forced labor and debt servitude in the nation's most exploitive migrant labor camps.

"Homeless people are sought by the most unscrupulous employers who have the worst conditions," explains Shelley Davis, an attorney with Migrant Legal Action of Washington, D.C.[9] "They're the most vulnerable. So contractors place them in conditions that other workers wouldn't accept and use force and coercion to keep them there." The testimony of Albert, which concludes this chapter, more than confirms such claims.

Being down and out is a daily fact of life for tens of thousands of employed homeless people. Indeed, this situation proves even more paradoxical than it appears: for not only did homelessness increase during the mid-80s upturn in employment, the percentage of homeless people who work rose when overall rates later plummeted for the nation.

Ultimately, it is an accolade to the industriousness of homeless people that nearly one in four do work, and that at least that many actively look for work, despite the difficulties they face. As the testimonies that follow make clear, many work for much less than the minimum wage and in conditions unimaginable to people with homes and the jobs, or resources, to secure them.

Ted
Atlanta, Georgia

> *Like many people, Ted is homeless only part-time, turning to shelters and soup lines when he can't get or keep the work he needs to make ends meet.*
> *Ted is white and in his fifties. Another part of his narrative appears in the chapter "Life on the Street."*

I'M A MASTER MECHANIC in the power train for eighteen-wheelers. I worked for Peterbilt Motor Company for seventeen years and I can right at this present hour tell you every piece of every cat engine Detroit ever made. I know the Ford, the Road Ranger transmission in other words, inside and out from the eight speed to the sixteen speed. I worked splicer boxes, the Eaton, rear ends, I rebuilt wrecks. But when you go out here and apply for a job, and they see that you're over 45 years old ... They got five applications lying there, and they got two that's 23 and 26 years old that's going to give 'em thirty years of their life ... I ain't got thirty years left to work.

So naturally you're not going to get the job, the younger person's going to get it. So that cuts you down there. And no freight line over-the-road masters like Trans Con, Time DC, and them can hire ya, no matter what, after you're 35. The union and the insurance people will not permit it. So even if you ain't got a police record or anything, you become a second-rate citizen because of your age.

And even though the application says no age discrimination ... bullshit. It exists. They won't hire ya; I had one man absolutely tell me that. He wanted to be honest with me because I was honest on my application. That's a fact.

Lost my job due to the same thing, that and a lack of customers buying trucks. 1983. They decided, "We'll save money two ways: cut the older guys who are the top men on the payroll, and cut 'em before we have to pay 'em any retirement."

That was Indianapolis, Indiana. And there's no work in Indianapolis, Indiana—outside of New Orleans it's the brokest city in the United States. They've overtaxed all the industry there and everybody left. Goodyear Tire, lots of companies. They've closed schools. Why I know only one labor pool that's left out there, out of fifteen. From say '68 to '83 all the labor pools, which handle two, three hundred men a day, closed up and left because nobody had any use of any men.

The labor pools exist to provide inexpensive labor for a company who only wants temporary help, and who doesn't want to pay a full wage. Instead of paying an employee $15 to $17 an hour, they pay 'em out of the labor pool for $5 or $6 an hour. The labor pool pays you $3.35 an hour and they put three bucks an hour into their pockets and become millionaires.

You are definitely exploited when you work for a labor pool. They think you're so damn dumb when you go out on the job that you can't even snap a chalk line or drive a nail. They treat you like a dog. Absolutely. Unless they get to know you and you repeat yourself over and over again. And you might have to eat shit for three months, until finally they realize that you're all right and they get off your back.

But every day they hand you your ticket—they ain't going to hire you on   and when bad weather comes you're the first one that don't go to work. If there's bad weather for two or three months, you just sit on your haunches. All it is is a cosmetic appearance of getting jobs to the people downtown who need 'em.

I only had a steady ticket once. It was with a stable, a riding academy. It was six days a week with the labor pool, all winter. Horses have to eat, have to be cared for every day. That's how I made last winter.

For eight hours of work out of the labor pool you get $26.76, to start with. They take out the ride, they take out if you take a draw—they give you up to $2 or $3 a draw. When all is said and done, with Social Security out and what else they can find to take out, it's between $17 and $18 for a day of hard, mean-ass sweat labor. And that's eight hours. We're ... we're not even blue collar workers. And the way most of these places will work ya, it's so hard that if you put two days in straight in a row—which we'll say is 17 hours—you are so fatigued that it'll take at least a day to let the body recover, especially if you're a bit older.

Once the labor pool sent me out to a hydraulic place where we was cleaning railroad tracks that come in off this ship from South Africa. I was using a hydraulic blaster to clean the tracks—a blaster with a wand, like you use at a car wash, only this one's a huge one and it's got 7900 pounds of pressure coming through it. The whole son-of-a-bitch exploded: took out two teeth, broke my jaw, busted my glasses. The only thing I got out of the g'damned deal was they replaced my glasses and payed the hospital bill. That was it. Pitiful. And I couldn't work. I was layed up, penniless for two months.

Another time I was out here at this place where they rebuild air conditioners, tearing down compressors, putting 'em in hot tanks of acid, like you do an engine block. I was on the tear-down end. When it got torn down I put it in an iron basket, put this little crane over it. You got these big tanks of 600 degree fluid, and you set the baskets down in there with the parts of the air compressor—the crank, block, the cylinders, heads—to cook the junk off. Then you take it outta there and take this high pressure water washer and get off as much as you can. Then it goes through this conveyor belt, where it's enclosed, and a pressurizer really cleans it.

It's so hot there's a blue flame underneath this tank. They keep it at 600 degrees all the time. And when you lift that basket out of there, if a part falls off and you're not expecting it, it hits that damn hot gunk and it goes all over you.

That's what happened to me. I was lifting it out—I had rubber gloves on but I'da been better off without 'em. A piece of the compressor fell off and splash waves came outta there. Burned my rubber gloves up, burned my face. Look at my forehead [he tips his head forward and points to the melted skin of a burn scar]. It went down in my shoes, screwed my feet up.

I was out of work for the whole summer from it, but I didn't get a shit out of it. Not only didn't get a shit, couldn't work! That's why they use temporary labor at it: they'll work at it for maybe a week or two, get hurt, or they'll see it's a hell hole and just leave. They can't keep permanent people there and they don't want to pay 'em much or insure 'em anyway.

And when one labor pool don't have nobody that'll go there anymore they'll change labor pools. And with the rotation of the people in the city—there's eleven labor pools here—by the time they go from one to another and back to the one they originally had they'll have all new people who don't know nothin' about it. So I know about that damn place and I won't go, even if I'm starving. And I'll tell anybody not to go.

Like I say it's a cosmetic deal. It gives a street person a little money to eat on. He can go take a couple of days off, get himself a couple of changes of clothes so he looks fair on the street. But to try and live on it as I do will just about kill ya.

But I don't worry about it 'cause it don't do ya no good to worry. You look at people today, struggling as hard as it is. They ain't gettin' by. And by the time I have to count on Social Security there ain't going to be none. SSI's going to be broke, welfare's going to be broke. There ain't going to be nowhere to turn. It's going to come to that, I really believe it, the way the cities are getting in trouble and all.

And you should see ... I'm working now out of this labor pool at this bakery that takes all the waste baked products from bakeries that bake pies, cakes, cookies. All the pastry products that are either missing ingredients and can't be corrected, or that have become waste. It in turn is recooked, filtered, and dried, and corn and wheat and barley—grain, in other words—and vitamins is added to it. When it come out the other end it will be dog food or somebody's chicken food.

I'm in the slop end of dumping all of that into the augur that takes it to the grinder that recycles it. Boxes and boxes and tons of overdated cookies, cakes, donuts—you ought to see the stuff that come through there.

One night we had candy bars. A load of candy bars that got wet. But only the top and maybe the sides was wet. Inside is maybe 35 tons of good boxed up Baby Ruth, Snickers, all kinds of candy bars. All going to chicken feed.

Tony
San Francisco, California

Tony works the streets, collecting aluminum cans to be sold for recycling. Though young, he is excessively thin and stooped, prematurely aged by days of endless walking and years of exposure to the wind and sun.

Tony's face, however, is warm and animated, friendly. Speaking with him, I can't help but feel that we should be drinking coffee in the cafeteria of a small college, discussing politics or art, perhaps a novel. Instead, we sit on the steps of a nameless alleyway establishment, our backs against a scarred and broken door, discussing his life on the street. Tony is 25 and an African American. Another portion of Tony's narrative appears in the chapter "Runaway and Homeless Youth."

THE REASON I DO just about anything for work is I don't believe in the food lines. I know where all of 'em are at, and I can go down there, but I don't depend on 'em. I believe in at least being able to cover my own so I can keep myself fed, keep myself clothed and washed up.

The way I work it now is I collect cans. I got all these cans [he holds up a large garbage bag bulging with them]. I got two other bags stashed in my hotel.

It's not a regular hotel, they call it Hot Line. To get it you have to wait in line all day, till 3:00. They're pretty bad, but I know the real bad ones and I stay away from 'em. I know a guy, a working-class guy, works with rent-a-cars, and he lives in one 'cause housing is so expensive in this city. He works but he's homeless.

And I know some people who collect SSI and welfare, and they're still out there on the food lines. Then there's GA—that's General

Assistance, a California deal. Three hundred dollars, I think. When you're on GA you can't live in a homeless hotel beyond eight days. That's how hard the city is. GA isn't enough to pay a month's rent with, but if you stay in a hotel they make you kick yourself out. Then you got to go back outside or try to get into another shelter. So if you can get used to it you save more by sleepin' outside than stayin' in a hotel, if you're on some kind of assistance.

But I'm not on SSI, GA, or nothing. I work. I do odd jobs—painting, cans. I've got this bag, in my room I've got two other bags. Tomorrow I go out around town again. Then I go cash them in.

If I work Thursday, Friday, Saturday—Saturdays are an option—Sundays and Mondays, I can make fifty dollars. You've got a whole bunch of competition, but if you know where to go you can get that many cans. They're out here.

I can work each day but Tuesday and Wednesday, 'cause that's when I have to do Hot Line to get a room. When you do Hot Line you can't go out and collect cans 'cause you'll miss your hotel.

I make Saturday an option for working because by Friday my legs will be tired, my feet will be tired. I need a rest. So sometimes I rest from collecting cans on Saturday and go back to it on Sunday. Then on Monday I turn the cans in, which sometimes is hard for me. To sell the cans you go to a recycling center. The one I go to is up on Church and Market, by Safeway. That's all the way up there, up in the Castro. After you work all day it's hard to walk over there and turn the cans in. But that's life. You know, there are some folks that work that hard every day.

But with cans it depends, some days are better'n others.

First I scan the area, like I've scanned this whole area already. The only thing I haven't scanned is that garbage can, the green garbage can over there. Out of all the garbage I should at least find one can. That's how I scan it. I scan the sides, underneath the cars, in the streets, all around.

You can also go into these nice places and restaurants and ask for cans. But I don't do that. I don't want to bother 'em. I mean there's a lot of places where I can go in and get cans, but I don't do it.

I look for cans as I go along. The most cans I've found so far is down by the Embarcadero. I was walkin' down there and I opened a garbage can up and I found about ten or twelve cans. I go down the road a little farther, I find fifteen cans.

One problem we have is that you have to always keep walkin', even if you're not workin'. Sooner or later you want to sit down. But they don't want us to do that, they want us to keep movin'. But think about it: we're gonna have to sit down and rest. But we can't. They keep on us to keep walkin'.

When they tell me to move, I move. But when they feel like harassing they tell you to get up and get in the wagon. If you're not drunk they give you three hours anyway. I've had two trips to the jail in my time like that.

Another thing that really gets me is never having more than an empty room for a few days. In the winter I try to get an apartment for longer but I can't always do it. And it's the same thing anyway, lonely.

I try to change everything up then, 'cause doin' the same thing I'm doin' now you can die out here. You spend year on year out here in the streets. You gonna get older, your face gonna get older, your ways gonna get more terrible. 'Cause as long as you stay out here you get tired. You get tired from just stayin' outside every day. I know a person right now, I see him every night on Powell Street when it's time to eat. I always do. But he be out here for a while and his ... his courage to go on and on, it goes down the longer he's out here.

And people get 86'd from these food lines and shelters. 86's mean that you can't come back. Let's say you go into a soup kitchen and do something wrong. Even if it's a little minor sort of thing they'll 86 you. For how long I don't know. But they'll 86 you. A homeless person, he don't need that. He's already been 86'd from everywhere else.

But me, I try to make the best of it I can. One thing I like is all the little kids talk to me. One time four or five kids came up to me and one kid said, "You're collectin' cans?"

And I said, "Yeah."

"How much do you get for a can?"

"Less than a penny." They laughed and I started talkin' with 'em some more and collectin' more cans.

There's other things you can do. Like Unemployment has this farm you can go and work at. But to go you've got to have trouble in one of two areas: alcohol or drugs. If you don't you can't get on the farm. Catch 22. That's why I'll never get to the farm—I don't use alcohol or drugs. It's a system, a city. For the homeless San Francisco is a city inside a city.

But since I've been homeless—as well as being homeless, being part of the mental health system—I've learned you have to have something constructive. Otherwise you can be what I call, excuse my language, ass out and shot to the curb—which means you're out there but you ain't doin' nothing. If I'm doing things constructive I feel good, at least I feel good that I'm doing something. 'Cause a lot of people they just hang out. There's a lot of homeless out here. And you know, I can understand the homeless who cannot do anything. Some really can't get on by theirselves. Others ... well, people look down on ya and ya lose hope. I see this every day.

But me, that's why in some senses I don't believe in it, in bein' homeless. I believe when you feel that you have the gusto to do better you can do better. But you know … I've tried. I really have. I'm still trying. That's why, even though I panhandle, I only panhandle a certain amount, I don't panhandle all day. 'Cause deep down I feel a person shouldn't be doin' this.

I've had different kinds of jobs. I've had painter jobs, I've had janitorial jobs, I got a certificate for being a master chef. Just like all these folks cooking around here [he waves his hands at restaurants and cafes]. I can do that too. But I don't get down 'cause they're workin' and I'm picking up cans, I think positive. The reason I think positive is I can never look down, 'cause then I'll always feel down. And I can't … I just can't do that. Now, even as I walk from here down to another soup line—which I'm not gonna eat—that's what makes me feel positive.

I went down there two days ago. I had five cents in my pocket and should've ate, but I didn't eat because I was fine with it and knew that I'd try to do as much as I can to feed myself by the time I go home. And, two, the reason I look so positive towards it is that's the only thing I can do. If I look unhappy towards it then I go backwards. And I can't afford to go backwards 'cause then I'll just be like everybody else, bein' down and not wanting to do nothing. I can't afford that.

But it's hard, you know. I'm always tired. I be tired before I even get to bed. From walkin'. Let's see, right now I'm way up here in North Beach. I have to go all the way to 16th and Michigan to get where I'm stayin'. Now if I don't have the change to catch a bus that's a long walk. If I catch a bus it's a short walk, but even though I get there I can't go to bed until I get all the way to this place where I eat that is way back by the Cow Palace, which is a long ways away. But the food's good there, and it's cheap. That's why I go to bed around twelve every night. I have to walk to sell my cans, walk to get dinner, walk to get my cans. By the time I'm done with all the things I do all day it be close to eleven o'clock. And then I'm too tired to do anything.

Elaine
Washington, D.C.

> *Elaine lives in the House of Ruth, a private agency that accepts a number of women who, like Elaine, are released from hospitals and mental health institutions, and find themselves suddenly homeless.*
>
> *Elaine is African American, perhaps 40 years old. Tall and strong, she carries herself with quiet poise and authority. We sit together at a table behind the shelter, a chain-link fence between us and the surrounding neighborhood.*

I GOT BURNED-OUT on nursing. I worked in hospitals, I worked in clinics, I worked in nursing homes. I'm a R.N. so I'm no slouch. I just can't work in it right now. Maybe in a few years ... and the doctor tells me I can go back. Don't think I won't. That's my first love. It's just ... you never realize how it can catch up with you. Then you start, you know, trying to overdo it. Overwork. Which is what I did.

Sometimes I'd work sixteen hours a day. And when they told me I couldn't work more than sixteen I'd find somewhere else to work some more. That's how involved I got. I got to the point I wasn't sleeping. I'd catnap. But I felt good because I liked the work.

See I've been divorced since 1979. And . . well I didn't have a family anymore, so I had to find something else to put all my energies into. And so I put it all into something I love—nursing. And I put too much energy into it. The whole world, I mean everything, just seemed like it fell apart.

I had money, from nursing, but ... well, what happened, I put some of it into my house, and some of it went to the children, and the rest of it went into the doctor bills—all that my insurance didn't cover. See, I went into the hospital after they ended my nursing career. I was in the hospital for three months because of stress.

It was like ... it went to the point of being just like a breakdown. But I refused to admit that I had ... okay, it was the stress, but I couldn't see it. Now I can. I've worked with a couple of people that this has happened to since then and it's like ... it's like I'm looking at myself. The same things that they were telling me, that was going on with me. But it's hard, you know, working at something you love and then not having any support ...

I was angry for most of the first month in the hospital. I was very angry about it. Then I guess ... well they gave me some medication, mild, that made me rest, and then I realized I have to bounce back. And I did have some good friends while I was at hospital. That sort of made me realize, "Hey, it's time to change. You don't have to work like that anymore."

They had workshops for us all. We [nurses] didn't rest, didn't take vacation time. And when you work in nursing—well, you get involved in families and you hear the piano chords ... but you can't do that, there's too much stress in that, in being too close to people at work.

So I'm kind of prejudiced when it comes to nursing [she laughs]. I take care of the sick but I could never get sick. That was hard to take. I mean you don't face it until you actually become sick. Then it's terrible to face.

But the thing that really hurt the most is when I had to rely on medical assistance to help with the bills. Being in the hospital, I used up all my insurance, all my money, all the money my house was worth ... then I had to turn to medical assistance. That was about the hardest thing I ever did in my life. But I couldn't do anything else.

I'm working again now. Different things. Telemarketing, selling things over the telephone. It's hard. Hard to try to start something new when what you love is nursing.

They say I would be good at teaching nursing because of all I've learned about nursing and stress. I didn't look at it that way before, but I am beginning to accept it. I guess I have to get over my resentments before I can say I'm gonna come out here and teach. If I'm gonna be good at something I'm gonna be darn good at it, or else I'm not gonna do it all. That's how I feel about it—it's something that Mom used to say to me. She said, "If you're gonna be something, you better be the darn best there is at it. Don't be halfway." And that made sense. But she never told me not to get hung up on it. There's a difference.

I didn't like coming here [the shelter]. I've always needed my own freedom and I've always worked for myself, never had a problem with that. But my doctors made me leave my occupation and now I don't have anything and I'm here.

And it's hard. These women [she sweeps her arm, indicating the other women of the shelter], they don't have anywhere to go either. When I sit up nights in here ... days, evenings ... listening to the women here, my heart goes out to them. They're very lovely people, and they're very lonely.

One lady, I think she's gone now, she can't get over her marriage. She and her husband broke up. Then her children were kidnapped from her, by her ex-husband. And this after they had gone through divorce court and all of that. Her husband had molested her youngest daughter. And then he took them again ... at night she kept talking, talking about molested children. Kind of babbling, all night long. But in the day she acts just like you and me.

My children, they didn't even know what happened to me. They still don't. The way I see it, they're still in their early twenties—there's no need to burden them with my problems, especially when I'm able, mentally and physically, to keep helping myself.

T
Philadelphia, Pennsylvania

> *Thin and neatly dressed, T strikes up a conversation with me as I wait for another man in the foyer of the Committee for Dignity and Fairness, a Philadelphia shelter. Thin and small, T is a middle-aged African American and an Army-decorated Vietnam veteran.*
>
> *"Given the opportunity to work," says T, "people will work. There is no such thing as people who won't work. They don't even exist."*

You know one of the worst things you can do when you talk about work? Not give a man enough. I worked for these people at this big luxury hotel. Sixty hours a week: I bring home eighty dollars. Eighty dollars. And then the lady decides she's gonna take twenty of that cause she felt that I wanted to take her job. So they abuse you.

And people don't want to pay you. You take factory workers, a factory worker welding used to make eight, nine dollars an hour. Sometimes more. Now they only want to pay them four dollars an hour. But me, I was hardly making a dollar an hour.

Now, if you got nothing, something's always better'n nothing. But who would want to work for that? Who would want to go to work for sixty hours and bring home eighty dollars? I tried to get a room. You can't even get a room on that, not unless you give up eating!

I could take you around the corner right now to a guy where I worked yesterday. We worked from eleven to seven last night. Made ten dollars. Worked! Wasn't no fuckin' playing. It wasn't nothin' where I sat down five of them hours. You see? I work. Yes, I do.

But he thought he had me over a barrel—I needed the ten dollars. When I got there I was grimy and filthy and nasty and tired from another job, but I went in and worked, worked hard. He wanted me to work today but I … I just made up my mind I'm not going to work for that, be treated like that. See this is the weekend. I'm going to another job tomorrow. If I worked today, for that ten dollars, I'd be in no shape to go to work tomorrow, where I hope to have a real job. All this work and I'm still living in a shelter. You see?

Today's society doesn't give a man or a woman an incentive. You've got people that absolutely want to work. We don't want no free ride. But let's just say you go into a job—and I'm saying this from my own personal experience—and the dude say, "Hey, I pay you ten dollars a day for an eleven-and-a-half hour day." But you need the job, you understand? You need the job. He knows that. Working your way up and all that is fine, but this guy knows full well that you're already capable of doing the same thing that he does. He knows that. There's no "up" in this job. He just wants to see how long you're going to linger with this.

And you deal with it. Even though you're not making any real money you do the job. Say you've a family to support, and everybody has to do their fair share. Then when you've been working there and it's time for a promotion, or time for a raise, then all of a sudden he gets amnesia, 'cause he's making money off of you. You understand? You lose that job and you gotta look for another one. Meanwhile he gets someone else to work for that ten dollars.

See, at one time real jobs were very easy to get in the city, but now jobs are very far and few between. And no employer I know is giving anybody any incentive—none whatsoever. They don't have to.

These guys go into shelters, go into shelters and say, "Hey, we need X amount of men." Man, I've worked three or four days for these guys and made twenty-four, twenty-six dollars. So from now on if they come in here I'm gonna say, "How much are you paying?" If he tells me something like that—three days, twenty-six dollars—I'm gonna say, "Sorry, nobody here want to work for that." Three days and twenty-six dollars! And these guys are not just gettin' jobs where you're pickin' up pieces of paper or cigarette butts, this is workin'! They're actually tryin' to work you in the hole. They've got people comin' to these places, tryin' to get people and to work 'em in the hole.

And I had—you know what they told me one time? I was lookin' for a job and Adult Services, they told me, "You got to know where your priorities are." And I looked at them and I said, "Well, okay, you tell me."

"Your priorities are gettin' here, gettin' a job, and gettin' a place to stay."

I said, "You're gonna tell me that my priorities are to come here and have you look down your nose at me every day, talkin' to me anyway you want to, tellin' me to get off my butt and get a job? Hey man, excuse me but I am workin'! Ten dollars a day, sixty dollars a week. I *work* for that! *And* I'm poundin' that concrete lookin' for something better. I don't need you to tell me I gotta come down here so you can tell me to get a job." I said, "I think you've got my priorities mixed up. Gettin' here is not my first priority. My priorities are to get a job and to get so I don't never have to come here again!"

Damn! ... Tell a man he has to come and be kicked in the butt by you every day, told to get a job, and then you look down your nose 'cause he don't have one. You understand? This is the way the system is run.

It's disastrous. You've got able-bodied men who are willing to do any type of work. And the way these people look at you is, "Well, he's a statistic. He don't have nowhere to go. Let's hook him up, give him a place to stay, three hots and a cot, occasionally give him some clothes. Let's wash his butt every day, then put him out on the street and let him come back in the next night."

Now is that incentive? Do you think that's incentive? I mean why can't that same money they're spendin'—and I really feel strongly about this—they're spendin' all this money on the B-1 Bomber, an' all these technological wonders for the elimination of the human race ... and I can say that 'cause I'm ex-military, some of this equipment I have tested myself. If they can put that kind of money into defense ... man, that makes me mad!

True, you know welfare rolls are staggering. You got individuals who abuse the welfare system. You have abusers everywhere, it don't matter what kind of situation you're in. I mean, you gonna tell me rich folks pay all the taxes they're supposed to?

But the people who're actually into doing something and doing it right are not being given the opportunity. Now the homeless people in my day, they were derelicts—the winos, the acutely mentally disturbed. But now you're looking at the designer-jean homeless, young men and women that are capable. But because of certain turns of events, that may not be no fault of their own, they find themselves without any bricks around them.

But they look at you and they say, "Well, where do you live?"

"Well, I don't have any.... "

"Oh no, we can't use you, you're a bum!"

See, that's the first thing they think—that we're all bums. Next they think we're criminals. Am I right? Or we're drug addicts. Or we're chronic alcoholics and don't mean no good to ourselves or anybody. Since we're homeless they think there's got to be something wrong with us, you know, stereotyping us. 'Cause you don't know how hard it is to find work when you don't have no place to live. Once you get in this situation you're lost in the sauce without the season.

These agencies, they care very little. They're so wrapped up in their jobs, their paperwork. You can push paper, but when all's said and done you're dealing with a human life, the most precious thing there is.

I mean they can look at you like you a piece of shit; they treat you like you the scum of the earth. And see it hurts, it hurts you. I mean ... man, I have a Congressional Medal of Honor ... You understand? A Congressional Medal of Honor! And it really hurts to have a person look at you as a subhuman. And then you look at yourself and go, "Why am I here? Why am I tolerating this garbage?" You understand what I'm sayin'? I'm still a man. I still have pride and dignity. Why are they doin' this to me?

Frank Robertson
Roanoke, Virginia

Mr. Robertson is a middle-aged man with thick, gray hair and broad shoulders. He is white and has lived and worked in Texas and California. We met at Justice House, a community of homeless people in Roanoke, Virginia.

Now ME, I'M A SKILLED STONEMASON, a stonecutter— not a bricklayer, not a blocklayer—a stonemason. In other words, I take native stone and cut it and put it together to build houses, chimneys, fireplaces, or art work.

But cement contains concentrations of calcium carbonate and lime. Because of constant exposure to it I developed an allergy to it: cement poisoning, what they call eczema dermatitis, which is a chemically caused allergy of the skin. My skin breaks open, sometimes clear down to the bone.

The allergy develops slowly, like you're being poisoned. An old mason told me one time—I was admiring his work, I said, "You do good work." He said, "No, the only good masons are either dead or retired." I thought this guy was joking but he explained it: "The good ones, or the ones that really love what they're doing and take pride in it, the cement poisons. It either kills 'em, or they have to retire from it and never do it again."

I worked for five years in masonry. For three of it I was a laborer for brick and blockmasons. Then I became a laborer for a stonemason and I worked myself up to mason. That's a skill I can go anywhere in the world with and get a job. Anywhere. And good money—up to $3,000 a week.

I worked as long as I could, but due to the cement poisoning I had to quit. Since then I've done very little but minimum-wage jobs. It's all I can get; being a skilled stonemason doesn't help me when I can't do masonry. And I don't know if you've ever been exposed to 'em or not, but a minimum-wage job is slave labor. The attitude is, "You have a job. If you don't like it somebody else'll take it." And there's lots of people that want it 'cause there ain't no jobs. So the oppression's not too far removed from the days of Rockefeller and the sweat shops. Only today it's not as nasty. But the attitude is the same, the whip is still there.

In a minimum-wage job you're treated like a dog. I'm a skilled mason and they push me around like I'm nothin'. I worked day labor for a solid year out of the Salvation Army up here. When they first started they said to be there at 7:00—first come first serve. Well I got there at 3:00 A.M. And I was either the number one man in line every day after that or no more than third. The officer there commented on it. He said, "Mr. Robertson, you've worked out of here more than anybody has."

But it didn't get me nowhere. They say take a minimum-wage job and work your way up. But raises in minimum-wage jobs come like fifteen cents a year. And within that year's time you've gotten so far in debt that your fifteen cents is wiped out and thirty more with it.

Oh, I don't know, I don't understand economics that well. But I do know if you ever get caught in the minimum-wage net it'll condition you to be poor. And with the rents and everything, if you have a minimum-wage job you get a choice: you can either get a place to live, and starve, or eat and have no place to live. So society oppresses the poor. In fact they keep us poor, they perpetuate poverty.

So I don't work day labor any more. I'd rather get out here and scrounge on the street; I don't care if I have a place to sleep or not. I couldn't afford rent if I was working anyway, so why should I care? And this way I'm nobody's dog.

Albert
Roanoke, Virginia

*Albert leads the advance team of the New Exodus marchers,
setting up tents and hauling gear for the homeless people who
have come from throughout the South to march to Washington,
D.C., for the November 1989 Housing Now! demonstrations.*

*Giving the campsite a last, late-night check, he waves to me,
smiling. "What about now?" he asks, referring to my request
to talk with him. "Sorry I didn't have a chance earlier," he adds,
motioning me into the cab of the pickup he's been driving.*

*I jump in, pushing the bags of camp equipment and clothing
aside. "Looks like you live here," I tell him.*

"I do."

Albert is African American and in his thirties.

I'M A HARD WORKER. I've always worked. I've held jobs in some of the
best hotels throughout Florida. I've cooked for hotels in the Carolinas,
Boston, Massachusetts ... my trade is cooking, but I can do everything
that needs to be done from mucking out a stall to doing masonry and
stuff like that. So it's not the lack of ability, it's just ...being homeless
you're thinking, "Is it because I'm not puttin' out enough effort, or are
the means just not there for me to make it?"

Like I was in Saint Petersburg, staying at this place called "We Care"
when this guy comes through to get workers to pick peaches in South
Carolina. This is in May. So I get on the migrant bus and I come up to
South Carolina with them.

I got caught up there for six months. Picking peaches, potatoes,
cropin' tobacco, picking cucumbers, picking squash. I was working for
like 30 cents an hour because, well, let's put it this way: they paid you

30 cents a bag for peaches. You pick 80 bags a day, and 30 times 80 is $24. And some days I would only pick 50 or 60 bags—so let's say on average I make $20 a day. At the end of the week your room and board was $35. And they had this place, where they served beer and wine, and crack cocaine. The crack cocaine was $35 a hit. The beer was a dollar and a half a can, the wine was $3 a pint. The moonshine was $6 a pint.

The first night I was there they passed out the cocaine, said "Do you smoke?" I said "No." The guy said, "Here, take this anyway." And then at the end of the week he said, "Remember that little package I gave you? That package cost $30." And you're so intimidated—'cause there's two guys standin' there with pistols sticking out of their pants—you don't say nothin'. Then he holds his hand open and says, "You want another one?" And clearly these guys want you to take it—and you've been high anyway—so you snatch it.

Pretty soon I'm gettin' me a rock every night. I'm gettin' me a can of beer every night, I'm gettin' me a bottle of wine and a bottle of moonshine, inviting everyone over to my cabin ... we'd party, get up the next morning and go to work.

So at the end of the week, instead of me drawing a paycheck, I have a balance due of a hundred dollars. I owed them a hundred dollars.

See what they do—a farmer hires what they call a contractor from out of Florida. The contractor goes around the street findin' homeless people, street people from the Salvation Armies, shelters, and rescue missions. They'll say like this here: "We're going to take you to South Carolina, we're going to feed you, free room and board, and you'll make anywheres from $150 dollars a week to $200 dollars a week, and all the money's yours, you don't have to pay for nothin'."

And most of the time when they pick these people up they buy 'em wine and beer, put 'em on the bus and everybody's so fuckin' drunk when they roll in you don't know where you are. Next morning you wake up, look around, say "Where am I?" and a guy's beatin' you on the foot with a stick, talkin' 'bout, "Come on let's get up go to work."

The farmer pays him so much a head—just for gettin' 'em there—they don't go through the state because they get around a lot of bullshit that way. They cut a deal with the contractor and say "I got a land of peaches here." He'll hire the contractor to pick 'em at $1.50, $1.75 a bushel. So the contractor pays you the 30 cents and he gets the rest.

And once you get on the camp—in South Carolina there have been some camps that got barbed wire fences around 'em. And they station guards on 'em at night, to keep the people from goin' out.

And if you try to escape from the camp you're liable to get shot, end up in the pond. I've seen quite a few people get hurt that way. One night a guy tried to leave this farm I've been tellin' you about and before he could get out the driveway with his backpack the contractor had his henchmen show up—his henchmen is like dudes weighing 250 pounds he keeps around to keep the place in order. He unleashed them on the guy and they beat the shit out of him, made him stay.

And the drugs—see the contractor has a trailer, and he has his cocaine there, his wine and beer there, and they pass it right out the trailer to you and write you down in a book.

One contractor so damn nasty, come payday and, say if you didn't buy no wine or nothin' during the week, he'll still write you up say you owe him and take your money.

See, it used to be the contractors were making money off of wine and beer and moonshine. But now that there's cocaine 90 percent of your field workers are hooked on cocaine. And as long as they can get the cocaine they'll do the work.

So if you're not hooked they'll try to get you on it. If you didn't make no money that week, and you owed him all the money, he'd give you a $50 piece, and you're so down and feeling depressed 'cause you didn't make no money, you take that back to your room and smoke that. So next week you've got another $50 bill. $50 plus $35 plus ... you know, so the cycle goes on.

There are inspectors. But when they come they usually pass out wine and beer and moonshine the days before and get everyone so drunk they side with the contractor. And if you get caught trying to speak to the inspector—the inspector ain't going to take you away from there with him, you know—then you're going to be dead meat.

This happens in Georgia, South Carolina, North Carolina, Maine ... see, 'cause when the peaches are done in South Carolina the contractors ship you straight into North Carolina. There you pick potatoes and you crop tobacco. You know, you're digging on your hands and knees, your fingernails be bleedin', scrapin' potatoes out of the ground for 30 cents a bucket. Carry them on the shoulder—a truck runs alongside of you—throw the bucket up and dump 'em. You work from sunup to dark.

Then in Maine ... rainin', just like it rainin' today. And you be out there choppin' broccoli with a paring knife. Throwin' it in a wagon as it goes out. And it gets so fuckin' cold up there. But up there they pay you $3.65 an hour, up there they sort of make sure the contractor is straight up. But what they don't realize is the contractor still has the wine and beer and the cocaine set-up.

But most of what I've been tellin' you about is South Carolina. Then last year I got stuck again. This other contractor came up, offered me a really good deal, said "you'll be driving truck, making really good money," and I thought, "Well maybe this year will be better."

I already knew what the scam was, but I was hopin', you know. And then again he caught me at a really vulnerable time. I was stayin' at a shelter, I was really feelin' shitty and I thought, "Well, this is a way to get out of Florida." And he made me believe him. You know, be a truck driver and all this. And it ended up being the same thing.

I mean this guy ... there were some stray cats there and he would take the cats—they had kittens—and every once in a while he'd throw one to this pitbull he had. I was standin' there and he said, "Watch this." I said "What?" And he took a kitten and threw it to the pitbull. The pitbull grabbed it, shook his head, and killed it. He's standin' there laughin', sayin' "Damn! Isn't he a great dog!" And I looked at him and said to myself, "Jesus Christ, what did I get involved with here?" And I watched out for that guy whenever I could. I kept up this facade, like everything was cool between him and me, and then I high-tailed it out of there the first chance I got.

CHAPTER 3

FALLING FROM GRACE

There is an almost infinite number of events that can push a person or family into homelessness. A murder, a jail sentence, a fire, and the closing of a coal mine are a few mentioned in this chapter. But whatever form the final blow might take, the underlying problem most shared by homeless people is poverty.

We have been slow to accept this fact. Indeed, only now, as research and studies begun in the early 1980s come to print, has the obvious fact that homeless people are but the most abject of a greater population of poor Americans begun to work itself into the larger public consciousness.[1]

The transition has not come easily. Popular notions of income, work, and housing give ground slowly, even in the face of living homeless rebuttals. Thus many people remain surprised to find homelessness among families, veterans, and persons who work, though such people represented significant portions of the homeless as early as 1982. Others stubbornly blame homeless people themselves for the crisis, ignoring societal trends that set the '80s apart from other decades, and the derivative effects of poverty, and other social problems, upon those most affected by them.

Contrary to popular stereotypes of poor people as lifelong indigents, fewer than half of the Americans who fall below the poverty level stay there.[2] The 1980s were no exception and turnover among people living in poverty was high. More people moved into poverty than out, however, and among the poor there was a significant increase in families, children, and people we might consider "extremely poor."

According to government "threshold" levels of poverty, the percentage of the population living below the poverty line increased by 3.8 percent—or 806,000 people—from 1978 to 1983, raising the poverty rate to 15.2 percent. Through 1987 and 1988 the poverty rate leveled off at just over 13 percent, which is roughly where it was before the onset of the current recession.[3]

Much greater, however, has been the increase in extremely poor people. Assuming "extreme poverty" to be personal income below $4,000 a year, the number of extremely poor people is now more than twice as high as it was in 1970—a full 224 percent increase from 1970 to 1987.[4] As Peter H. Rossi has pointed out, if the ratio of homeless people to extremely poor people is considered constant, this increase alone would account for more than a twofold increase in the number of homeless people.[5] Given the current recession, it would also predict a great surge in newly homeless people through at least 1993.

The increase in extreme poverty can also be considered geographically. While only 39 percent of the nation's poor now live in areas marked by high concentrations of poverty (rates greater than 20 percent), most of these people have become concentrated in our large urban centers. While predating the crisis in contemporary homelessness, this trend reached its point of "critical mass" in the '80s when, combined with other societal patterns of the last two decades, it so filled these concentrated pockets of poverty that people began to spill out and into the streets of the broader, urban community. This was particularly true of areas of extreme poverty, where more than 40 percent of the population falls below the poverty line. For Chicago, Detroit, Los Angeles, New York, and Philadelphia, for example, where almost half of all persons below the poverty level lived in 1980, the total population decreased by 9 percent over the '70s, while the number of poor people living in areas of extreme poverty increased by 182 percent.[6]

In contrast to traditional shifts in demographics, this trend accompanied the *removal* of jobs from these very areas.[7] This occurred as our central cities made the shift from goods-producing to service-producing industries, a change that transformed manufacturing centers into hubs of information services. New York City, for example, saw the removal of 492,000 industrial jobs in the fourteen years between 1970 and 1984. Roughly half that many jobs were added during this period, but the majority of these were jobs in the new economy of information and services—one that required significantly more education for career positions, and paid significantly less at the "entry" level.[8]

The obvious upshot of these changes is that there developed a growing mismatch between the economies of our central cities and the work force of their poorer, less educated residents. Together with sweeping reductions in low-income housing, this mismatch pushed great numbers of once-employed people into areas heretofore home to a smaller population of the very poor. This overcrowding engendered violence. In turn, the violence and crowding forced more of the employed residents to leave, thereby increasing the concentration of the very poor.

Another result of this concentration is the extreme isolation that characterizes these communities today. This isolation removes such residents from the larger, urban community, thereby restricting their access to the institutions and networks that form avenues to economic success, thus perpetuating the vicious circle.[9]

This isolation can become inculcated within the community itself. Residents of large housing projects sometimes have trouble recognizing their neighbors, for example.[10] And skid row residents learn early to regard each other with fear and suspicion. In each case the effect of such settings is to heighten the isolation and alienation that those who live in such places already suffer.

Ironically, it is homelessness itself that has begun to erode the isolation of these communities. When the poorest of the poor spill out of such areas, the larger community becomes forced to recognize their presence and accept them as neighbors. This spillover, while emblematic of the great division of our society, creates an opportunity for the kind of reintegration needed to offset the economic dislocation described above. As is demonstrated in "Solutions," the final chapter of this book, the reestablishment of community ties is key to this process.

Other characteristics compound the difficulties of extremely poor people, whether concentrated in our central cities or not. While less likely to have adequate medical care and decent schools for their children, they are more apt to be single parents, to be victimized by crime, to be "precariously housed" in substandard or crowded apartments, and to have few recourses for bettering their situations.[11] In many cities, as many as half of the people who rely on food and medical services for the homeless are extremely poor people "precariously housed" in this manner.

And though our larger cities have received the lion's share of attention concerning such problems, residents of rural districts who find themselves extremely poor are yet more likely to live in crowded and substandard housing.[12] In fact, the rural poor are also less likely to have access to food and other assistance programs than their urban counterparts.[13] Many of these people end up in cities which, like the farm belt they left, no longer need the labor they once provided.

The slip from these tenuous positions into homelessness is often gradual as people lose their livelihoods, homes, and family connections piecemeal. In this way homelessness, whatever its final, precipitating cause, marks our society's point of most abject destitution and isolation, the last stage in the downward spiral of poverty and abandonment.

That this spiral should have gathered breadth and momentum in the 1980s is hardly surprising. Claiming that assistance programs bred patterns of dependency, which locked people into lives of poverty, the Reagan administration came to power seeking drastic cuts in social spending.[14] Ultimately (and together with Congress), the administration dropped a million people from food stamps, nearly half a million families from welfare, and two million children from school lunch programs.[15] Such cuts slashed the resources of low-income individuals and families at the very moment when the trend in employment had begun to crest.

Beyond reducing benefits and dropping people from assistance programs, social service cuts weakened the safety net for those who fell into poverty for the first time. These so-called new poor included more women, children, and previously employed persons than ever before.[16] More numerous, too, were people who fell into poverty through accidents, injuries, crime, violence, and other unforeseen circumstances.[17] Coupled with the rise in income among the very rich, these changes made for the widest recorded gulf between rich and poor American families—a gulf that further heightened the isolation of the poor.[18]

But "poor" is a relative term. The 1980s saw housing costs rise as construction of low-income housing fell and thousands of existing SRO units were removed from the market.[19] Altogether, the supply of low-income housing shrank half a million units for every year of the Reagan administration.[20] Inflating prices for the low-income housing that remained, these trends dumped yet more of the precariously housed and extremely poor into the street, swelling the ranks of homeless people faster than increasing rates of poverty would predict.

Consequently, as many as half of the people now homeless may be "economically displaced," people pushed out of their jobs and squeezed out of their homes by unemployment, underemployment, and the low-income housing pinch.[21] Others are homeless because they can no longer rent a home and buy food on the amount of government assistance they receive. Worse off are those with difficulties compounded by their poverty: people with physical disabilities, mental illness, histories of substance abuse, poor educations, weak social skills, and tenuous family ties. Such characteristics contribute to homelessness among individuals and are a chief cause of chronicity among homeless people. Sadly, they seem also to be perpetuated in families, particularly those with multiple problems. Thus while societal shifts in income, housing, and health care determine how many people become homeless, personal characteristics determine who among the poor is most likely to be affected.[22] Interestingly, no one has yet fully analyzed the degree to which such characteristics are themselves a manifestation of extreme poverty.

Nor has the international nature of homelessness been fully explored. The same period that saw the explosion of homelessness in the United States also saw soaring budget deficits and a huge increase in military spending. These factors, while linked to a domestic policy that gave great momentum to homelessness in this country, exacerbated shifts in the global economy we are yet to fully understand. Indeed, the "new" homelessness of the 1980s was a multinational phenomenon that continues to affect a wide variety of countries with disparate economic and political structures.[23]

Finally, research and data on homelessness can obscure the role of poverty in the problem. One of the most recent status reports on hunger and homelessness issued by the United States Conference of Mayors, for example, lists "poverty or lack of income" as one of six principal causes of homelessness reported by its participating cities.[24] But four of the six—the cost of housing, unemployment, poverty, and inadequate levels of public assistance programs—could be summarized as "poverty." And the final two—mental illness and substance abuse (and the lack of affordable services to deal with them)—are said by homeless people to be associated with the stress and difficulties of their economic situations.

Similarly, poverty—and the isolation it engenders—forms a common denominator for the narratives that follow. Each is set into motion by a distinct event, but each reaches the street for the same reason: lack of money or other resources of assistance.

Understanding the balance of personal and societal factors that create homelessness for these people is a delicate act of framing specific stories within larger social and economic contexts. Fortunately, the achievement of this balance is a common feature of human life: it occurs each time we sit across from someone, open our minds, and listen.

Molly
Bremerton, Washington

I roam amid the buildings of a housing project, searching for the unit that houses a cooperative shelter for women. Three young girls tag along beside me, each sure that she knows where it is. Finally, matching my map with building numbers, I find the shelter and knock. Molly lets me in to an apartment dark with thick curtains.

Molly is in her late twenties. She is tall, white, and broad shouldered. Strong. "Let's talk outside," she suggests. "It's such a nice day."

I WAS ADOPTED and raised up in Gary, Indiana. I got two horses back out there. I've been in Washington State, let's see — three years January 31st. My adopted dad had a heart attack—that's what brought me out here—and I just kind of got into a rut.

And I want to go home. Every time I get down like this— this is the second time in two years I've been down this far. The first time I didn't have to stay in a shelter, it was because of what happened to a friend — and I usually have a job, I usually got more than I've got now. But since I've been here I have gone completely down.

People would think a big town like Gary would be rougher than a little town like Bremerton, but it's not. Yeah, we've got all kinds of people back home, too. But I have seen more violence here, and I have had more violence done to me here, than I ever heard of back home.

I came out here to see my dad. He had his heart attack here and was in an intensive care—a cardiac unit. I walked into his hospital room and he looked at me and he goes, "What are you doing here?" It just, that really freaked me out. I mean I had come out to see him, because of the heart attack.

So I left. I went to downtown Bremerton and walked into this restaurant and met this girl. She goes, "Well, how long you been here?" And I go, "Oh, about seven and a half hours." And we talked and talked and talked and talked. The next thing I knew we were roommates.

Two days later I was raped by a guy who said he was an ex-deputy sheriff. He pulled into this service station just as I was trying to walk across, jumped out, and pulled a gun. He told me either to get into the car or he was going to kill me.

He took me out someplace — raped me, beat me — bragged about being an ex-deputy sheriff. Coming back he pushed me out of the car over these railroad tracks when he was doing about 35 miles per hour. The police found me wandering around and took me to the hospital. I told them everything about the guy. They did a sketch of him and everything, but nothing ever came of it.

But my roommate, she helped me through this. She was a friend. We were real close, and we'd only known each other a little while. I mean we thought alike. We didn't never argue like women do, we sat down and discussed things. She wouldn't say, "Let's do it this way." She'd say, "Hey, can I make a suggestion?" And I'd say, "Yeah" and we'd sit down there and we'd think about it and talk about it, discuss it. We'd discuss the good points and the bad points, and then we'd make our decision from there.

Then I was workin' one night and the police came and told me she was stabbed in our apartment. Someone told me they heard it, said it sounded like a woman was screaming. Then it got real quiet and they heard the door open and they looked out and saw this guy shutting the door. The police went over to investigate and had to kick the door open. They found her in the room, stabbed to death. They still haven't caught the guy who did it. They don't know for sure but they think he was in the Navy.

I went through a lot of changes behind that. I felt guilty, because it wasn't me instead of her. And if I had been home it wouldn't have happened. Both our names were on the lease and when I went up to the office to get her name off the lease—that was the hardest thing I ever had to do.

I left and went to stay with my mom. It was supposed to be until I got my paycheck, but my mom and I do not see eye to eye on anything, and in three days I was a nervous wreck. I'm twenty-seven and they treated me like I was seven—they forgot to put the twenty in front of the seven.

I got other jobs. I was a bartender, a grocery store clerk, a nurse's aide, a telephone operator in a motel. But it started wearing on me after a while. It just seemed like anybody say anything to me and I'd just bust out and start crying.

And I let people start moving in with me. They'd say, "Molly, I'm down and out and on my luck. Can you let me crash here?" And I said, "Yeah, sure," cause I had a two-bedroom apartment still. And sometimes, you know, I didn't want to be alone. But the more people I let stay with me, the more my stuff would be going out the door. I had my color tv, my stereo, all my clothes, my own place, and I lost it all. And then work, you know, I just couldn't keep it together.

Then I met this guy who lives here in government housing. He said I could stay with him till I got back on my feet. He was an older guy, a disabled veteran, and I thought, "Well, I don't have nowhere else." Only he started hounding me. And drinking.

Then one night I was lying on the couch and he came in, drunk, and started talking to the dog. He's pettin' the dog and he starts sayin' "Looks like I'm gonna have to rape Molly. Yup, gonna have to force her legs open and rape her."

I got up like I had been asleep and didn't hear him and went to the kitchen, told myself it wasn't gonna happen again! I got a butcher knife and kept it behind me. I would'a run only I didn't have no place to go! Luckily, I didn't have to fight him. He'd drank too much and by the time I got back out into the living room he'd passed out.

I found this place and got out of there as soon as I could. Now I talk to some of these young girls around here and they say he messes with them.

And I hope you put something in your book about these places, these shelters for women. Because if it wasn't for the women here I don't know what I would have done. I mean where would I have gone? Places like this, they do so much good.

Coal Miner's Daughter
Roanoke, Virginia

She sits on a dusty couch in a dark corner of a shelter and smokes. White, aged, and nearly blind, she seems to focus her gray, tired eyes some distance beyond me as we talk. "I've had jus' about everything happen to me," she explains. "But I never thought I'd end up here."

I'M FROM WEST VIRGINIA, old coal mining town—way back in a coal mining town. 'Course I've been here since 1963, in Roanoke. You know where Switchback, West Virginia, is? Well you go down, like you goin' into Bluefield, and you go down through Bluefield into the old coal mining towns. Very small places.

My father was a coal miner, and he was a drunkard. My mother had eight children to raise, and she took in boarders to feed us. On the farm it's not easy. So I reckon that's the reason I respect these shelters more than most do. I was brought up the hard way and know how hard it is to take care of what you're provided with.

My father was sent to prison when we was real young. My mother did all the takin' care of everything. It made me think, I wanted to get out and make somethin' of my life. I liked to be a tomboy. I reckon them was my good days. I remember goin' around the depot, pullin' on little overalls, and goin' up and down the track like I was the conductor. Or I could go out there on those crates and play in the coal.

As a matter of fact, the black and whites there looked almost alike. I reckon that's the reason I get along with black people so well, 'cause I was brought up in a coal mining town where everybody was black with the coal. I went to school with black kids, eat with them, played with them, and when our daddies came out of the coal mines they all looked alike. That's something my mother always taught me: never be prejudiced—we all come here one way and we're all goin' out the same too.

But it's always been pretty hard here, especially in the Hoover days. That's when there just wasn't no work for the miners and we had to live on what you now call salads and beans. That was Hoover days back then. Once anybody experience that they know what it is to come to a shelter and have somethin' handed to 'em free. You really can.

But as years went by I went on my own. Just like most everybody, I wanted somethin' better out of life—and found out it wasn't any better. There wasn't anything better out of life, though people think there is.

I got married and that didn't work out. I was real young. I went in the service, tried to make it my life, the service life. But that didn't work out. It just wasn't suited for me. I had a brother there, and they came and told me that he was missing in action. That's what really put the fuse off. So I went out on my own, over the fence, that's what you call it. AWOL.

In '71 I was married again; lost my husband in '78. Remarried once more in '85 and now, since '85, seems like hell's broke loose for me. No work. Drinkin', me and my husband both. I'm almost 80 years old. And now I'm here.

I walked into this church and I never was so shocked in my life. It's more like this bad flood we had when I was girl. People layin', beds everywhere. Made me think a bit.

But now at my age, it's very hard. I'm disabled, permanent arthritis, all through my body and my legs. All crippled up in one leg. And it's goin' up in my back and off into the body. And that's permanent.

Some's died out that used to mine the coal. You know, the ones that had to do it to raise a family. But there's still coal, it's just so dangerous. And once you get black lung you got it for the rest of your life.

'Course I guess it'd be different now because them days—I know when my daddy's leg was cut off, it was nothin' compared to now. Now you get somethin' permanent when that happen, to go on. In them days it wasn't like that.

But people still marry, start havin' kids when they're so young and everything, say they'll just work harder and it'll all be okay. Then when it isn't they drink, tryin' to cover the past I reckon. They try to drink and forget, but it don't work out. You got the same problem next day. Always been that way for me.

Batman
Roanoke, Virginia

Batman wears a face deeply scarred with the hazards of prison and street life. Barely 30 years old, he is a testament to the ease with which a jail term can become a life sentence of homelessness.

Batman is white; he makes his home in and about Lexington, Kentucky. Another portion of his narrative appears in the chapter "Life on the Street."

I WAS BUSTED in Daytona, Florida. Went down there for spring break when I was 17. Got partyin' with some friends, got drunk, passed out in the back seat of a car they used to rob a drugstore and I'm an accomplice. They tried me as an adult, said, "Well, we got a place for you son and here it is." Three years.

I got out of prison March the tenth, 1982, with $200 and a bus ticket to the Alabama state line. Dropped me off at a rest area. I walked to the next town. But $200 don't last but two or three days. Stay in a motel room, buy your food. It wasn't long till it was all ate up.

So you get out, you pay your price to society. But society acts like it never wants to let you get started again, it always wants to make you live this moment down in your life. I've been out of prison eight years, but you got a thing on your application where it says, "Have you ever been convicted of a felony?" If you don't answer this the federal government can come and arrest you for lying on an application. And if you do answer it's, "Uhmn hmn, I see you've been in jail — I'm sorry sir but the position you're applying for is currently being filled." The people won't hire you, they just ball up the application and throw it in a garbage can. Or there's a sign in the window and I apply for the job and they tell me the job's already been filled. I've had that happen a lot of times.

And it's like — as soon as they find out you've got a record they either tell you to leave town or tell you they're gonna trump-up charges on 'ya if you don't. They say things like, "We're going to have these 43 unsolved burglaries solved within the next month if you don't leave town." I've been told that a number of times.

I mean every little thing that happens—even if somebody breaks a window out in the next town over—if you're an ex-con they'll come and drag you out of bed at 2:00 in the morning tryin' to find out where you was.

Like I was in California when they had that Hillside Strangler thing going on. I got jammed up for that for about two weeks in the LA county jail. 'Cause I was homeless, I had a record, and my record contained violence. I was hitchhikin' down the freeway and they picked me up. Then it was like, "Look here, you cop-out to ten of these murder charges and we'll give you a life sentence."

"What? Excuse me, but did you say life sentence if I say I killed ten people?"

Another time I got stuck in the Madison County jail, in Kentucky, on these bogus charges for driving while intoxicated. I was publicly drunk, that's all. I didn't even have a car. But while I'm there they stick me up in this one-cell block. There was a big drug bust in the jail at the time and they needed a scapegoat to get their anger out on. So I got attacked: lost my bottom teeth; they stomped my back and my rib collapsed, deflated one lung.

They took me to the hospital, put a tube in my lung. While I was there they dropped all the charges on me. Gave me a piece of paper to sign saying they weren't responsible for what happened. I told 'em I wasn't signin' diddly. Got out with another bus ticket and haven't heard anything about it since — get your life almost taken and it's like sayin', "Hey man, you ain't nothin' but a bum. You don't count. You ain't got no rights."

See I'm from a broken up family, so there ain't any help there either. My mom and dad got a divorce when I was ten years old. From thirteen on I've been on my own. Every Christmas, November, something like that, I cruise in for a day or so. Things aren't really cool there anyways. So you go once or twice every couple of years, "Hey man I'm alive. Remember me?"

"Who are you?" [he laughs].

I wanted to go to college, be a teacher, maybe a veterinarian. But your dreams — it's like your life's over, man. It's gone now. I'm thirty years old; I've been on the street for nine years. And it's been downhill all the way.

It's just like they say, a revolving door. Once they put you in they ain't gonna give you a break. One in a million get a break. So you got one of two choices: you either go out and live on the street, or you go back to stealin'. You got a good choice there.

But me, I've got to the point where it don't really matter anymore. I've decided that I don't care if I starve myself, I ain't going back to jail. Nobody give me a job? Okay, I'll eat garbage, live in dumpsters, scrounge — pick up cans all night, cash 'em in next morning and eat that day. Don't look at me like I'm scum 'cause I live that way. I didn't make the rules. And I tell you, I like it a whole lot less than you think I do.

Raymond
Philadelphia, Pennsylvania

Raymond is intelligent, small, kind, and gentle. An African American, he looks 30 but is much older. A scar, distinctly out of character for him, runs like a raised wet welt from his forehead to his chin.

THE MAIN FACT of being homeless is being displaced. I'm a displaced person. I don't really live here, in this shelter. This — how do you say, this level of existence is not my habitat. It's a nonexistence. I don't really live anywhere.

My problem is that I can't apply for anything because I have a problem identifying myself. And the agencies that require the identification do not know how to assist me in obtaining identification. I can't get my birth certificate, my social security number, my high school transcript—and that keeps me stagnated.

I've been to college, I've had all kinds of jobs. But being displaced —well, it's no place for—homelessness gives you no foundation for one thing, it gives you no platform. And then there are the problems of it becoming permanent. You know, it's supposed to be a temporary situation, but not being able to identify myself keeps making a temporary situation a permanent situation. Year after year after year.

This has been going on for nine years. Before that I was going to school. I had my identification as a student, my birth certificate and all that kind of stuff. I'm a veteran too: post-Korea and pre-Vietnam, between '58 and '62. After the service I was studying here in Philly.

I was studying social services—like homelessness—computers and mental health. I'd worked with the Youth Study Center, the United Fund, the Jewish Allied Appeal, the Red Cross, and all those kinds of places, even to the Bowery, where we studied services that were supposed to have reached the homeless there. That was part of our practicum. Now it looks like I got so involved in the practicum that I'm part of the practicum.

Then I was studying religion. After the service I had a scholarship, because my SATS were so high, but I turned it down, thought I needed another year to study religion on my own. A little later I took a break, went to New York again, just to look around. But that situation, my friends and contacts there, had changed. The things that I was involved with were no longer there. So I got on the bus and came back to Philadelphia. But the things I was involved with in Philadelphia were no longer here. People had moved, you know, between semesters, over the summer.

Then my high school burned down and all my records were lost there. I tried to get back into college but the scholarship wasn't there anymore, and I couldn't apply for anything new without my high school records, which had just been burned up. Traveling to and from New York I lost my birth certificate. Now I can't get anything—birth certificate, army records, anything. Even stuff I should be able to get. So since then I've just gone around in a displaced circle.

I assumed the situation would just be temporary, but I was just stranded. Then I started getting into incidents, with kids in gangs who would hassle me. Then I was cut up, and locked up. And the next thing I know my whole previous life had just vanished. And now I'm here, homeless, stranded in this situation of not being able to attain my identification to change my situation. And it's been like that now for nine years.

Hell
Philadelphia, Pennsylvania

Hell has brown hair, round, dark eyes, and a hearty, rasping laugh. She is Puerto Rican and 28. Another portion of her narrative appears in the chapter "Life on the Street."

IT WAS MY FAULT I dropped out, I know it was. Things wasn't right at home when I was growing up. You know, things wasn't going right. If your home life is tough you just, you lose interest in the things that are going to make you into a better person. Like your diploma; I lost interest in that and in going to college. I lost interest in my dreams.

My mom had emotional problems, some type of mental disability, and drug addiction and alcoholism on top of it. And everything that went wrong in her love life, or home life, or anything else, was my fault.

When I left home I was put into different foster homes. But they had their own children and their children were great and I wasn't shit. So I had to—I kept running away from home and everything. And nothing went right.

I was strong, that's all I had. I walked into my own world and now we're doing good. Spain [her partner] and me, we're sort of happy together most of the time. I mean like I get tired of seeing his face every day [she laughs]. I do, and he gets tired of seeing me. He hates the way I wake up in the morning. He says I wake up evil. You know, I figure I'm sleeping, it's peaceful, I don't have to think about anything—no problems, no nothing. And when I wake up, boom! There's our problems all over again. So I wake up cussing him out. 'Cause he's there. If he didn't love me he wouldn't be there.

See I work for myself. We've been homeless—I've slept in shelters with cockroaches you wouldn't believe, I've slept in the streets, the subways, all over. It's been tough, especially if you're a woman. But we have a home now because I showed a friend of mine this abandoned building that I used to rent a room in. He went downtown and he's paying back taxes on it. Since I showed him where it was he lets us stay in it. We did electrical work, put new locks on the doors, new glass in the windows. We've worked hard there.

I have a daughter, she's spunky. She failed first grade, but she's going to pass this year though. Because I did get one good foster parent when I was growing up and she's taking care of my daughter for me. My son, he's two years. About like this [she holds her hand out from her waist]. We call him "He Man." He's big. He stays with his daddy now, while I get the plumbing in my house. When we get the plumbing hooked up then he's going to come stay with me.

For food and stuff we get by panhandling. You know, where people ask people for their spare change? I do that. I do that when I can't get work. I figure it's better than begging for handouts in a dirty shelter or going out here and sticking up somebody, or robbing somebody's store. When panhandling's illegal it's tough, the cops push you along.

And I get robbed as it is; I was robbed the other day of what money and food stamps I had. That left me broke and hungry, and so I had to panhandle.

It keeps crime down, plus it keeps a little money in my pocket. It feeds me on the weekends when the soup kitchens aren't open, and it buys my cigarettes for me. And if I want a beer I buy myself a beer. I'm not robbin' nobody, 'cause I been to jail too. I spent ten months in jail when I was 16. In a woman's prison, you know. That was hard. It was; that was very hard. Most everyone downtown's been in jail at one time or another.

I don't know whose fault that is, it all depends on what they get arrested for. You know, if they get arrested for sleeping in a public area, I call it society's fault. If they get arrested for beatin' up somebody, it's their fault. If they had a bad childhood and threw away all their chances and got arrested for stealin' something, I guess it's their fault—though society sure didn't make it any easier for them.

It all depends on what color you are too. The darker you are, the better chance you got of being arrested. I'm Puerto Rican, my dad's Puerto Rican and my mom's a Chicano. Puerto Ricans come in all colors. A lot of people think I'm white. They say, "What are you doing here?" They look at my man and think he's black. He's every bit Puerto Rican too.

Oh yeah, one last thing. I'm Hell; that's my name. My mother called me that.

Jaime
San Francisco, California

Jaime works at St. Anthony's, a large shelter, soup kitchen, and referral service in San Francisco's "Tenderloin." Born in Mexico, Jaime has lived in the U.S. since the mid-seventies and has been granted resident alien status. He is 35.

THE FIRST TIME I CAME to California it was an adventure. It was "The North." I came with passport for ten days. I lost the permit and everything, stayed in Riverside for actually ten years. You know, like off and on. Going to Mexico and coming back to work. I had pretty steady jobs.

I lost my last job where I was a janitor, supervising these other guys. They found out that I was an illegal alien they had to, well, kick me out. And so I said, "Well what the heck am I gonna do?"

In LA I knew there was a turmoil—assaults all the time, immigration in the factories and stuff, go from LA to Mexicali in a week. Then something kicked my mind and I said, "I'll come to San Francisco." And I did. I came walking. It took me fourteen days altogether.

I came to San Francisco in '81, stayed on the street about two years. In San Francisco everybody tells you the main source of jobs is the restaurants, hotels, you know, all these tourist things. But that's hard if you're illegal. And there is not too much about factories and other kinds of places. The chances are less and less.

I came here all dirty and everything. Then this man at St. Anthony's, he extended his hand. Gave me food and I said, "Free?" 'Cause in Riverside this Mexican-American family teach me that in America there is no such thing. It can't be. And I was like in shock, 'cause I was dirty. I ended up in Chinatown and it's just a bunch of tourists and all this, they see you all dirty, you know, "Oh, look at this guy!"

You sleep anywhere you can. I ended up the first time at Embarcadero Center, by the bushes. I slept like everybody else, the freeway, places like that. I had to come to churches and missions for food. I had to find my way around.

The worst day was when I found out I had lice. There were like five other Mexicans. We were scratching and we said, "What the heck is wrong with us?" You know, maybe the food and maybe this and maybe that. But it was lice.

It's incredible now the number of kids that come here. You know, looking for this—promised land. I never thought there was a promised land because, well, what brought me here was I had problems with my family and I had to get away. It's not the case with these guys from small towns in Mexico. They tell me sometimes they have to work from dawn to night, just to eat. But me, I'm from Mexico City. Now the city is a mess but it's better there than in small towns. So they go from the countryside to Mexico City, and when they find there's nothing for them there they come to the United States. Only it's tougher than they ever think.

And I found out in a hard way that being in groups doesn't work out that much here. Because immigration, they know for a fact that Hispanics like to be in groups. So when they see a group I mean they go get 'em.

But the Mexican-Americans, you won't find them on the street for the same reason. You won't find them homeless. They go with their uncle, or their sister, or whoever, if they have to. They will always get help 'cause there's more togetherness in Mexican families, even those "Born in the U.S.A." [he laughs].

Like I was in Riverside with this Mexican-American family. The youngest son, he was always in trouble. But they always tried to help him out. He had problems, but they went for it, they always welcomed him back. And I can tell you this, I hear many Americans tell about their family and that's not the case with the American culture. I mean you fail and you're gone. That's why they're here [in this shelter]. There is, I guess, less communication and family—togetherness. I don't think there is too many ties in American families. More like me in my family.

And Latinos don't—they'll come here, sure, when they need something. They'll come here for help when they have to have it. But they don't—they want to get by on their own, they don't want to have to need someone else's help. So they do all they can on their own.

Like when I went to Riverside they told me, "Here are the jobs you can have: you can pick, and you can wash dishes." And you know, I want to say I know the situation I'm in, I know I can't do every job. But you don't have to humiliate me either. Just like here on the street, people look down at you already, you already have enough problems from not knowing the language without being looked down on as dirty scum. That doesn't help either.

But when I found out I had lice I felt low. That was the worst. You know, my mother had always said, "You'll go, you can leave, but someday you'll be so low you'll regret it." And she was right.

John
Iowa City, Iowa

John says he "falls into that gray area" of people who "have a hard time working, though they're not quite disabled." Homeless, manic-depressive, dyslexic, living with AIDS—his problems are many. Like most homeless people, it is through the combination of his difficulties, rather than any one factor, that he has become homeless.

Like many homeless people who are gay, John first became homeless as a runaway. He is white and in his thirties.

ACTUALLY, MY FIRST EXPERIENCE of being homeless was when I was 18. I was having lots of problems at school and ended up quitting the second semester of my senior year. It was one of those, "If you're not going to school you're not living in my house." And so I came here.

It was being gay in a small Iowa town and being restless and being lonely. I mean school was a nightmare. It was the most awful experience I could ever imagine. Homeless is nothing compared to the ridicule and abuse I got in school. Constant.

They had this word for me, "Gayboy." It was used as an offensive word. I was a timid freshman and I'd be sitting in the lunchroom, all these hood upper-classmen slimes saying, "Oh there's the gayboy," screaming it so everyone could hear, picking things to throw at me. Going down the hall it would be, "Gayboy, Queer, hey Gayboy!" And being very insecure and not very muscular, not a jock ... I mean I was in home ec., the typical sissy. And being dyslexic, troubles in school, manic-depressive....

I had been experiencing depression since I was a child. I had psychological treatment—my father died when I was ten—and I had a lot of problems in school, but most of it stemmed from my sexuality. I don't know why adults are so afraid to accept the fact that a 10-year-old boy could be homosexual. It's like, "You don't have sex yet, you can't be a homosexual. You must be crazy."

The school actually committed me to a mental institution. They brought me here, to Iowa City, for a year. I wish I could dig up those records because I really don't understand what that period of my life was about. Then I moved back to Cherokee [Iowa]. Learned some coping skills and faked my way through school all those years. And now here I am.

I still think I can work. I'm in that gray area, you know, people that have a hard time working though they're not quite disabled.

Finding a job is the hard part. First, I have to find something where I don't have to write, because writing is a self-esteem nightmare for me on account of my dyslexia. I don't even like to leave notes for people. Then there's the AIDS. I don't feel I have to tell an employer I'm HIV positive—that shouldn't matter unless there's a danger of exposure. But I take AZT every four hours and that's pretty hard to hide. I'd rather be honest anyway. Then I have to go to clinic every couple of weeks, so I have to have those days off. And insurance, hell, I don't even dream of getting covered. But lots of places won't hire you unless they can.

As far as treatment goes, I'm on the State Papers program, which covers me through the University of Iowa. I never have problems with waiting lists, but I have to be here on certain days for clinic. I don't really fear getting cut off because I feel grateful for any medical treatment I get. I guess that's kind of the last thing on my mind. I mean when you don't have a home and don't know where you're going or what you're doing, medical care seems to be the last thing you think about, let alone worrying about how your health is going to be down the road.

And don't think I don't know my situation. I watched a friend of mine, Ron, die of AIDS. He was a dynamic person, one of my favorite people in the world. He was witty, humorous, handsome, you know, kind of an idol. He started coming down to the bar and getting drunk. And his behavior, like he started drooling. He only lasted six months. And it was really freaky because his body never deteriorated, it was his mind. Meningitis—but it affected him like Alzheimer's. He got to the point where he didn't recognize people. He couldn't go to the bathroom by himself. His brain just rotted. That's when it really kicked me in the stomach. "Oh, that's AIDS."

But now, it's like the last of my worries. I mean I would give anything just to be someplace where I feel I'm in control of my own environment, and where I don't have to worry that it's going to be gone. See I just stay with people now, anyone who will take me in until

I find work and a place. And I'm so tired of living in temporary situations. You know, one bedroom to the next, one living room couch to the next. You don't have a choice. It's that or suicide—suicide is always just a convenient device away. I mean if I could rig a tube of exhaust into the back of my car without having to buy anything to do it I'd probably have done it a long time ago. Still might. That feeling of desperation, ready to give up, it's always hanging there. But so far something has always come along that gives me that jerk of hope.

Fortunately I've been able to keep my car. It's the only sense of security I have. At least I have a roof over my head no matter what. It's the one thing I have. It's the only link to freedom. And living in it, sleeping in it, that doesn't bother me. It's payed for; nobody can legally take it away from me. It's kind of weird getting a sense of dignity from a '76 Honda Civic, but I do. These days it's the only real home I have.

CHAPTER 4
RUNAWAY AND HOMELESS YOUTH

Like the homeless crisis at large, the population of runaway and homeless youth has changed as rapidly as it has expanded. Nearly twice as likely as adults to be poor, more than one million of our nation's children now become unaccompanied and homeless each year.[1] Those who work with them describe these youths as increasingly younger and more troubled.[2] In some areas of the country as many as 90 percent may engage in prostitution or pornography.[3] And whereas the homeless youth of earlier eras were largely "runaways," more than half of today's street kids have no home to which they can safely return.[4]

Many of these children are considered "throwaways," kids pushed out of homes or encouraged to leave. Others are "system kids" who flee institutional and foster care, or who are simply the children of homeless families. One youth shelter, Covenant House of New York City, has already begun to serve the grandchildren of teenagers they first housed in the 1970s.

And while the percentage of runaways among street kids is declining, their raw number has also increased. The Florida Department of Law Enforcement now receives more than thirty-one thousand reports of runaways each year, more than triple that received in 1984.[5] While many of these youths live on the street, others return home after long weekends away. Typically, they run from short- or long-term family strife, much of it associated with death, divorce, reconstituted families, communication problems, school, and difficulties occasioned by their sexuality. A remarkable number of them are gay boys who run from harassment in their schools and families to find acceptance and companionship among others like themselves.

Regardless of category, the conditions of life regularly faced by homeless and unaccompanied youth are dire. Contrary to lingering notions of street kids as Huck Finn prototypes or anachronistic hippie/rebels, the vast majority of street youth eke out lives of violent desperation. Staff members of runaway shelters in any of our larger cities commonly speak of addictions, rampant sexually transmitted diseases, rape, homicide, and the tragic mistreatment of the children of children.[6]

Why children and teenagers choose to live in such environments becomes more understandable in the context of what they have left. According to the National Network of Runaway and Youth Services, as many as 70 percent are physically or sexually abused in their homes.[7] Drug and alcohol abuse are likewise rampant in such families. Estimates of "neglect" range as high as 100 percent.[8]

There are few alternatives for such youths. The hardest age group to place in adoptive or foster-care homes, teenagers are more commonly placed in group homes, state hospitals, or detention centers. All too commonly they are mixed with adults, the severely mentally ill, or hard-core juvenile offenders. Placement decisions are frequently made on the basis of resources, rather than a child's needs. Many spend years being bounced from one care setting to another, or are returned to neglectful or abusive families. One Boston-area study determined that half the teenagers in its sample were returned home despite the determination by service providers that it would be "inappropriate" to do so.[9] Small wonder teenagers frequently run from the "system" instituted to protect them.

And street life, for all its dangers, can be alluring. The rush of freedom, drugs, money, and excitement can be both an addiction and palliative for teenagers with much to forget. Prostitution can seem lucrative, as can pornography and the various scams and hustles endemic to street life. And the teens who band together in groups or pool belongings to squat an abandoned building often report finding more love and family in each other than they have ever known.

But even a street family is unlikely to make up for the damage such youths have already suffered. Those who manage to survive the emotional trauma of their lives can suffer neuro-physiological impairment due to injury, substance-abusing mothers, drug use, and inadequate prenatal care. Consequently, many homeless youth exhibit learning disabilities, antisocial behavior, and developmental lags that promise to work against them for the rest of their lives.[10]

We are only now beginning to come to a sense of the adults these children become. Some find work, of course. But others remain in the "system" or turn to crime after maturing and losing the "innocence" so marketable in their early teens.

A few find help and guidance from a friend, service provider, or police officer. Some get back together with their families. Of the rest—hardened, denied any normal sense of growth and development—few stand much chance of entering the "mainstream."

In fact, it has already been determined that homeless adults show a disproportionate chance of having had foster or institutional care as minors.[11] Given contemporary rates of poverty among children, the existing shortage of low-income housing, and the prevalence of drug addiction, violence, prostitution, and crime suffered by homeless and runaway youth, it must be expected that the homeless children of today will be yet more likely to become homeless adults in the years to come.

Lana
Seattle, Washington

Tough, resolute, hurt, Lana is a self-described "survivor." A Native American from Washington State, she shares the most common of runaway pasts: a childhood of abuse and neglect. Lana is in her late teens.

I WAS ADOPTED AT FIVE. I was physically abused by my biological family and then adopted to a Christian family where I was sexually abused for nine years.

When I was fifteen I finally figured out it was wrong and left. I spent from fifteen to eighteen just running around. You know, went to a lot of group homes, went to school once in a while, ran away a lot. Ran away to Seattle, ran away to California twice....

You get lost in the system. People forget you're there. And they move you around so much. I was in almost every single foster family in Skagit County. I've been in CRC's, they're Crisis Residential Centers. You get ten days to stay there, usually, and within that time they're supposed to find you a place to stay. I went back like seventeen times. And if you run away from there you go to a detention center for two days. So that's where I spent a lot of my time, in detention.

I spent time in an institution after I tried to kill myself. My case worker...well, I ran away and my case worker said she was tired of it and going to quit. She was the person I trusted most, you know. And when she said that I tried killing myself. The first time it was just for attention, I just marked up my arms. The second time I was in for three months. It was in Tacoma. I got out one weekend and got a bunch of girls drunk on Mad Dog. You know, I'd been having a hard time but I'd kept it together. Then as soon as I drank I just lost it. I tried to put my head through a window. This lady that was trying to get me not to do it, I dislocated her shoulder, broke two of her ribs.

They made me go back to CSTC, that's a Child Study and Treatment Center. It's a crazy hospital. Their system's so bad they put the crazy people in with the depressant kids. I mean we had schizophrenics there, we had rapists there, all sorts of stuff.

It was never any good. One time a friend escaped. He was running and I was yelling out the window, "Run, run! They're after you!" They put me in this quiet room, just cement walls with a drain in the floor, and shot me up with Thorazine. Under law they're not supposed to do that unless you're being harmful to yourself or others. And Thorazine is really bad stuff. At first it makes you really hyper, and then it makes you real hot, like you want to rip all your clothes off. I had it twice. They did it another time when I assaulted one of the staff.

Next I got out and found my real family, my biological parents. See I'm Indian, and when I went to court over running away from my adopted parents they wanted the Indians to represent me. They had to find out what kind of Indian I was so they got my mom's address and contacted her.

It was awful. You wouldn't believe how bad. So after it didn't work out with my mom and dad I went to Job Corps. It's this vocational school where you live and all this. I didn't make it there either.

They put me on a bus at Job Corps, said I was supposed to go back to this hospital. I was seventeen. I rode the bus as far as Seattle and just got off. A friend loaned me $400 and I got a place to stay. Then it didn't...I ended up on the streets.

I never got into whoring, like a lot of girls. But I got into things, like with crime and stuff. I got into it with a guy who ran this gang. They steal brand new cars and take them to Oregon and repaint them and sell them. He also had a string of whores out on Aurora. He wanted me to start collecting his money from them and stuff. I wouldn't do it.

One night I was on cocaine and drinkin' and I stabbed this guy and almost cut his fingers off. Then I went to a shelter, lived there for a while, went back to Snohomish state, to a foster home. And I would stay like with my dad for two weeks and we would get in a fight and I'd end up back downtown. When I turned eighteen I went to this Young Adults in Transition program and spent two months there. They give you two months to get your act together and, well, I didn't get my act together [laughs], so I ended up back on the streets. And I mean I actually slept in the alleys. And I drank a lot, you know, drank constantly.

Then one night this girl I was going to stay with, these other girls were trying to beat her up. They were drunk and my friend was drunk. She couldn't even stand up and they started dragging her around. I tried to stop them and this girl she hit me, so I put her up against a taxi cab. All her friends then jumped in on me. I ended up in Harborview hospital. They thought they were going to have to restructure my eye socket. I wear scars from that now.

The only thing that finally got me together was a cop. She arrested me and then when I went to court she got me off. She just said, "Well, this kid's changed a lot and she isn't in that much trouble." So they gave me six months probation. If I didn't get in any trouble in that time they wouldn't press no charges. So that's what happened. I seen her again 'cause my friend got raped. We were together and talked for about an hour that night.

I'm off the streets now. It's hard at first because you don't have anybody, you know. At least on the street you have people and you're so scared for your life that the conflict is always making it exciting. And on the street you don't have to live someone else's life.

So it's harder now, trying to get my life together, to go to school. I don't drink at all now. Can't. I gotta make it this time 'cause I'm pregnant. I was working up until my sixth month but I couldn't keep my job after that so I'm on welfare.

After having my baby I'm going to work with a play at the Orion Center [a drop-in resource center for street teens in Seattle], we're doing "West Side Story." After that my EMT—Emergency Medical Technician—class comes up in the spring. I want to take that and then, when I turn twenty-one, I plan to go back to the reservation to become a tribal cop. Later I'll move back here and become a Seattle PDP. The state and my tribe will pay for my education.

I want to work with kids and show them, "Hey you can do it!" You know, give them an incentive. But I don't want to have to be there all the time. See, I don't want to become a DSHS worker or a social worker. I don't want to have to be there all the time. I've been damaged in too many relationships where it was supposed to be long-term and it ended up not being long-term and it was ... it hurt. No, I want to be a cop.

See this cop helped me figure it out, 'cause when this girl scarred my eye I wanted to go and slice her face up. And she said "No, let the law do it." So I did, you know. And I see now that if I had cut her I'd have ended up in the same place she is now. She helped me realize that.

There was one kid, I met him at the YMCA. He was twelve. Twelve years old, runnin' down in the streets. The thing about it was that he was so much like me. He needed love. He needed someone to reach out and say, "Hey, I love you for what you are. Who cares if you're a renegade." Just someone to recognize him. That's what I tried to do for him. But this kid, he's already gone. All of a sudden he just disappeared.

I've always been a survivor. I almost died when I was a child, but I didn't. I've always survived. I was always going to show everybody else, show 'em I could do it. And it was just, "You fuck with me and I'll kill you." I was born that way, born a fighter. Some people are born a fighter, some people learn to be fighters, and some people just don't have it at all. Those are the kids that don't make it.

There was a girl that used to come here. She wanted to die. There was nothing—you could lock her up in a hospital and she would die anyway. She didn't want to live. She wasn't just crying out for help, you know. That's the thing: if you don't catch it by that point you can't stop it. You can't turn that around.

That girl, she shot herself. And you know that kids are serious about killing themselves if they use a gun. But pills, you know, or cutting your veins or something, you don't really want to die. You're hoping someone catches you. I know; I did it. I would never have shot myself in the head, but I cut my wrists up. Another time I took pills.

See, the people I've seen killed or hurt, it's because the other people are hurting. Inside. It's not because you need money, or food—you got enough places to eat down here. It's more the hurting. People downtown don't need to be fed, they need to be loved.

You're downtown and people they...business people, they look down on us. You see white people looking at you like you're scum, and you just want to turn around and shoot 'em. The things that I have seen, the people that have gotten killed, or beat up, the people who were drinkin', drugin', whatever happened down here, it was 'cause people were hurting.

Like I had a friend that killed someone downtown. She got raped and I helped her go to the hospital. Then we got in a fight this one night. We were drinkin' and she picked up a bottle to hit me and I layed her flat on the ground. About three weeks later I find out she's killed a girl, strangled her to death. It happened in one of those programs where you can sleep the night. She was angry at the world.

Rape's different. You got rape from the tricks that don't give the girls the money and rape 'em, and then you got the guys that force it on you. It happens down here mostly over drugs and drinkin'. Girls get too drunk to defend themselves, you know, or they get in a car 'cause they want a place to stay. Me, I was drinking at this party and these guys took me out on this hill and raped me. Both of them.

It all starts when you're young ... everything starts when you're young. Like I remember being abused. I remember it all the time. I would be in bed with them when they were supposedly making love, having sex. Or I would come in to see them and then it would happen. She physically abused me but he totally abused me. Physically and sexually. He was a pervert.

But I've learned a lot. I've learned about my heritage, I've learned singing, how to sing Indian. I can do a lot. I'm proud ... I'm proud of my heritage. You know, I just decided that I was going to get off the streets. And there was someone there for me, to be tough with me. Now I live with the director of another street youth program. I'm stayin' with her.

But it gets scary. Before it didn't matter if I did it, if I made it off. Now I have to do it; I've got another life. I don't want my baby to see what I've seen. I don't want my baby to go through the hurt ... of what I've seen ... the hurt that I've had to overcome. And I want my baby to be able to accept love. Sometimes I can't. And that's ... real hard. You see, I don't think I'll ever be able to marry, to have a long-term relationship. I'll always be single. I've been hurt too much, especially when I was down. I know that about myself. I can't. Not anymore.

Martin
Seattle, Washington

Like many homeless teenagers, Martin is gay, having first run to find more people like himself. Once downtown the excitement, drugs, and money became as alluring as the new freedom he'd found there. Martin, now 18, is an African American.

I WAS SIXTEEN when I first went downtown. I had a friend I was goin' to school with, then I didn't see him for like eight years. Then I seen him and he tells me about downtown, so I started goin' down there. I was gone every weekend that first year.

I was gay back then but I didn't know any other gay people. He was gay and we went down there and all these other people were gay. It was mostly just findin' other people like me. I started to go to the Monastery [a night club] and then that place like closed down. I'd do drugs. I did MVA, people say it's a sex drug, but it's like speed. Then I did acid, and like total speed—seein' all these people, all the stuff that was goin' on. God, I just couldn't believe it. People gettin' robbed, people havin' sex all over, people gettin' robbed while they were havin' sex.

And then I started prostitutin'. I remember my first night. My friend Larry said I could get easy money just goin' in and talkin' to a guy, lettin' him do stuff. And so this black car pulls up and he says, "Get in, girl, he likes black guys." He drove around about four times, and then I got in.

I drove around and talked to him for about an hour. I said this is my first time and he said, "If this is your first time I don't know about this."

But pretty soon he said, "How about forty bucks?" So we went to his place. He was friendly but he was an old man, in his mid-forties.

But see when I was first doin' it I was stayin' at home. I was goin' to school Monday through Friday. And then Friday when I'd come home from school I'd go out, go downtown, and not go home until it was time for school Monday.

Then my dad wanted to take me 'cause my mom told him what I was doin' and stuff. So I stayed with him for a month and went to school. He did this to me [he points to a long scar on his face] and I went back to my mom.

Back then I'd get out of my mom's apartment, see my friends and leave for about four days. My mom would see me and say to me, "Martin, let me look at you. Martin, you need to come home and take care of yourself." I did that for about a year and Mom got tired of it. So she said, "You're gonna stay home or you're gonna stay out in the streets." So I moved out into the streets.

I remember the night I made the most money. I started knowin' men I'd see regularly. So this night I'd see one, jump out, run over to my friend. He'd say, "Girl, check out who's here." Then I'd see another one, go see him. Then I'd see another one. I seen three of 'em that night; I had $125. And then that never happened to me again.

I've met some nice men down here ... some guys get fortunate and they get a sugar daddy—that's an old man who'll pay for your apartment. And you do sexual favors, or keep his house clean, something like that. Most of 'em want somethin'.

Then, well my friend Larry who I was tellin' you about? The one I hadn't seen in six years? Well, one day he left his school bags over at my house and then went on downtown. And two days later my mom was sayin', "Martin, isn't that your friend—what's your friend's last name? I think he got killed." I didn't want to believe it. She showed me the article and I just freaked out. I had to go over to his mom's house and bring his bookbag and things ... he got shot, five times in the head ... I don't even know what for.... I always thought I was different but I could never really tell. They wanted me to go to ... uhmn, psychiatric help.... [He pauses long and thoughtfully, then continues.] My friend Larry, I seen some guys charge him and take his clothes, leave him downtown with no clothes. He had a Guess outfit on: jean pants, jean jacket with leather patches all over it. They took it right off him. How could someone take the clothes off a person? Then he got killed ... another time I seen these two guys get in a knife fight, and this one guy got killed ... that was the first person I've seen dead.

Then I got busted, for prostitution. I had to get checked [for venereal disease], 'cause ya got to worry about that, too. But now me and my friends, we be sayin' to each other—'cause we tell each other everything, who we had sex with and what we did, everything—we'll come up to each other sometimes and say, "You guys, let's not have sex for two months." Then maybe one of the other two will be honest and say, "Chile, I already had some last night," or somethin' like that [he laughs].

But we try to keep each other safe. Come and get rubbers—I'm good for that. I'll walk around and give everybody a rubber. I'll say, "Girl, what are you doin' tonight?" If they say, "I'm gonna look for some fun!" I'll say, "Well try this."

At first I didn't like using one but now, hey I know that's going to save my life one of these times. I'm gonna put it on the right one and that's going to be the one that's gonna save me.

But see some men, they don't like 'em. I'll pull 'em out—sometimes I'll be funny and put three out that're different colors and say, "All right, choose your flavor," something like that. Then they'll probably say, "You want to use that?" I'll say, "Yes sir." They'll say, "I don't like them, you don't get the real feeling." And I'll say, "Well, you just have to get used to 'em."

Tony
San Francisco, California

> *"I don't keep track of the hard times. I don't keep track
> because as I went along I just kept goin'. Not too much thinking
> back in my past, not too much thinkin' in my future, I just kept
> goin'. I mean there are times in my life when I sit down and
> think, Was it all worth that? But then those times don't come
> up too often. I do a lot of what you call puttin' it on the back
> burner and leavin' it there. 'Cause I try to keep goin'."*
>
> *Tony, now 25, is an African American. Another portion of his
> narrative appears in the chapter "Work and its Discontents."*

THE WORST TIME I've had was sleeping in the rain. Sleeping in the rain
when I was thirteen years of age. It was the first night I was ever
homeless.

I was going to Treasure Island, that's a school. It was bussing time
and they had to bus us. A good friend there said "Come and visit me,"
and I said "Sure," and went down to see him. When I got back home I
got whipped with an extension cord. That's when I decided to run
away.

I'd sleep in places that ... little doorways, or a crack in the side of a
wall where trees would block me. But that was my worst time: that first
night when I first ever met downtown San Francisco, being rained on.
I slept right in the rain. I woke up being rained on and I just went back
to sleep.

Momma wanted me to take care of my sisters, to feed them, and also
to go to school. I was a house slave and I was only ten years old. My
mother did some work, I'd say minor work. But she did a lot of foolin'
around. I mean she'd go out and party just like everybody that lives up

here [he sweeps his arm, indicating the upper-class neighborhood]. They go out to these little pizza places, party, drink their beer—that's the same as my momma did.

I was doing all the work: cook, clean, change diapers—there were three girls—and also go to school. When did I have time to myself? I was ten years old.

So at thirteen I decided to walk away from home. I got picked up by a police officer, picked up because I was a runaway. They took me to juvenile hall, on the top of the hill. They called it Beyond Parental Control.

So then I became a ward of the courts. That's when I learned a lot about the city. I mean I was in boys' homes, foster homes, group homes. After my last foster home I ended up back out here. I'm back where I started, on the street. The only difference is now I got a little knowledge. I didn't have any the first time. But I wouldn't want to do it all over. Not on my life would I want to do it all over again.

The hardest part was going through the group placements and foster homes. Did you ever see a ball bounce around from one person to the next person? That's the way I felt. Once I wanted to move in with an ... oh, how do you say ... with a Caucasian family, in a foster home. My social worker said I couldn't because they only lived around white folks. I wasn't worried about that, I can handle myself no matter where I'm at. The family was fine with me ... they wanted to take me. But my social worker said, "Oh no, no." It made me mad. Not only mad, it made me take off and I ran away again.

The only time I didn't feel like that, like a ball bouncin', was when I was fifteen. That's because I went back to a group home that kept me. They said, "OK, you can stay with us." Originally I wasn't supposed to stay. I liked it there. They made me comfortable.

I stayed with them until they were going to move me to another group home. That's the way the system work, the system make you bounce around so you don't get used to one place.

It was the night of the Beach Boy concert. I was supposed to go to the concert but instead I came back over here to the city. I went to this place, between a halfway house and a hospital. I was sixteen. I wanted to leave the placements, foster homes, all of that. I didn't go back to one until I was seventeen, after I'd been to Napa.

Napa is a state hospital. I asked them to let me go there. And not because I was crazy. I went there on a volunteer basis. I feel good about that. I was under a lot of stress, a lot of stress. After all this I was real fast, hyperactive. So I went there and stayed a year.

After I got out of there I went to three more places. Three more foster homes, just like I knew I would. The last one I went to was across from Marin, Golden Gate. That's my favorite because I had a good foster mother. She trusted me. She gave me a place to stay and said, "You cook, you feed yourself, and you go to school."

The state was going to pay me to go to school and so I said, "Cool, I'll go to school." I like school. And so I did this for three years. And as I was doing this, the foster mother I had there, we got real close. Even right now, if I wanted to go all the way over to Marin County and talk to her, see if I can stay back in her place, I can do that. That's because she's nice and, aside from me being a soft person, I do handle responsibility well.

But I've changed from there to over here, and it gets a little difficult. I mean try to leave San Francisco and go back over there after you've been out in the streets for a few years. I know that sooner or later I have to leave the streets. I know what the homeless got to live through; it makes you old, being out here. But I've got to do it myself, I can't just ask to move back in with her.

Some people think all homeless people are the same. I go through it every day, having them look down on me. But I can only say some. There's others—like I came up here this morning and this guy, he was saving me some cans. He knows I'm trying, he knows I'll try anything to do better than stay out and down here.

Billy
Minneapolis, Minnesota

Billy's clothes are big, as if bought to grow into: stone-washed jeans and jacket, unlaced high-top basketball shoes with pink laces. Her hair is straight and fine; she clears it from her face by leaning back and shaking it behind her shoulders as we talk.

Billy is 16 but looks younger. In her short life she has been a drug addict, mother, and a runaway. Billy is white; at the moment she lives with her own mother.

MY MOM, SHE KICKED ME OUT of the house. I was doing drugs: blue pyramid acid, mickeys, cocaine—B ball rocks—hash, speed, uppers, downers, all-arounders. But then I got off drugs; only she didn't believe me.

I remember I came home and I was playing with this pen, tapping it on the table. She didn't like that so it made her mad and she said, "Why did you have to go to that drug place?" [a rehabilitation center].

"'Cause you told me."

"No I didn't."

"The hell you didn't! ..."

We were arguing like that so I went to my room, smoked a cigarette, came back. She thought I had been smoking pot. I told her it was just a cigarette but she went back in my room anyway, looked around. Didn't believe me. Got pissed off some more. So I left.

I went back later and asked if she was cooled off. She said no. I told her I really wasn't doing drugs anymore—at least then anyway. But it didn't do any good.

She was still pissed so I went upstairs and my sister came in my room. She said I had taken this thing of my mom's, but I didn't. She told me to give it to her and I said, "I don't have it!" Then she started hitting me, beating me. I was screaming and hitting myself...a nervous breakdown. When I was done I sat balled up in the corner of the room, rubbing my temples for hours; I remember they were raw. When I was coming out of it I called the cops and they took me to the hospital.

When I got out I moved in with my dad, but he beat me. I moved out, had a baby, gave it up for adoption, and moved back with my mom. When you're that young you can barely provide a place for yourself, not for another life.

But my mother was a little whore. There were ten guys and one or another of 'em was always over. After they were done with her they'd come to my room. Once I woke up with this guy on top of me, all drunk. Man, did I scream. They don't bother me now 'cause I have a guard dog, my little brother. He's thirteen but he's big. He's got muscles and he can fight. All I have to do is call him.

But I still couldn't live with her so I ran. The first night I ran I was scared. I was so scared I got three friends to run with me. We got a ride out to this bridge where we hung out. Then the cops came and found us, took two of the girls home. Me and the other girl walked seventeen miles home.

I've been in temporary homes, foster homes, shelters, everywhere. They can't control me if I don't want to be there. This one foster lady, she didn't want me to leave, was trying to talk me out of going. She said she wouldn't let me go. I spit in her face and just left.

Another time I lived with my uncle, but that didn't work out either. Then for quite a while I lived in this parked van. Or I'd stay with a friend or just stay up all night. I never had to sleep, you know, in the street. But the question "Where would I stay?" was always with me. Somehow it always got resolved, but it gets you down, worryin' and carryin' that with you all the time.

The only good times then are when you're on drugs, trippin' on acid and drinkin' at a keg. It's fun then 'cause we're free of all our problems: free of our parents and all our pressures. Just to forget about it all, kick back stoned in a red room, and feel like you can just flip out for the rest of your life.

Our parents don't care. We go to friends and other people and they teach us things. Some parents are so fucked up. I have this one friend and her mom goes shopping late at night. When we're there we have to get up and go with her. She says that's when all the single men are shopping. She'll be shopping and she'll look at some guy and say, "Uhmn hmm! He's sure got a nice ass." She does this like all the time.

But another friend, her mom and dad are great. They taught me how to do laundry. Now I'm a clean freak. I wash everything. I come home, do the laundry, and my mom says, "Who taught you how to do laundry?" She's all pissed 'cause someone else took the time to teach me.

But these parents of my friend's I was telling you about, we want parents like that. Parents that would let you decorate your room anyway you want, and who wouldn't bite your head off if you brought a friend home. Parents like that. Yeah. My dream is to have my mom raised by my friend's parents.

CHAPTER 5

VETERANS

The homeless American veterans who regularly converge on the capital as part of demonstrations demanding housing and job assistance for the homeless are by no means the first to do so. Contrary to accepted notions about the benefits of military training, and the patriotic respect and care with which we like to imagine we treat our veterans, American veterans have been overrepresented among the homeless and unemployed since the 1700s.

Demonstrations by homeless veterans followed the Revolutionary and Civil wars, as well as World War I. Unable to pay whole regiments of the men responsible for our revolutionary victory, George Washington faced several contingents of poor and rebellious soldiers. In one particularly gruesome instance, Washington sent six hundred federal troops to crush a demonstration of some two hundred veterans.[1] After being overwhelmed and disarmed, the veterans were forced to execute their own leaders. Washington called it "an example."

A hundred years later, Civil War soldiers from both armies foraged their own way home from the war as transients. Some of them remained homeless for years. And following World War I, MacArthur led troops against some twenty thousand homeless and destitute veterans who had assembled on the outskirts of Washington, D.C. Their demand? Federal assistance they had been promised.[2]

Fortunately, economic growth and new federal programs reduced homelessness among veterans following World War II. By 1982, however, veterans were once again overrepresented among homeless people. In 1987 New York City mayor Ed Koch urged President Reagan and the Veterans Administration to find shelter for the twenty-five hundred veterans he calculated were among the homeless of New York City.[3] A Long Island City shelter for veterans opened later that year and was overrun with requests for housing and services.[4]

Today service providers throughout the country report high concentrations of veterans in shelters and food programs. In Florida one group of more than sixty homeless Vietnam veterans live together in a forest encampment. Others have taken up residence in a wilderness area of Washington State. And veterans of Desert Storm have already begun to appear in soup kitchens and shelters. Overall, veterans are generally considered to constitute one-third of all homeless men.[5]

Given the increased range of educational, health, and disability benefits offered veterans, and the preferential treatment they receive in civil service employment, figures half as large would be remarkable. And any substantial figure flatly contradicts popular and recruitment notions of the military as a springboard to jobs and opportunity.

Despite their greater numbers, veterans are homeless for many of the same reasons other people are. Their work histories resemble those of other homeless people, and they share similar rates of substance abuse. Homeless veterans are more apt to be disabled and to suffer chronic health problems, however, and they are more likely to have been hospitalized for psychiatric treatment. White veterans are overrepresented among older homeless men, while black veterans are overrepresented among homeless men in their thirties and forties.[6]

As might be expected, historical explanations for higher rates of unemployment and homelessness among veterans cite the debilitating effects of injuries and emotional trauma caused by war. Less to be expected, it is also argued that veterans fare more poorly due to the educational and job-skill opportunities they miss out on while serving their country. Armed service advertising notwithstanding, military service appears to impede rather than enhance future educational attainment. A study commissioned by the Veterans Administration puts it this way: "Vets tend to hold lower status, less secure jobs than comparable non-veterans," since veterans, regardless of their prior background, are less likely to continue their education than they would have been had they not joined the service." "This tendency," the study notes, "is particularly significant among veterans who served in Vietnam."[7]

And just as conscription laws allowed wealthy patriots of the Revolutionary and Civil wars to hire substitutes or avoid military obligations altogether, Vietnam soldiers were disproportionately drawn from lower socioeconomic classes. Frequently disillusioned, alienated, injured, and three to four years behind their compatriots who did not serve in work experience and education, many poor Vietnam-era veterans returned to find themselves worse off than before the war. Unemployment, substance abuse, rising housing costs, and post-traumatic stress syndrome, among other difficulties, contributed to their hardships.

Consequently, the second quarter of 1982—when homelessness first began to draw national attention—saw unemployment among young veterans approach 18 percent, nearly twice the national average. Unemployment for young minority veterans rose to nearly 25 percent in the same period.[8]

The Veterans Administration also contributed to the homelessness of the era through participation in the widespread deinstitutionalization of the seriously mentally ill.[9] Like those released from state hospitals, some of the veterans who had been deinstitutionalized later became homeless when unemployment, shortages of low-income housing, and cutbacks in federal assistance came to a head in the early 1980s. Unfortunately, the present recession has created the same conflation of factors.

Consequently, and despite eligibility and obvious need, great numbers of homeless and precariously housed veterans continue to receive scant medical and psychiatric care. One Los Angeles study reported that while 37 percent of the homeless in their sample were veterans, no more than 2 percent claimed to be covered by VA-sponsored health benefits.[10] Advocates for homeless veterans blame the VA for such figures. The VA argues that many homeless veterans do not receive services because they have either not applied for benefits or can no longer substantiate military service.[11]

Of course, no one is homeless because he or she is a veteran. And the role of military service in homelessness is best understood in terms of all the factors that have worked to bring about the present crisis. The high rates of homelessness among our veterans warrant specific attention, however. And it should also be noted that many homeless veterans view their military service as much more than simply one of many precipitating causes of their present difficulties.

Stacy Abner
Washington, D.C.

Stacy sits beside the main visitors' entrance to the Capitol. He sits in a chair, a large sign next to him explaining that he is an injured WW II veteran who can get no assistance from the government. He lives in the corridor that runs underneath the main steps. Which is to say, he lives there until he is arrested. Once released from prison, he returns to resume his protest. Stacy has lived this way for thirteen years.

Stacy's clothes are neat, clean, and worn. His hair gray and short. He wears an expression of intense, firm anger and is an African American in his early seventies.

I THOUGHT I WAS a United States citizen till I went to the army and find out I'm a slave.[12] Stayed over there three years and three months, had rheumatic fever, high blood pressure, heart trouble. Had something else they called dropsy then. Had gout. That was in '44.

Then when I got 39, 40, 41 years old, my ankles, hands, and wrists would swell up, my knees would swell up and the doctor would have to draw water off 'em with a needle. 'Said every time he had to draw water off, my health would go down and down. 'Said if I wanted to keep my knees I had to leave off tryin' to work. I went to another doctor and he told me the same thing. All these doctors sayin' this and the army wouldn't give me no help.

Just like Russia said. Everything he said is true, true, true! He told Roosevelt, he said his mens wasn't goin' a'fight 'side of no slave. If slaves were gonna fight—and he knew Roosevelt was usin' 'em—he didn't want no part of it. 'Cause he said wars are not for slaves, wars are for free people, for people who fight for their own country. The slave ain't got no country. He gonna be a slave when he go, he gonna be a slave when he come back. What has he gained?

This was in 1943. LeGaule, he didn't have no country to rule if he had been the ruler: Germany had France—and just about had England too. Both of 'em, LeGaule and Churchill, they was just representin' France and England. Both of 'em became elected after the war ended. They needed Russia. And they all practically cried like babies and begged like coons for God knows how long before they could change his mind.

Roosevelt told him he couldn't free us, said if he didn't send MacArthur some he was gonna lose Okinawa, said, "I have to send him more soldiers, black and white." Then Russia said, "Well if they're so important then you free 'em." He said, "I can't free 'em, I'd have to call everybody home from Europe to Mississippi to control the race riots," said this and that.[13]

And now, 44 years after the war, everything Russia said is the truth, the whole truth, nothin' but the truth. Stalin of Russia. The only difference now is it's worse 'cause they says we're free and we're not. The only difference between me and an animal is I've been treated a whole H-E-double-L worse than an animal, for 44 years, by the United States of America.

There's a lot of pain, misery and sufferin' in wars—pain, misery and sufferin'. What we do all that sufferin' for? I went through there with pains, aches and pains, with all these diseases, workin' and sleepin' and fightin' with these diseases. I'd like to die several times. And what did I get? Nothin'.

I've been kidnapped and sent to jail twenty, thirty times for standin' out here, and ain't no law been violated. It against the law to stand on the steps of the Capitol building? It against the law to carry a sign in this country? Now if I ain't no slave what am I? You get three years for kidnappin' a monkey, but kidnap a black man and nothin' happens. A negro can kill a negro and go to his funeral. *You* can kill one and nobody do nothin' about it. What you kill? A man? He ain't nothin, he a slave. Shit, we still "skills." Why you can't even kill squirrels and possums all seasons, but you can kill a slave twelve months 'round.

I just came out of jail, forty-nine days. Kidnapped, right from here. Convicted, a hostage. Sent to jail! I was standin' here in front of Congress, and they come and say I had to stay off until the president come in and make his state of the union. Well, I'm not good enough, I'm not fit enough to be around here...I was protestin', I was demonstratin'. And no, I wouldn't leave. Hell, he the man I'm protestin'.

Roosevelt, he passed a law, make me go over there ... If I didn't I could go to jail, and that just same as shootin' me down like I was a rabbit.

But I went to my draft board, I served my country, I fought, I helped save this country. I worked and slaved and fought. Jumped up all through the nights, duckin' and dodgin' bullets and bombs, goin' out with nothin' but your shoes on, and sometimes you didn't have time to put them on. Six and eight inches of snow, duckin' and dodgin' bombs, fragments. Tryin' to stay alive.

Now my G.I. rights says anybody that went to the army and stayed ninety days, anything that happens to him in one year after he come out is "service connection." Now how come all these diseases I just told you I had, and suffered with for three years in the army, how come they're not "service connection?" And how come I can't get soldier disability, service disability? I suffered from them when I was in the army and I'm still sufferin' from 'em. Can't work because of 'em. And I haven't got any assistance since, to be specific, January 14, 1946. How come? 'Cause I'm a slave. Three years, three months, and eight days. Went all the way through England and France, Belgium and Germany. Got back home and weren't nothin' but a bunch of tramps and bums.

The doctors I have seen, public health doctors, you know, they tell me, "You need a heart specialist, see one and do whatever he says." But I can't, I can't do none of that 'cause I can't get no VA help. And I'm livin' on street. So I stand out here.

And since I been here a book sergeant, a staff sergeant, a second lieutenant, a captain, and a full-fledged colonel came up to me and told me to do just what I'm doin'. They said, "Your G.I. benefits are yours, it ain't no charity, it ain't no gift."

But all I got for it is seven, eight years in the federal penitentiary, for standin' out here protestin'. That's all the federal government's given me since January 14, 1946. They tell me, "Son, you born with that problem, government don't pay for that. Oh you had that when you went to the army. You was gonna have that if you hadn't went in the army. You got to be wounded, shot, or broken leg, broken arm, your body got to be broke, that's all they pays for."

So I get by now just like Russia said, just like an animal. Just by whatever I can grab and find, what I can get and what people give me. People that I never seen before, never heard of before, they come up and give me a quarter, or 25 cents, or a dollar. And I don't ask 'em, not for money. All I ask is that they read what I have to say. People from Germany, France, they come read my sign, think about it. They say it's a shame, low down dirty shame. People from Switzerland, England, France, all over the world, they say it's the biggest disgrace they ever heard of in their life. Japanese and Germans, they come up and say this country don't have sense enough to take care of its veterans. A Japanese man said to me, "Everybody knows if it weren't for World War II there wouldn't be no such thing as the United States of America."

He didn't say, "we would have it," but that's what he meant. But we stopped 'em from takin' it, we saved it. And we stopped the Germans. And seems like to me they should be appreciatin' people like me.

I've been stayin' right here for the last 13 years, when I ain't been in jail. Sleep here too. Put me in jail again and I'm comin' right back. I want people to know what the United States of America think about you losin' your health helpin' to save a country like this. It ain't worth savin', and it wasn't worth savin' then. Like some of the guys said in Europe, said maybe we're fightin' the wrong people.

Guys would say, "Japan and Germany, they never did nothin' to us, either one of those countries never did have no slaves. America's the only one of the bunch that had slaves, they're the ones we should'a been fightin'." Heard that all through the war: when we was in England, France, Belgium, and Germany, always someone would say it. I was in with a negro outfit. But we had a white lieutenant, a white second lieutenant. How come? 'Cause we all slaves. And all the way from Mississippi, everywhere we went someone would say it. Some even said we should be helpin' the folks fightin' America, that way when we got home we'd be free. They said when we get back home we're gonna be treated just the same as we was 'fore we left—if anything it'll be worse. They was right.

So I stand here in front of the United Sates Capitol. I have a sign, it says "I lost my health in WWII." Crummy heart, gout, can't get no help from the US of A. But I'll stay here until they lock me up, or kill me. Until I die. They told me in England I was sick enough to come home, but I kept on fightin' and I'm gonna keep on fightin'. I could'a come back again when I was in France, in '45. I could'a come back. But just as quick as I was able I kept on goin', went back to fight again.

I tell people from all over the world this story. I don't tell it for money, I just tell it because it's the truth.

Bridge Man
Roanoke, Virginia

Young, clean-cut, white, and angry, he speaks while marching with other homeless people en route to Washington, D.C., on the New Exodus, Housing Now! march.

"I can get by. I can make it. But you've got veterans, you've got families, you've got veterans with families that ain't got no place to put 'em. It's for them that I'm marchin'."

The Bridge Man has lived in Atlanta, Georgia, for most of the past year. He is in his late twenties.

WE WAS PLAYING POKER at Fort Bragg, North Carolina. It was $50 a hand. This guy had an ace of spades up his sleeve, okay? And what it was, I caught him, threw him up against the wall and held a knife to his throat. Right then an MP came in and threw me in the holding cell.

Two days after that I had a court hearing. The judge asked me why I did it and I said, "Your honor, the man cheated in a card game." Gave me thirty days in the stockade and then I be throwed out.

They gave me a bus ticket. No back pay, no eatin' money, no nothin'. I went 'Atlanta. Heard a lot of people saying Atlanta's got jobs and stuff. But I didn't have no ID—I kept it in the sheath of my knife and they took it with the knife. And if you ain't got no ID you can't get no jobs. And going into a new town, you know, you got to have ID. All I had was my birth certificate and my social security card. Had my certificate and army papers but that's not ID—you got to have something with your picture on it.

So the first day I got to Atlanta I went to jail. I was lyin' on a bench—didn't know where else to lie down. These cops handcuffed me, carried me to jail. They said I had to get ID. I said, "Well, how am

I gonna get ID if I don't have money to get one?" They said, "Well, work."

I still don't have ID. I live under a bridge in the West End. It's hard but I'm used to it now. You got people comin' up there throwin' bottles at ya, gettin' cut, callin' you a tramp, bum, a hobo, and all this kind of trash. You can't earn an honest livin'. You get robbed. 'Guy pulled a 38 on me under that bridge.

I sleep up top, in the corner. You got rats and all comin' through there. You got to watch 'em or you get bit. The first train comes by at 4:30. I usually get up then 'cause when you're asleep somebody could come up behind, hit you in the back of the head. So you're always afraid.

There's eight of us on one side and sixteen on the other. In the daytime you can hang around, but night time you can't trust anybody. Even you best friend can mess you up.

And everybody's got their spot. You walk up to your spot and there's somebody in your spot? You're expected to kick his ass. Ain't no good sayin' "Hey, get up and leave." You've got to defend your spot. If you don't they're going to go off and say, "This here's a whimp," and run over you. That's how it is. Word gets around.

Once this dude came up and there was an Indian on his cardboard. He had one of these liquor bottles, broke it, and cut him up under the belly. Ambulance picked the Indian up and the dude went to jail. Stayed there for thirty days, came out and took his spot back. Blood still sittin' right there. All he did was turn his cardboard over and go to sleep. That's what you got to do, to survive.

And we got veterans livin' under that bridge. We got one that came out of Vietnam, he's got two ears missin'. Can't hear. Another one's got bone disease, can only walk two or three feet before restin'. He can't make it to the soup line so I usually bring stuff up to him. There's another veteran, he's got a wife and two kids livin' up there. They go to this church 'bout half mile down the road, for sandwiches and stuff. I try my best to help 'em out too, even though I ain't got a family. Try to be a part of somethin', you know.

It was hardest for me right when I got there. I was used to workin', coming home, eating a good meal, going to sleep, get up and do it over again. I mostly did guard duty and drivin' heavy machinery. I liked it. I was hopin' I could stay, hopin' I could retire from it some day. This was the National Guard. They were supposed to give me a good education, self-respect, good job, and money when you come out. I went in, I got that. Then that one man messed me up.

But bein' in the military's just like bein' under that bridge. You don't stand up for yourself and they call you a pussy, pick on ya. And, like, let's say you snitch on somebody, then you're gonna wake up with a rag over your eyes. Everybody's going to have a soap in their sock and you're gonna get messed up—what they call a soap line: hit you right in the stomach, one time a piece.

See Fort Bragg is a Marine base. You got to stand up for yourself there. The National Guard and the Army comes there to train, but Marines run it. And they're tough. I've seen Marines—when I was on guard duty once I seen Marines slice a man's throat over a cake. This guy took another man's cake and they sliced his throat, killed him. Put the knife in his hand to make it look like suicide.

So like in this card game, what I did was the only thing to do. I needed that ace of spades myself, make me two pairs. But I was just the one that saw it, if it hadn't been me somebody else would have done it.

But if I had the chance I'd go back right now. I'd go right back. When my mommy and daddy died, and when my grandparents died, I went into the Guard to make something of myself. Now I got no family to go to. It's the only place I know where I can get my life back in order. I want an education, I want to be somebody. I don't want to be a deadbeat. Too many deadbeats around this world already.

Johnny
Washington, D.C.

> *I'm on the third floor of the Community for Creative Nonviolence, walking among the dividers that separate the cot and locker afforded each man. I come upon Johnny, a middle-aged African American and Vietnam-era veteran. He lies on his cot, reading.*

I'M HERE BY CHOICE. I don't have to be here, I could leave today or tomorrow. I'm here because things that used to be important to me aren't important anymore.

I had the typical male American dream: married, a home, two cars, a kid. What really hurt is our system. Our system puts more emphasis on materialism than on family ties. So my wife, she just became obsessed with materialist things. Before I could pay for the Refridgidaire she call for the dishwasher. And what does it do for the family? I mean hell, I could wash those dishes. But it's keepin' up with the Jones', you know.

It's like I tell my brother. He says, "Damn man, as smart as you is, and man you done been to school. All that shit's bein' wasted."

He wanted to see me go and do the things that he do. But the things I've seen in the working world I just don't have the heart to do to other people any more. I think it's morally wrong. But society and this system, they condone things ... pay people as little as you can and charge people as much as you can—that's the American way, enterprise. You know what I'm talkin' about. My brother, he's in the export business, that's how he makes his living.

Everyone does. When I worked in construction, like when I would get help, I'd get somebody who only wanted ten or fifteen dollars to get a pint of wine, or a McDonald's hamburger. If he was sensible I didn't want him 'cause I couldn't manipulate him. So I used to manipulate people, and I did quite well.

I did concrete—steps, patios, porches, things of that nature. It paid damn good. I had a house in Fort Washington. You don't know nothin' about that, but that's the elite black district. At that time the homes were rangin' from a hundred and fifty thousand on up. I had a dumptruck, pickup truck, the wife had a car. Then I had a little, I laugh about it now, but I had a 'vette. All these motherfuckin' vehicles; but you couldn't drive but one at a time.

Now it's my turn to have minimum wage jobs. So I know how they feel: they use me just like I used the men that worked for me. I don't blame 'em, it's the system, the American way. But you can't live that way. Hell, by the time you get paid, you pay rent, you get some food and pay for transportation, you in the hole. You got to live in a shelter to get by on a minimum wage job. Either that or eat in one. So why bother? You gotta be usin' somebody to make any money. You gotta either use people or be used by them.

A whole lot of times now I just have to say, "No, this is not too important." Like the other day, I went to work. This dude couldn't find four people, so I said, "I'll go, man." Twenty bucks for a day of hard diggin'. But once I got there I said shit, I don't want to do this. What I doin' this for? I mean I could see if I was getting paid for my labor, but I wasn't getting paid for my labor, I was getting paid for my ignorance. So I left. I demand respect, 'cause I'm going to respect you. And I deserve it. If I don't get no respect I'm gonna bow out gracefully.

I mean I consider myself as part of this system because, after all, I was born and raised in this United States of America. But I can't manipulate and use people no more. I won't do it. And I ain't gonna be used and manipulated by nobody either. Shit, the world's mad. I ain't mad, that's why I'm here.

The system's so messed up now there's no unity in families anymore. I have a home—I mean my ex-wife and I. She lives there now with my daughter. I didn't want her to come up like I did. You know, eight of us, two or three rooms. And then my aunt and her three kids were also there. But you know, we got along better than we do today. We didn't have a tv, we didn't have a radio, so we used to sit and entertain among one another. Nowadays we don't have time for that. We used to have family reunions, we don't even do that anymore.

My uncles and aunts, they got along. On a weekend it wasn't nothin' for two, three uncles to come by the house, "Come on boy, let's get one!" Go down to the wharf, get a bushel of crabs, sit in the back yard, cook the crabs. They looked out for one another.

Nowadays, you don't see that happen. People'll leave their own momma on the wayside and never look back for her, just say "Get out of my way!" Bein' selfish, greedy, that's what happened to Rome. And Hannibal came across the Himalayas with the elephants and destroyed them big fat motherfuckers ... layin' around in jacuzzies, suckin' grapes ... I mean he run over the biggest empire in the world at the time ... they got so fat and lazy from greed—the ones with the money. The slaves, they weren't going to fight for 'em. That's what's happin' here now.

See, sometimes I get a little carried away with the world's problems, but it's too much weight for me to carry alone. So that's when I prefer to read or talk, it tends to relax and calm me down. I mean in Vietnam I seen how those people live, because of turmoil. I mean those kids, they don't know nothin' but devastation.

And then I come back here and see everybody with their asses up on their back and their head stuck there. I'm sayin', "Hey you all complainin' 'cause you can't have steak everyday. A bowl of beans is better for you than a steak. Yeah, get yourself a bowl of beans and a piece of cornbread."

That's why I don't have the headaches a whole lot of other people have. This world turns people against each other, it's too crazy—I don't play that game anymore. I don't live above my means. I make it a business to not eat but once a day. My system is already geared to eat that way. I try to be simple. And if I can go a day without a meal I know I can go three days without a meal. Somewhere down the line I'm gonna find something to eat before I starve. And I'm very healthy, mind and body.

So now I spend my time reading. If I get frustrated or something like that, I just pick up a book. I don't mean no sex book, that's the last thing I need up here 'cause AIDS don't have no respect for nobody. I read things that will teach me something. That way I keep my mind tuned and sharp.

What's important to me now, seriously man, is socializing, takin' a little load off one another mind. Like I might say to you, "Hey man, are you married? Tell me about it." That's what's important to me now.

I went over in '65, with the first troop movement. We didn't know our ass from a hole in the ground. We had to learn everything the hard way. '65, '66, I imagine that was your largest death toll. They had the "Big Red One," they just cleaned out the whole Iron Triangle. We just didn't know the guerrilla tactics. Booby traps, things of that nature. Men got killed; wiped out near the whole battalion.

That's how I got this eye busted open. I came up on a young boy, he must have been about fifteen. You know, just walked up on him and we startled one another. I looked at him and I dropped my weapon—I don't mean on the ground, I just pointed it down—and he came up with the butt. Smack! Busted the eye right open. Then took off runnin'.

Man he could'a killed me, but he didn't. I imagine he said, "Hell, he could'a killed me." And I didn't. I didn't want to kill him. But, I mean after that, I didn't take no chances.

I used to couldn't talk about it, but now I can. I used to have nightmares, you know and ... I think that's another thing that's causing me to be a little more ... humane. 'Cause there was a whole lot of things that I participated in there ... there's a whole lot of things I did. I've seen men crush newborn babies. Two-weeks-old, three-weeks-old, just kill 'em—that's what we 'spozed to do. Burnin' down the huts, search and destroy. Just kill everything: the chickens, the pigs, the ox, you know, the old men and the old ladies and the babies. Kill everything. Then you don't leave nothin' to come back to. Pour kerosene in the fields, put a match to it ... burn it all down. Don't leave nothin', make it burn. Yup, fuck up the fields. You'd be surprised—you've never been in a war, have you? It was just like the Civil War here. I mean, would you appreciate a Frenchman coming over here and joining the Southerners?

They say age brings about wisdom. Well, I can agree with that. Some people can understand these things but nevertheless they use their wisdom to step on people, to use 'em, even though they understand some things that they do is wrong. I try to stay outside of that. That's why I wear my watch on my right hand—I don't want to be like the average man.

But you gonna have to follow me fifty miles in my footsteps to really know what I mean. Then you could begin to see what I'm tryin' to say—after you know what I've seen, what I've been through. Sometimes you just can't explain things in their fullness.

Joshua
Washington, D.C.

> *Angry, tall, compelling in voice and countenance, Joshua*
> *approaches while I speak with another man in a D.C. shelter. "I*
> *got something to say," he begins. The man I have been speaking*
> *with nods, indicating that he would wait and that I should*
> *listen. Joshua is an African American, and I could not*
> *determine his age.*

I GOT SOMETHING TO SAY. What about the people who went to Vietnam
and got out and can't get a decent ... a decent living! You're lookin' at
one. I didn't choose to go, I got drafted. And what did the army offer
me? Not a dime. I ain't got shit.

They ask me what my MOS is and I tell them I was an infantry
soldier. What's an infantry soldier? A trained killer. They ain't trained
me for nothin' else. A bush soldier.

So when you come back who want to hire a killer? Then they don't
give you no education or nothin' out there. You stand in line, you fight
like mules, and you come home. That's a hell of a thing for somebody
to think about.

Society. Society sends me over and society brings me back. And I ...
society says kill people and I kill people. I kill people. You understand?
And what I get for that? What I get for bein' made to kill people! What
I get for ... for ....

You dig a little hole, you use your own ... your motherfuckin' own
shirt off your back to wipe your ass with ... And man, I come back and
man ... it got so bad I did time in the penitentiary, state penitentiary.
And hey, you want to know what I went to the penitentiary for?
Murder! I killed somebody. You know why I killed him? Because he

came fuckin' with me and he was fuckin' with the wrong person. Killed him just like I was trained to do.

I've had two wives since I came home from the military, and I ain't with none of them. I got four kids: I ain't with none of their mothers, and I ain't with none of them. You understand?

They drafted me and they tell me they're going to do this and that for me—they ain't done a damn thing. I be layin' down in my bunk sometimes and I dream about the shit that happened to me over there. I dream about it. Sometimes, man, I go out. I just flip out—like that, like that! [angrily snaps fingers]. And I ain't gettin' no help! I need some help and I ain't gettin' no help.

It wasn't like that before I went in there. Now my mind, it can click off like that! [snaps fingers], in a heartbeat. I ain't gettin' no help, and I need some kind of help, you know, some kind of psychiatric help. 'Cause I feel like … I … I feel myself that I'm not right yet. I want to get better; I don't want to get worse. Yea, 'cause I know I got a problem. I got a very big problem. 'Cause I could be standin' up here man, and somebody talk to me, tell me something, and I go off.

I jumped on a boy last night outside and I beat him up real bad. I took a stick and start to whippin' on his ass. See, I know I got a problem. I want 'em to help me, I don't want to get worse [he pauses to look at me, pleading]. But every time I go to the VA they want to drug me up! [slams his fist on the table]. Last summer I was in there and they had me so drugged up and all... Man, I got some friends they helped and they walkin' around like zombies now.

But I need help man, I know it, or I'm going to hurt somebody! I don't want to, man. 'Cause... I can feel it, man … I'm gettin' ready to flick off now, I can feel it comin'....

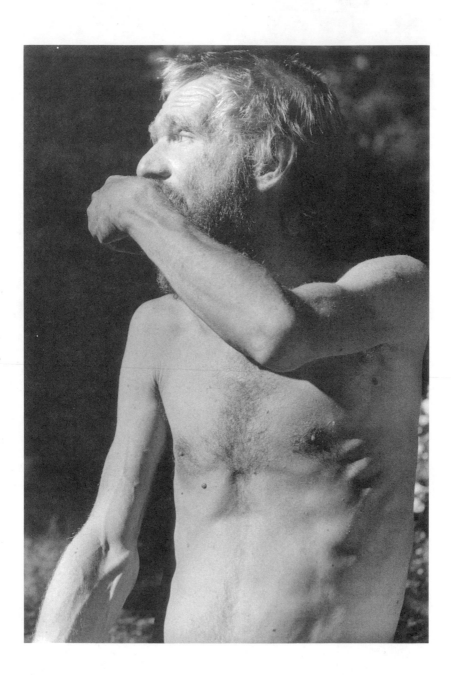

CHAPTER 6

THE HOMELESS MENTALLY ILL

More of the mentally ill now live on our streets than in our public health hospitals.[1] This number—which does not include alcoholics or drug addicts—appears to be increasing, as is the fear of such people, and the number of voices raised to demand we "do" something about them.

This is not to say that most homeless people are mentally ill. They are not. Nor did the much debated deinstitutionalization of mentally ill patients create homelessness—though homelessness would be much easier to understand if it had.

Rather, and like all segments of the homeless population, the homeless mentally ill are a diverse group, more varied than alike. Understanding their situation is a delicate matter of avoiding these and other generalizations, and of accepting multiple truths: truths that may at best yield a pastiche—rather than a single tidy portrait—of the problem and its causes.

The argument that deinstitutionalization created homelessness goes like this:[2] psychiatric institutions released more than half a million patients between 1955 and 1984. The Community Mental Health Centers (CMHCs), originally designed to provide outpatient care for such people, failed to do so.[3] Adrift from their institutional moorings, and unable or unwilling to take the medications they need, hundreds of thousands of these people now live in our streets.

But the crisis in homelessness did not immediately follow deinstitutionalization. State hospitals released most of their patients before 1978, the greatest percentage of patients having been released in the 1960s. Homelessness did not begin to be recognized as a national crisis until the early 1980s, when families and the working poor—as well as the seriously mentally ill—began to overrun shelters and social services heretofore dominated by street alcoholics and transients. As Jonathan Kozol has remarked, if a significant number of the homeless were institutionalized "before they reappeared in subway stations and in public shelters," one might wonder "where they were and what they were doing from 1972 to 1980."[4]

Furthermore, formerly deinstitutionalized patients constitute but a small portion of the present population of homeless people. In fact, while deinstitutionalization did remove more than half a million patients from state hospitals, the bulk of these people ended up in nursing homes—not the street.[5] This is documented in numerous studies, all of which show a direct correlation between deinstitutionalization and nursing home admissions.[6] Reporting on data from across the country, for example, the U.S. General Accounting Office (GAO) announced in 1977 that deinstitutionalization would be more accurately described as "reinstitutionalization," because the nursing home had replaced the state hospital as the "largest single place of care for the mentally ill."[7]

Finally, up to one-fourth of the homeless people in our nation may be children,[8] and the median age for homeless adults is 36—still too young to have been released from state hospitals in the 1960s and 1970s.[9]

Certainly, some deinstitutionalized patients were discharged to homeless shelters and did end up homeless. Others may have become homeless after being pushed out of low-income housing, or tenuous situations where they lived with and were cared for by a relative, during the more significant current of homelessness that struck in the early 1980s. But while deinstitutionalization and the subsequent failure of the CMHCs contributed to homelessness, these factors can hardly be considered the precipitating cause of such a widespread, national crisis.

Nevertheless, it is true that rates of mental illness among homeless people are extremely high, many times that of the general population.[10] A portion of that figure can be attributed to the deinstitutionalization of ex-patients,[11] and another can be ascribed to the fact that some of the homeless mentally ill would have been hospitalized under the previous system. This would account for the many homeless schizophrenics who can be shown to have been genetically predisposed to mental illness. But even these considerations do not account for the roughly 30 percent of homeless people who appear mentally ill—especially those who demonstrate no sign of mental illness until after they become homeless.[12] Hence, if the so-called myth of deinstitutionalization is dismissed, one is left with the question of where so many homeless, mentally ill people come from.

One approach to this question is to examine the role homelessness may play in mental illness. This is the approach that most homeless people themselves take when considering the issue. Simply put, they think homelessness can drive you insane. In contrast, the great bulk of the psychiatric literature on homelessness assumes only the converse: that insanity can drive you to homelessness.

This occurs because the present psychiatric view considers most serious mental illness as the result of biological rather than environmental factors. According to this view, schizophrenia and manic-depressive psychoses, among others, are genetic illnesses—more like diabetes than emotional stress or the residual effects of traumatic childhood experiences. The underlying theory is that serious mental illness is located in the individual, rather than in the social context of the individual's experience. Accordingly, mental illness is seen as preceding (and thereby causing) homelessness for the mentally ill of our streets and shelters.

Homeless people tend to disagree. While acknowledging that many mentally ill people do become homeless, they stress the debilitating effects of their situations as a chief cause of mental illness among them. "When you're homeless your mind kind of wags," says Tanya, a homeless, college-educated woman who was hospitalized for depression and schizophrenia after losing her children to the state. Cyrell, a homeless man working to create a cooperative survival center in Philadelphia, explains it this way:

> People become self-absorbed in their own minds when they're homeless. People say they're insane or psychotic, but a lot of people are neither. What happens is they become absorbed in theirselves and their problems. I call it "mental inwardness," because nothing on the outside matters to them.

> If you don't have decent clothing, or you're dirty and have no money, you're looked down upon. People turn their heads, say "Get away from me, scum!" So you don't fit in. Society rejects you, doesn't care for you, and you begin to lose hope. When that happens you just sit alone, thinking about your problems. Dejected. And with no human contact you just totally block everything out. The outer world gets canceled out. You get up off the grate, look this way and that. Self-absorbed.

This rather commonsense point of view is frequently corroborated by mental health clinicians like Dr. Anne Braden Johnson, a clinical social worker who oversees mental health services for women in New York City's Rikers Island Jail. As she notes in her widely respected book, *Out of Bedlam: The Truth about Deinstitutionalization*:

> Something that has not been studied to any appreciable degree, surprisingly, is the relationship between life without a home and mental status. Living on the street or in a shelter, as many homeless people do, cannot possibly have a positive effect on one's self-esteem or provide much in the way of gratifying experience; and homelessness itself is a

state of such unremitting crisis that one would expect it to provoke some kind of emotional or mental disorder, in and of itself. For the most part, though, the detachment prized by science has allowed researchers to look at specimen homeless people so objectively that the possibility of their having been driven mad by worry, fear, grief, guilt, or shame has not seriously entered the observers' minds.[13]

The lack of research on this question is particularly egregious because documentation to support it has existed for years. Examining whether mental illness might be best understood as a "response to conditions in the social environment," Johns Hopkins sociologist and epidemiologist M. Harvey Brenner studied the relationship between economic conditions and admissions to mental hospitals in New York State. He found that "instabilities in the national economy have been the single most important source of fluctuation in mental-hospital admission rates" for the last 127 years. This effect of economic conditions on rates of mental illness, Brenner notes, has been particularly strong "in the last two decades."[14]

Not surprisingly, rates of homicides, suicides, and deaths from alcohol-related illnesses also correlate with some periods of economic decline.[15] Similarly, unemployment among men has been associated with a myriad of emotional difficulties and psychiatric symptoms, while women in unemployed families have been shown to be inordinately depressed, anxious, and phobic.[16] Homeless people have also been shown to be significantly more "demoralized" than the general population.[17]

This research does not deny that factors predisposing certain people to mental illness exist. Rather, it demonstrates that economic stress correlates with the appearance of mental illness. Thus while mental illness in a dormant or mild form may precede homelessness, the stresses of poverty and homelessness activate or accelerate the disease. As Brenner puts it, "the appearance of mental illness is seen as *the* maladaptive response to the precipitating stress situation."[18]

The ramifications of these findings are startling. First, rates of mental illness would naturally be expected to be higher among those for whom the stress of economic change has been greatest. This would certainly include people who have lost their jobs, homes, friends, and families. Second, the stress of homelessness explains why many of the homeless mentally ill demonstrate no sign of mental illness until after the onset of their homelessness. Third, to the extent that this view is accurate, such rates of mental illness among homeless people must be understood in societal terms, for it is in response to conditions in the larger society that homelessness has occurred. Finally, it follows that any treatment of the mentally ill must address the socioeconomic sources of the stress responsible for the rise in mental illness among those affected. For homeless people such "sources" would include the unavailability of low-income housing, cuts in disability and assistance benefits, unemployment, low wages, and their acute isolation.

Homeless people also question whether the conditions of homelessness could generate responses that may be mistaken as symptoms of mental illness. That is, while the conditions of homelessness might elicit or exacerbate mental illnesses, is it not also likely that any "normal" response to such experiences would be apt to include depression, phobias, rage, and other behaviors symptomatic of mental illness?

People who work with homeless people find this a rather obvious assertion. In fact, one counselor has commented that she has learned to treat the displaced rural homeless she sees just as she treats East Asian refugees suffering from cultural displacement and post-traumatic stress syndrome. "Their conditions are surprisingly similar," she remarked.[19]

Common sense deems that one should be cautious in designating a Cambodian refugee as mentally ill for behavior that seems out of place or odd. Adjustment and behavioral difficulties would be expected in such a situation. Similarly, one should be cautious when interpreting the behavior of homeless people. In point of fact, however, the exigencies of homeless life are rarely considered in examinations of mental illness among homeless people. In this way, psychiatrists and other researchers can misinterpret symptoms and misdiagnose the disease.

Alcoholism, drug abuse, and other medical problems also confuse psychiatric profiles. Homeless diabetics, for example, often lose their insulin, have syringes stolen, or fail to find the proper balance of food they need. Unable to control their disease, such diabetics can appear drunk and severely mentally ill.[20] The same is true of lesser maladies. Soiling oneself may indicate mental illness, or it may indicate a lack of toilets. It may even indicate an attempt to fend off rapists. Sleep deprivation, another common effect of homelessness, also manifests itself in symptoms identical to those of mental illness.

But even if it were accepted that the treatment most needed by homeless people—the mentally ill included—is an income, a community, and stable housing, the question of what to do with those who do need greater psychiatric care would remain unresolved.

Lithium and antipsychotic medications, for instance, control many of the symptoms of mental illness. Regular treatment with such medication could enable some of the homeless mentally ill to hold down jobs and gain greater control of their minds and bodies.[21] But a large proportion of the people who could benefit from medication will not take it. Typically, they are either not aware of their illness (people who are paranoid, for example, do not believe their fears to be delusions), or they fear the medication itself, some of which causes drowsiness, confusion, and tardive dyskinesia, a condition marked by tics and facial contortions.[22]

Joshua, whose testimony concludes the preceding chapter, is a good example. Joshua's problems may be endemic to the trauma of his experience in Vietnam, or he may have acquired them through physical injury or inherited family traits. Regardless of cause, the debilitating conditions of homelessness and unemployment, and the rejection he has suffered as a poor, black veteran exacerbate his frustration and anger. Brenner's research would suggest that the stress of these factors triggered or activated the symptoms of his illness. Homeless people might say the stress caused them. In any case, Joshua is demonstrably violent, having been convicted of murder, and says that he is apt to "hurt somebody" again. For Joshua's good, as well as that of society at large, some kind of assistance is urgently needed.

Fortunately, Joshua is eligible for health care through the Veterans Administration. But he will not accept the treatment (read "medication") they offer. Whether such medication would help him is beside the point—too many of the other "treated" veterans "walk around like zombies" and he refuses to.

The question of whether Joshua should be forced to accept medication occupies much of the debate surrounding the homeless mentally ill. The issue is largely moot, however, as the facilities and funding needed to (re)institutionalize such people do not exist. Even homeless people who seek psychiatric hospitalization are routinely denied it.[23] Nor would forced medication create affordable housing, cure substance abuse, or provide education, counseling, a supportive community, and job skills—most likely the "treatment" Joshua actually needs.

Ultimately, helping the homeless mentally ill means understanding both their homelessness and their illnesses. While not a mental illness in itself, homelessness is complicated by mental illness and the manifestations of homelessness frequently mirror those of schizophrenia and other psychoses. As the following testimonies make clear, solutions to the difficulties faced by homeless people who are mentally ill must address both issues and acknowledge the extent to which mental illnesses are triggered and exacerbated—perhaps even caused—by the conditions of homelessness itself. One step toward this end is to do what has not yet been done: to consider the mental illness of homeless people in the context of their lives, as well as their genes.

Chuck
Philadelphia, Pennsylvania

Chuck comes forward to meet me—the first person I speak with on this visit to the shelter. He is thin, well-groomed, educated, noticeably ill at ease in the inner-city shelter. It seems he thinks I, too, am homeless: a middle-class person like himself.

Chuck is Puerto Rican and perhaps 28 years old. He seems to have at least partially completed a college degree.

THINGS BEGAN TO GO BAD for me when my mother died. My mother died and then, you know, well, being in America can be a little overwhelming. Facing obstacles and all. Trying to get opportunities, like getting a good job, or living in a nice neighborhood without any trouble.

It's hard to be accepted in certain circles here—black, white, Puerto Rican. And it's a matter of being poor in a lot of directions. I have the problem of not ... sort of not having any particular group to identify with, even though I'm basically black. I don't seem to fit in exactly with anybody. You know, everybody has different ways and they don't always mesh together. And so it makes it difficult for me to be focused on any one group, or to be in an office with a certain type of clique. For example I've been in a law office, working, and then have had to come back into the ghetto, deal with the people there. There's so many things going on that you're really ... you sort of get confused about what you're about.

Like you can be in the ghetto for twenty years, though years before that you have traveled all over the world. So it's like up and down. And that really ... it doesn't seem like you can stay—for whatever reason—in a niche. It's confusing.

For me it was depression, depression over things happening in life—a chain reaction of things. My mom died, new family situation, adjusting to new types of jobs, being away from home, problems dealing with people, females, things like that.

Maybe if I had the mentality I have now I wouldn't have got upset and would have been able to deal more effectively with all this. But if you're sensitive and you come up against those kind of things ... well, they can bother you when maybe they shouldn't.

I can't think of the word but I heard it the other day, it means out of control. I was out of control. And when you're out of control you can't do anything.

Nancy
Washington, D.C.

I am taking notes at a table when Nancy sits down and begins talking. She speaks for nearly an hour, rambling, crying, exclaiming. While the names, facts, and details of her narrative cannot all be real, the pain clearly is. So are the photos of her daughters she shows me. It strikes me that the stories, when delusional, are metaphorically true—true to the experience of her suffering.

Nancy says she will soon be 38, which seems reasonable. She is tall, white, blond, and must once have been thought very beautiful.

Nancy lives in the House of Ruth, a women's shelter. A staff member tells me she was released from a state mental hospital some time ago. Nowhere to go; no family to claim her. Luckily, the shelter took her in.

WHEN I WAS four years old Jesus gave me God. That's nothing to lie about. My morning star of David came two years ago, in Indiana, he baptized two of my daughters. Right now what I'm going to do is in Ecclesiastes 3:1. A time for getting into heaven, a time to forewarn, a time to die, a time to tear down, a time to rebuild—you have time for all this? I tell you, you could write a book about my life.

I woke up on the delivery table three years ago and my twins were gone. Two children. I have one daughter that's been murdered. I've been paid off by courts, lawyers, judges, and psychiatrists from Elk Heat, Indiana, to the Pacific Ocean. I was blackmailed by this girl that works in Senator Byrd's office. I had to put my two oldest daughters—my very miserable and very unhappy...this is my Tammy, she'll be seventeen [she hands me a photograph of the young woman]. She's in the Indiana Soldiers and Sailors Home.

I cannot keep track of all of it, but Jesus came to Harvard University, and when the Lord comes to the earth he comes out from the heavens in a white cloud.... There's a right, a wrong, a true and a false, and I cannot deal with anything else, with anything but truth and righteousness, it makes me mad! [she pounds the table in her anger]. I cannot deal with drugs and abortions, I cannot deal with this kind of stuff, with these whores, Las Vegas tramps, Jim and Tammi Bakker—and if you knew ... they took me, and I'm angry about it. I'm not going to kill them. But I'm going to kill the murderer of one of my children, I'm going to kill two psychiatrists....

I was in Indianapolis, with a doctor Joyce. She says I'm schizophrenia, paranoid, mentally ill, and crazy. But like I told her when she gave me my commitment papers, I told her she would have to go before God to take her papers, take 'em before God.

I lost three children. Do you know what a mother would do, what in hell would she do? If you woke up and your kids—I mean my children ... they were gone from me! My three, I don't know where they're at—and President Reagan flew into Indiana—remember? Brakes went out on Air Force One. Do unto others as they do unto you.

But Jesus Christ this is no way for a woman to live: to wind up in sanitariums, and in and out of hospitals, lose the kids ... I have an underground filming of all this. I also have the filming of Satan the serpent. In the end the girl in Senator Byrd's office is Satan. She followed me when I was twelve, after I went to the inaugural dance of John Kennedy.

This is real, this is not fantasy. And I'm going into the Congress and Senate shortly and I'm gonna kill—I've got a sword from Bush. In the Bible you know God asks for twelve swords. I don't know how many they've gotten, but I do know Bush has a sword for me.

But I'm love, too. I love Iowa, Oregon, Wyoming, Colorado, and like if I could do the whole world with God I would want it all perfect, like Tom Sawyer ... I love Mark Twain, and hats, and fishing pools, not dumpy chlorine pools. What's the name of that song Johnny Cash sings, "Little Baby Ducks." I love that record, and I love "Sunday Morning I was Drinking Beer" [laughs]. That reminds me of one of my brothers that was in Vietnam. He got messed up over there.

See a psychiatrist gets a hold of a woman—instead of a minister or a priest—gets her on Medicare, Medicaid. You know the money they rake off on each one of us people? They take our kids, stick us here, put us on welfare, food stamps, we're a burden to taxpayers. My bills were a hundred and thirty thousand. They sent the bills to the state. Hell yes, they pick that up. And I'm just one patient.

Aaron
Atlanta, Georgia

Sunday morning. I sit in the courtyard of a church I had been told is a large soup kitchen. There is no meal today, however, and I rest for a moment, looking at my map of the city.

Aaron approaches, hobbling slowly on crutches, his leg in a cast. He is young, white, pale, and thin with whispy blond hair. He sits down by me, tired, his arms red from the crutches, and asks about the meal.

"There'll be one at this place further downtown this afternoon," he says. I wonder if it will take him until the afternoon to get there. We begin to talk. His voice is soft and steady, never falling or rising.

I WAS HIT in the back of the head with a baseball bat when I was three years old. That brought on brain damage. I'm epileptic.[24] So for me, basically it's been a hard time finding work with people afraid to hire me because of my seizures. When people see ya having seizures on the job they don't want to have anything to do with you 'cause they don't want to take the chance of having to pay workman's comp. Like I had this job one time when I was doing some dishwashing work, and I was getting some good remarks from my employer. But unfortunately I had a couple seizures on the job and he laid me off—didn't want to see his insurance go up. And you see I try to be honest with employers, so sometimes I don't even get a chance.

I work anyway. Even if it's out of these labor pools. But at the labor pools you end up making less than the minimum wage. You take that and you've not only got to find a place to stay, you've got to take care of your clothes, you've got to eat—you know, the whole nine yards.

And if you're out working during the day you aren't going to make it to the soup lines 'cause they're closed at night.

You can't get as much work at the labor pools as you used to 'cause they only put out a certain amount of work, as opposed to the people they're gettin'. And in the last two or three years it's really gotten bad in Atlanta because the poverty's gotten so bad. I've been a victim of the crime myself several times. Last month alone I got robbed four times.

That's how bad it is for people to get money around here. Even poor people mugging other poor people. Like during the week you can come down here and you'll see this soup line's crowded with people trying to get food. And you ought to see what the winter shelters are like down here, they are loaded with people. They get a bunch of cots and just line 'em up wall to wall.

Summertime it's nearly impossible to get something to drink. Lots of times they won't even let you sit down. And you have to walk around all day long. Between the heat and carrying things you start to get worn out. Most of the guys have big heavy bags they carry. I just mainly have my books.

See right now I go to Atlanta Area Tech. I'm taking accounting. My doctor told me I need to get into some kind of office work 'cause that would be the safest thing for me. And I've always had a pretty good math aptitude, so I'm taking accounting. I hope that when I'm finished with it I'll have enough training to get a decent job.

I live at the Union Mission, or if I don't have the money I sleep out in the woods by the school. It's kind of in the suburbs so you find yourself a great big ol' patch of woods and just fall off in there and sleep some place, hope you don't get rained on or bit by a snake or somethin'. One night I slept out in front of Grady hospital, and I had several nights when I slept up here at a church on the corner. But that was one of the times I got robbed. I went back up there a couple of weeks later and tried sleeping there and got robbed again, so I quit trying.

Usually I try to go some place like the Samaritan house to shower. Or they got another mission down on Coca Cola Place, run by the Central City Park area. You can go down there during the day if you want. Sometimes they're able to help you find work and they got a big restroom they keep open. You can shave, take a shower, use the restroom, take a nap. Just, you know, just to get inside—get away from all the nonsense—study if I can.

Then about three weeks ago I was coming home from this shelter and I had a seizure walking through the park. When I fell I banged my leg up against the side of the curb. I walked around with it like that for a couple of weeks, then finally decided to go to Grady. They told me it had been broken and put a cast on. So now I've had this cast for two and a half weeks.

I had to go to the recovery center, 'cause of the cast. I didn't want to take a chance of being robbed so I slept with my wallet. But one guy apparently got the smart idea of rolling me over during the night. I have a hard time waking up because the medicine I have to take for my seizures makes me extremely sleepy. So I woke up the next morning and my wallet was gone.

That put me up a creek 'cause see, I'm paying for school. I applied for a grant from the government, but that was six months ago and I still haven't heard anything. So it looks like I'm paying for it, me and a person in this church that's helping me out a little bit.

Duane
Washington, D.C.

"People treat homeless people like they idiots, they treat 'em just like trash. I mean if you think about it, you gotta realize that homeless people are not stupid. Nobody stupid gonna survive the street. And maybe if you think about it ... maybe it was a loved one or somethin' that put 'em there ... My mother is deceased now. We were real tight. When she died my mind just zapped out."

Duane is 27 and an African American.

MOM HAD IT HARD. She was a social worker, had to quit her job 'cause things got too out of hand. She used to always tell me to keep the family together. She was everything...without her there I wouldn't of survived.

My father wasn't...he'd beat on ya, punch on ya. And then the things he did to my mother...so there was all that, all that inside of me....

But what really put me uneasy was the way she died. They pulled the plug and all I could smell was her waste comin' through her bottom, comin' through her mouth and nose. I couldn't believe it was happin'....

I guess it was just too much pressure. Half the time I didn't even know who I was. Then it got worse, where I never knew who I was. I used to go to the park after she died, just sit back, rock back and forth. My girlfriend used to call me by name. I didn't know who I was, didn't even think about my boy. My mind had just snapped.... You stand there and see somebody die, see them pull the plug out and all you smell ... that's enough ... push you over the hill.

The night of my mother's funeral I slept in the street. I had on my suit and I layed across the bench with a fifth of liquor on my chest. My mother had a place but after she died my sister, she just threw all of us out. My baby brother, he was sleepin' in the hallway of an apartment. And the look he had in his face ... oh man, that look could of killed me.

I kept feelin' like I was reachin' out for help, but I didn't know how to reach out for help. It was like I sometimes knew what was happenin', but I couldn't do nothin' about it. I was out of it—that lasted a long time, lasted to the point where I became mean, violent, so violent that I was punching my girlfriend. Here I was in jail one day, didn't even know I'd done it. They said I was mentally disturbed. I got myself back together but ... then, like I was goin' to say, these are things that really put people where they are.

There came time when I slept in a box. I had two quilts, two blankets, the snow was knee deep. I wrapped it up with trash bags, anything to keep myself warm. One time it was rainin' and snowin', I was so cold my brain started to ache like a popsicle. Cold, my clothes all wet, shivering, wishing that I had some place to go, somebody to come say, "Hi, you're wet. Come on, I'll take you home, dry your clothes." And I said, "Wow, is this the way it's gonna end? Am I gonna die? Am I gonna freeze up?" I really didn't know.

I slept down by the State Department. I'd take a bath right on in the street 'cause they had a big ol' pool. I'd wait until about 1:00, when I knew the place was closed, take a bath, wash my clothes. And you know, people stop and look at you. Stuff like that really knocks over a man, or woman, or whoever it may be.

I was 19 when the girl got pregnant, 20 when my boy was born, 24 when my mother died. Now I'm almost 30 years old. And I wish that ... I was an honor role student, and I always dreamt that I could have half of what I wanted by the time I was thirty. I always dreamt that when I had my son—when I was a father—my boy would want for nothin'. So far I've felt like I haven't givin' him nothin'. He says, "Daddy, you take me home tonight?" I say, "I can't son, Daddy got to work tonight." 'Cause I'd give anything in the world for him not to ever know I live here. But I don't want to make him think I don't want to be around him.

It was my old man. If he'd a treated us like somebody, not abusin' ya all the time.... He used to make you sit in the middle of the floor—if you moved, if you scratched, he'd knock your head off. We were so scared.... It got to the point where I said, "What the hell, he done beat me up so much I don't have no reason to be scared no more." It just don't matter no more.

But being here [a shelter]... it's like it kills me. You can't concentrate, the lights go out at a certain time. If you read, you know, you don't have an outlet or anything. You go to the TV room you still can't concentrate because of all the noise. I'm stayin' here to get a little money, keep my body clean—I didn't like to be dirty and stinky. But it's somewhere I don't want to be, somewhere I don't belong. And the drugs here, man: acid, snort, the pipe, lovely—that's PCP—herb, anything. They're here. I just wish, if you were—I'm not prejudiced or anything you know—but if you were black I could get you a cot and you could stay here a few nights. You could see exactly what I'm sayin'. You don't have to go through it you won't understand.

A couple people have died. One guy got drunk and layed down on his back, threw up and it just went back down into his lungs, and he was smothered. Another guy OD'd in here. People have been found dead—killed, stabbed, shot ... people dyin' around me, I can't take that.

All I want is a piece of this crummy world—a piece for me and a piece for my boy. 'Cause that's what it is, a crummy world. When you're not workin' you have to go out and hustle to get money, this and that. I'm so tired of it. See people don't understand the things a homeless man has to do just to keep things together. Me, I don't know what's going to happen from day to day; I don't know if I'm going to be alive.

My mother danced with us, she participated in everything we did. She was a father and a mother. Sometimes all I can hear is her talkin'. I hear her sayin', "I'll be back Monday morning, Dingy"—that was her nickname for me. She never come back. And the way she died....

I got no money in my pockets right now, I got nothin'. I'm working with a food service, washin' dishes. Last paycheck I put half in the bank and took care of my kid. Now I'm two weeks behind in child support. The court don't have nothin' to do with that, I do it 'cause he's my son and I know I'm supposed to. I don't need nobody to tell me to take care of my boy, my baby—my only baby. He's six years old. His mother, my ex-lady, she grew up a lot, she quite mature now.

I know what must be done. Right now I eat out in the street to save money, and I work as much as possible. I figure maybe on my off days, Saturday, Sunday, I might be able to find another job. I need the money. I keep only what I have to keep. I take care of my son, I pay for my mother's cemetery plaque, the rest I put away. That way I can get out of here.

Tanya
Philadelphia, Pennsylvania

When the sisters of Women of Hope found Tanya she lay huddled in a blanket on a Philadelphia street corner, depressed, nearly catatonic. Four years earlier she had been a college student, bright and ambitious.

Tanya is African American and perhaps 30, though she looks much older. Like many homeless people who are mentally ill, she demonstrated no signs of her difficulties until she became homeless. And like many homeless women, the loss of her children is by far the greatest factor in the stress she has had to deal with.

Another portion of Tanya's narrative appears in the chapter "Life on the Street."

I WAS TEN YEARS OLD when my father died. My mother was goin' blind at the time and her sister came and got her, moved back down South. Back to Georgia. She wanted me to stay up North. That was in '85. My father, he was from Little Rock, Arkansas. If they were alive we would all still be together.

But from the age of ten until sixteen I was in a foster home. The people they were nice, but they never had any children. The man died in '81. The woman, as far as she's concerned when you're sixteen you're grown: you can get a job. That's how she raised us—which we did. We had little part-time jobs, here and there and everywhere. And we got a little apartment when she put us out. I still had two years of high school to complete. I completed it livin' on my own. Then I got brainwashed and thought I could go on to college.

I got a grant to an out-of-state college and I figured, well, "If I could work and go to high school here, I can work and go to college there." I'd work summers and go to school the rest of the year. It worked, for a while. I would get good jobs. One of my jobs was in a metal company. In another one I was in a VA Administration hospital that's over here on Baltimore Avenue.

But when you go to college you need somebody to rely on, you really do. I thought I could live there, on campus. But that's not the way it is. After the term we had a break and we had to go back home. It was for people—like if you had a family, you know. Somebody. Christmas break and all of that stuff. A couple of times I went with one of my girlfriends. I went with a roommate from Chicago, I went with a roommate from Ohio. Other times I didn't have any place to go.

Then there wasn't enough money—even with my grant and working in the summer—and I had to quit. I came back to Philadelphia. But whereas I could always get a job before, I couldn't get one this time. And, you know, I didn't have anyone. I was homeless for a while. Then I met a guy, got a room. Had my first child.

I had this thing with my first child where I had to stay in the hospital, with depression. The word was schizophrenic—they say you have a split mind, but I don't consider it a split mind. I consider it depression.

Everybody have up and down days. Some people have up and down days where they have to have somebody to talk to. If they don't those days keep going down, down, down....

I was alone. The man, after the first baby was born they put him in jail. He wasn't working ... well he was working as a security guard, but he went to jail and had to quit. They put me in the hospital and I got needles and medication. They looked at my work relief record—I ain't got no income—and ... that's sort of it.

I had a room, but they said it was unsterile to raise children in a room. Said there wasn't enough room for them to run around. So I went out and applied for the project house. Then as soon as I got to the project house they took the child away from me.

So I was stuck in the house. Not that it was too much room for me, I could have stayed there forever. But I was on public assistance then and they cut that off because I didn't have the child: I went from a room to a house to keep the child, then they took him and pushed me on out because I didn't have no kids. They said it was a family dwelling—you're supposed to have a family to live there. I went and explained my situation, but they never returned him and they didn't want to hear that they had just put me out.

After I had the second baby by him they put him in jail again. He came to the hospital, to help me come home and help the baby come home. Before he went home that night they put him in jail, and before

I left the hospital the next day they took the baby and put it in Catholic Social Services.

I was left alone, no children, no job, no place to stay. I had to live on the street, in a blanket, got real depressed. The sisters, they found me, took me in.

I've been without them four years—you know, not seeing them. My youngest one, he'll be six this year in October, my other one'll be nine this year. In September. And they say that's the law—that if they take your children away from you they can just say anything.

You see, when they see you're homeless the first thing they think is you're sick. You are sick, you're mentally sick, being homeless makes you that way. But you're not as sick as they think you are. I mean they could pull you off of the streets—which they have done for a lot of people: pulled them off the streets and given 'em a job, and they've been on that job ever since, every day. It's just that they had to have something there to hold on to, especially all these single people. You need somebody.

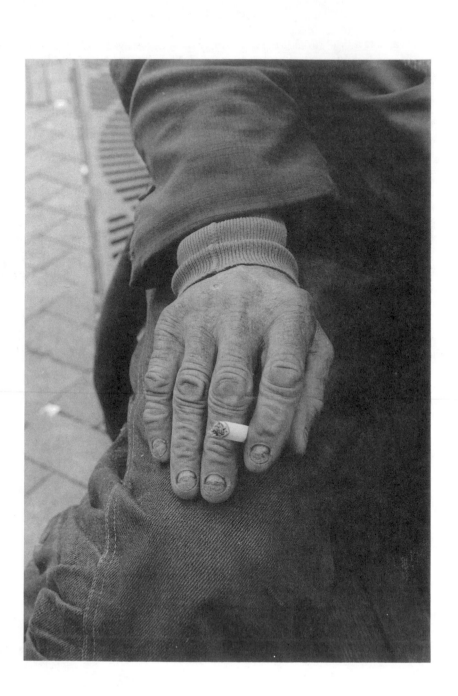

CHAPTER 7

DEPENDENCIES

No issue causes more difficulty for homeless rights advocates than the great prevalence of dependencies among homeless people. Social assistance programs target the "innocent and needy," deserving victims who suffer unjustly. Street alcoholics and drug addicts, by contrast, elicit little sympathy. And raising concerns about substance abuse among homeless people often does little to help their cause.

Advocates for new shelters, increased federal housing programs, and greater homeless services thus tend to play down the issue of substance abuse.[1] They argue that the percentage of drug and alcohol addicted among the homeless reflects that of the population as a whole, and that, in any case, restricting assistance programs on account of those who may abuse them punishes the many for the transgressions of a few.[2]

Given the recent history of "poverty" legislation, fears of "punishing the many" are understandable. By raising the specter of supposed "welfare queens," ghetto mothers who bought Cadillacs by abusing the welfare system, the Reagan administration was able to justify dropping hundreds of thousands of families from food-assistance and welfare programs. Little did it matter that no one demonstrated many such "queens" actually exist, nor that—assuming a few could be found—needy, deserving children might go hungry to better root them out.

Similarly, detractors can reduce the problem of dependencies among poor and homeless people to name-calling. "Wino," "junkie," and "drug addict" are loaded terms, cues to stop thinking about a person or problem that marshal deep-rooted fears and prejudices. Regarding homeless people they are particularly seductive because they allow us to blame them for the crime of their situation, thereby removing any responsibility or compassion we may feel. Small wonder such terms are more frequently applied to poor and homeless people than, say, Kitty Dukakis or Betty Ford—women whose substance-abuse struggles are viewed with respect and admiration.

The problem is also one of ignorance. Notions of substance abuse among the poor stem largely from Puritan concepts of free will and just deserts, concepts that were never fully relevant to alcoholism and that prove particularly inadequate when applied to contemporary drugs, such as crack, and their impact on communities.[3]

Both tendencies—to avoid the topic and to blame the victim—perpetuate the problem. The issue is not whether homeless people are more dependent on alcohol, drugs, or gambling, but that we as a society suffer these compulsions and some of us are homeless because of them. And once homeless—isolated, uninsured, commonly removed from the support of friends and family—the impact of such dependencies is greatly magnified.

The victim/perpetrator distinction, moreover, while customary, and attractive in its simplicity, obfuscates any real understanding of the problem of dependencies among poor and homeless people. It is true that, as one street alcoholic told me, "It's the person who has to stop. Don't nobody make you bend your elbow." But it's also true that "addiction is a disease," that "Society make it easy,"[4] and that lack of economic opportunity, and other factors, contributes to the problems.[5]

Fortunately, the task of understanding becomes easier when substance abuse and other dependencies are considered in the context of people's lives, and the history of their communities and families. We are less apt to judge those we know and, consequently, more apt to see them in terms relevant to their lives and ours.

Joe Dee
Washington, D.C.

Joe panhandles the side streets along 2nd Avenue. Walking with the help of a short cane, its handle wrapped with aluminum foil to help prevent calluses, he limps and shakes a small, tin cup.

Joe is an elderly African American, friendly and articulate. As happens to be true for all the men whose stories appear in this chapter, he is a veteran.

I'M JUST STANDIN' HERE tryin' to get me a little hustle. I'm an alcoholic. I don't like to mention that, but I am. I be fifty-five tomorrow, God be willin'. June 21st. First day of summer and longest day in the year. Plus Father's Day. And I'm out here on this street corner.

I'm from up here. Born and raised in Silver Spring, Maryland. Went to school in D.C., Brightwood Junior High. I started drinkin' in the army. But it was a minor thing, you know, a little thing. After I got out I worked at the grocery store for fifteen years. They had twenty-one stores, now they got about three. Consumer Supermarket, called a co-op. They still owe me money right now, from shares. They're holdin' it in escrow [he laughs]. I ain't worried about it. I ain't got but twenty dollars left there. I took all my money out when I left. I seen it was fallin'.

I did the produce and parcel pick-up, something like the "all around" you know. But it was in the union, you was makin' good. Then they started losin' stores to everybody—Safeway, A & P; they'd knock 'em off. The last of it was they had me in my car, goin' from store to store moppin' floor. And the guys that were managers and assistant managers, they was puttin' groceries on the shelf.

Before there was a shelter we stayed over at this flea-bitten school. You get lice and everything on you. You can see the marks on me from the lice [he rolls up his sleeves to show me his forearms]. Scratch, scratch, scratch, 'cause you don't get the same bed each night.

When I lost my job at the grocery store I went to the Gospel Mission. Then I went to the Central Mission: the Gospel Mission's $2 a night. Then when I learned about the school I went over there, that's where I caught the lice. There ain't no linen there either. I decided to go on downtown, find me out where I can find a job. I do and I break my ankle: drunk, tripped over a piece of ol' sidewalk, goin' down the street. And the doctor say, "You gonna get arthritis." And dadgonit if he wasn't right! I got arthritis.

That was in 1980. And I can't work now 'cause I've got arthritis in the back, leg, neck. See that? [he slowly turns his head a few degrees]. Can't hardly turn my head. Back aches and everything. Sometimes it comes and goes.

After I got out of the army I just started to drink. I don't know why. Drink, drink, and drink. After a while my wife left me. I don't blame her. I see things really good now, things I should've seen twenty-five years ago.

But it's bad down here. There's dope habits, alcoholics, people are robbed when they get their check. It's a month to month thing, you know. Day to day and month to month. I don't socialize around the people that drink incessant, or them that use the drugs: herbs, coke, PCP—they use everything. You see 'em usin' it in their car, in the street. That's no mystery. No sir.

You don't have a week go by that somebody don't get killed over drugs, or get fightin' over drugs or somethin'. Guy just shot his old lady this week. He was on drugs and jealous. Kill the baby in her stomach and kill her.

But just like alcohol, it the person that has to stop. Don't nobody make you bend your elbow. No sir. That's the 100 percent. Once it grasp you, you got to have the will power to get off it. You can go to all kinds of programs, all kinds of shelters, but it don't do you no good if you don't got the will power.

Now me myself, I don't drink nothin' till the evening. Now somedays I might drink in the mornin', say if it's Sunday and I see some of the fellows have got it. You always see somebody's got it…. But I don't know, don't know if I would quit if I could. It's kind of an enjoyment, kind of a let-out, you know. Kind of a get-away. That's why a lot of people use drugs. They get the habit then it kind of … well, it ease your mind, your livin', ease your mind from society. But what you tryin' to get away from?

It's just like a guy told me, he said, "I'm going out here on the truck today, make a day's work." It's called a labor pool. He might bring home about thirty dollars. I said, "That's better'n nothin'." He said, "But man, you know one thing?" He about forty something years old, "I don't know nothin' but slop and mop."

'Cause that's where, when you talk about people in poverty, that's where it goes. Ghettos, poverty—men don't know nothin' but slop and mop. Or sweep the streets, you're lucky to get one of them jobs.

See, if you don't know nothin' you can't do nothin'; the paper's full of jobs every day. It's where you come from, your parents, your background. You ain't got some background behind you, or somebody got some money to send you to school, or help you go to school, you're lost. You'll never make it. Somebody got to have money to get you started unless you're an A student and can get a scholarship.

One of my daughters is an A student. She got a scholarship. She wound up a paralegal, works at group hospitalization, Blue Cross. She went to school. My mother helped her, my sister helped her. I didn't even know it.

David
Port Orchard, Washington

We sit on the stained, recovered couch of a cooperative family shelter in Washington State. The room is large and stuffy with the smell of people and their bedding. A variety of toys litter the floor. In the adjoining kitchen a young woman makes tuna sandwiches while her children rest in the family's bedroom upstairs. It is a warm place, the atmosphere clearly that of the respectful tolerance those who live together well learn to achieve.

An African American in his early thirties, David has a thin, tense body, and eyes that reveal the determination and strain of his war against addiction. He speaks with conviction and energy, needing to talk. "We always had a place," he says. "Food, money, we always had everything we needed."

His young son dances in and out of the room, occasionally hopping onto the couch as we speak. David keeps an eye on the boy, noting where he has gone each time he leaves the room. But the boy is always quick to dart back, glowing in the warmth of his father's protective gaze.

DRUGS BROUGHT ME DOWN: kickers, acid, PCP, crack, crank, anything you can name. Me and my family. And where we were everyone took drugs. You go outside, you see it. You stay home, they come to your door. We had to leave to escape. That puts us in this shelter.

Now crank, it's synthetic, it's something they make. It's like, well crack is supposed to be cooked cocaine. But it's not. Crack is something you have to make out in the middle of nowhere, 'cause it makes such a smell to cook it. But crank, it's propanol, you can look that up and find out what's in that—they use it with animals somewhere. Also Benadryl, yeah, that stuff that comes in nasal inhalers, they can make a cheap type of crank with that. It's not a high, it's a stimulant. You can be up all night on it.

But this synthetic cocaine, crack, it's like when it gets inside of me ... it's crazy man. It's so crazy, it's just so insane. You think it's a drug. It's not; it's a poison. When I get it inside of me it totally takes control; I feel like I've got an alien inside me. Seriously.

I mean I can't even touch it—not without getting an effect from it. Just touching it, you know. So if it's inside of me what does it do?

I'm not sayin' I don't want it, I'm not sayin' I have quit—that's something I've learned not to say. I just deal day by day, week by week. And hopefully one day it goes right into forever.

Then I'll see it, have it around me, maybe I'll go out and somebody give me a little drop. I'll just let it sit there in my hand. That's what I'm looking for, looking forward to being able to be around it and not use it. That would mean total control. You know, if someone said, "Here, this is yours." You might want to try some, you know, from past experience. But then you'd look at what it would cost you, and you'd say, "Can't do it." But if I felt like I do now I'd shove it right in his face, or grind it in the street beneath my heel.

That's why now, if I knew who was making the stuff, I wouldn't have no choice—there'd be nothing I could do but go and waste him. I know how hard it hurt me, so I know it hurts other people. I'd kill him; I'd have to. It'd be self- defense. It'd be stoppin' a murderer.

Because crack ... crack man, it's not even cocaine. It's poison. It's more poison than cocaine. You know it can't be cocaine because it's too cheap. Guy shows you this rock and says five, ten bucks, you know there can't be no cocaine in it.

You know what the main ingredient of most crack is? For the stuff we used to make we'd use Raid. Roach spray. That's right, poison. 'Cause it's oily, cooks down real nice with a little coke, dries hard and white. And it gives you an effect. It's not good, I mean you know it's got to fuck you up—it's roach spray.

I swear to God I think someone's trying to take over the country with it. Think about it: People so poor now they can't afford cocaine. So what they do? They take a tiny bit of cocaine and they make something this big with it [he makes a circle with his thumb and forefinger the size of a large marble], sell it for five, ten bucks, so everybody can do it. Get everybody hooked on it. A little bit of cocaine and a lot of poison. Make everybody come back for more and more of it, make 'em fight and steal for it. See what I'm sayin'?

Sherry
San Francisco, California

We meet in the soup kitchen of a Methodist church, introducing ourselves over the clatter of silverware on soup bowls and the relieved laughter of children glad to be back indoors for the evening. Sherry has been in the area only a few days, having fled Los Angeles and the life of crack addiction she led there. Though excessively thin she is young, vibrant, and athletic, and jubilant in her escape.

Now homeless and alone with her young son in a strange city, she spends whole days window-shopping. The child, Kareem, sleeps upon her shoulder as she wanders by storefronts, passing the daylight hours in which her shelter remains closed.

An African American, Sherry is in her early twenties.

IT'S ME AND MY LITTLE GUY KAREEM. Kareem's three. We just moved here to San Francisco; we've been here about three weeks. Moved down from LA. Too much of a drug scene there. The apartment, the area … it's all the drug. I just had to get out.

There were robbings, a lot of people were smoking crack; hiding in corners, holding pipes.…

They got nice parks and stuff, don't get me wrong. They got a park with a fountain and everything. It's beautiful for kids to play there. But it's all drug related. The drug dealers use the park. A kid goes to kick a ball behind a tree and there's somebody hiding there smoking rock. It's no good. They snatch bracelets off little kids' arms. Anything. They'll sell their shirt, their shoes, anything to get that rock.

When you're smoking that rock there are no worse days. It's only bad when it's gone. That's when you're like, "Oh, I gotta get more!" It just makes you want more and more and more. But you never really get anything high up after that one first hit. That's it. But it's in your mind. People just keep going and going, thinking they're getting this hit. It's not so. You never get as high as you do when you take that first hit.

In the daytime I was always sleepin' because I was up all night smokin'. Then it's okay to stand on corners, light the pipe. You take a hit and you blow it out and it's like… spaced, for a minute. You just sit there. You blank. And then you bug out and look all over the floor to see if you've dropped any rocks. The next thing you know a couple hours have passed. The whole night has passed. If you've got enough you'll stay in the room. You'll smoke, you will not come out. You won't drink water, you'll get dehydrated; you don't want to eat, you lose weight. You lose all aspects—forget the rag, forget food, forget clothes, forget baths, just forget everything but the rock. That's all the rock makes you do. It just keeps goin' around, just keeps goin' and goin' and goin'. It makes you want no other drug but that one.

I mean I've stood out on corners and made fake rocks. And I'd go up 'the nearest dealer, say "Yo man, let me see a rock." And see I got so slick 'cause I wanted it so bad: I'd be able to switch that rock in his face and take the real one, give him the fake one. I'd use a piece of plaster, anything that I could find that looked like one. I'd wrap it up in foil.

Or I'd say, "I don't want this one, it's too small, let me see another one." Then, "let me see another one," until finally I've got a big one. That's the one I'd switch. Very dangerous. And then sometimes I'd say, "give me a rock." Then, chooom! Take off and run. But they know you, you live in the neighborhood. Especially rock dealers, they know you. Stuff like that I used to do all the time.

I didn't care, that's the thing. I feared for my safety when I was straight, but when I was high I didn't care. I would do it, come right back downstairs when I was done with it and do it again.

They had this one dark alley … they'd take people who didn't know the scene, like who wanted to get high but didn't know who to cop from? 'Cause there's a lot of trick dealers that sell phony stuff to get real stuff for themselves. They'd bring them in the alley, rob 'em, beat 'em up, take their money. Leave 'em bleedin' in the alley. They beat this one guy with baseball bats. I know 'cause I'm lookin' at this from my window.

And this one particular case, this guy asked this girl for, you know … for a blast, and so she set it up with her boyfriend. She left the door unlocked when her and the guy are in the room. So they're doin' their little blast and everything and the boyfriend comes in the room and it's, "What's goin' on?!" It's a set-up. So they beat the guy up. The guy only had twenty-two bucks but he had a lot of rocks on him. The guy said, "Don't beat me up. Look, I'll give you a hit, you don't have to go through that." They beat him up anyway, took everything. Then the guy ended up smokin' all his rocks with them. This is happenin' inside the hotel where I stayed.

Then the dealer that lived in my building, some addicts broke in and robbed her: beat her really bad, tied her hands and legs behind her back, gagged her and everything. Took all her drugs, her money, her gold.

Also this hotel, the owners know. The people that work there, when they get off they go in the drug dealer's room and get high. I saw this one guy say to the dealer, "Let me see eight rocks." So she puts them in his hand and he puts them in his pocket. So she looks at him, you know, and he goes, "The hell with you. Call the cops," and walks out. No problem, you know. "I let you be here so you got to pay me." They all get their palms greased, every worker in there.

As long as they're gettin' their money every month they can care less what's goin' on in the building. They don't even take care of the building. They keep the lobby nice and pretty, but the inside—the walls, the apartments, the rugs—dirt and garbage. It's bad. It's not worth what they charge. They run that place ... and the rooms look like... like a camp where they would keep prisoners. And all women and kids. You know, a welfare place. It's a shame the way they have ya living.

But I can't really put the blame on anybody, you know. On the hotels or the dealers. It's the drug. It alters your mind, makes people do things that they normally wouldn't do. It changes you.

Like I have a friend, she'd do anything for you before she'd take care of herself. But when she got a hold of the drug she didn't care about her kid, she didn't care about me. Because when you're high, and I know from experience, you will do and try anything to get that drug. That's it. And it's mainly crack, other drugs I really didn't see there. Crack, period.

Ron
Arlington, Virginia

*We meet in a community clinic and shelter as neat and tidy
as the town's colonial storefronts. Ron seems ill-fitted for such
a place, his features sharp and rough against the newly paneled
walls and padded office furniture.*

Ron is white and of Irish descent. He is perhaps 40 years old.

I'VE BEEN HOMELESS for years. This time it's by choice. I had a hassle
with my roommate and rather than knock the shit out of him and go
to jail, I left. Before that I'd been an addict and didn't have a choice. I
had a choice, but the choice was I'd rather use than get straight. If I do
use I don't have a choice: I'm a slave to whatever drug I use.

See, an addict's an addict's an addict, whatever your drug of choice.
Some people go from pot to beer to heroine to coke to everything. Some
people kick alcohol to get onto heroine; they substitute one drug for
another. They say, "Hey, I'm not an alcoholic. I might be a heroine
addict, but I ain't no wino." And any of those guys will cut your throat
for a roll of dope!

I used to go into liquor stores and boost it right off the shelf. My
buddy'd keep the guy busy and I'd grab a bottle of Jack Daniels, stick
it in my jacket. A lot of times they see you steal it, but they'd rather
leave you alone 'cause they don't know how nuts you are.

I think what happens to a lot of people ... well, there are a few things
in life that can really hurt a person: loss of a loved one or spouse, loss
of a job, and divorce—or losing your kids. I know this girl just recently,
her child was killed by an electric garage door. It's done something to
her.... She's separated from her husband now, and she's a coke addict.

See when you want to ease the pain or feel better you take a drug, everybody does. Look at TV. I mean Christ, everybody's taking aspirins or Tylenol to ease the pain of reality or whatever. There are a million people out there that went over that line—tried to ease the pain and crash! You've got the disease of addiction.

And if a person don't want to stop you can't do anything to make him stop. I know it; take it from me. I've lost it all man. I've had houses, cars, boats, two wives, fantastic jobs.... What I do is I make geographic changes. I leave a problem to get away from it, to run. I go from coast to coast, North to South. But there's no running away from yourself. You can throw your guts up in a toilet in Seattle as well as you can in Boston. If you're sick you're sick.

See addiction is a disease, that's all I've ever known it as. People are just beginning to accept that. As for whose fault it is, it's definitely genetic. My father was an alcoholic, my grandfather was an alcoholic. All my cousins on my father's side are, my uncle was. But it's killed my sister, it's killed my father, and my brother's in the penitentiary. That's the way alcohol goes. It's a physical obsession and a mental passion. It is. It hits you and man it's pretty fuckin' sick.

It isn't even how much you drink: it's what it does to you. There's a guy I knew, he drank three times in his life. The first time he got a DWI, got in a wreck and wiped out. The second time he did something crazy and the third time he killed himself.

And it's tough. I work construction, all the guys think they're hot shit and I get a hassle about it. They'll say, "Hey Ron, let's go get a drink." I'll say, "I can't drink, you guys know that." "Then let's smoke some reefer." "Hey I can't do that either man." I'd like to, doesn't mean I don't want to. But I can't. I smoke a little dope and two weeks from now I'll be drinking. And when I'm drinking ... bam! I'm in trouble. In a heartbeat. One time I went through $1,855 on an eight-week drunk.

I got started in Nam. It was something I never realized was happening.... You're nineteen or twenty, and you see a lot of John Wayne movies. And then you get off the plane and you see a whole lot of body bags and it's for real. It ain't another story, man. This is real, this is fuckin' real! Everybody just looked at you and said, "Hey man, you got thirteen months here: get used to it and keep your ass down."

I did heroin, Mexican Brown there. And every time I fired it up it took me out of this world. That's why I did it, I didn't want to be in reality. Not that reality.

Later there was the excitement—going down to cop it in the bad part of town, seeing if you could outsmart the cops, a lot of excitement that. Then finally getting it and getting the high, getting the rush. That's why I always relapse so much, I like the excitement in my life. If I wasn't getting in trouble in one form or another I was walking steel eighteen stories in the air on a construction job. I was always in the air because I liked being on the edge.

But when I was in the war it was fear, peer pressure, and to ease the pain, to try to feel good. You didn't know when you were going to die, and your life was so completely maxed out. '67 to '70. It was a pretty heavy time. Then when I got home everybody was calling me a baby-killer and all that shit. And the heroin....

There's a guy in D.C. I knew. He's an addict and he says, "G'damn, did you hear about those eight people that died shooting up that smack this weekend?" I said, "Yeah, that was pretty bad." What it was, the stuff wasn't stepped on, stepped on means it's cut. It wasn't stepped on enough and these guys fired it up. It was too strong, gave 'em a hot shot and they died. Anyway, this son-of-a-bitch, he says, "Man I'd like to find that shit, that's some good shit."

That's insanity, isn't it? That's a disease, man. Insane. See addiction is the only disease there is that tells you you don't have it. It's not like anything I know of. If you have a bad appendix you know you have it and you had better do something about it. If you get in trouble with alcohol or drugs you forget the pain and you figure, "Oh, I can handle it." The cops told me, the judge told me, people told me, "Hey, you're addicted." But I kept on going. All my friends are using it, and how else are you going to fill the void? What else are you gonna do when your whole life revolves around drugs, or alcohol, or both?

I know four guys this year that couldn't take it. One guy got a bunch of librium on his birthday, and then he drank. Yup, on his birthday killed himself. Another guy got in a fight with his girlfriend, then shot himself. One guy jumped off a bridge, missed the water and hit the rocks. He lived for a day or so. That's a hell of a way to go out.

See you get to a point where you ... hell, there's a lot of times I'd like to die. Either I didn't have the balls or a gun handy. I ain't no hero; I've had some real, real bad times.

It's a sad thing. People start out trying to use drugs socially and end up a slave to them. And end up dying behind them, or in prison beyond them. Losing families.

Like right now they're doing a lot of PCP. I've done it, but not very much. I know a lot of people who're PCPing, who smoke it. You sprinkle it on parsley, or on pot. It's an hallucinogen. Or what you do is you buy the stuff, it's liquid, then you dunk your joint in it, let it dry. Then—well, you know what it does—it blows you away. It's the worst shit I ever smoked. But a lot of people are doing it, a lot of people. It makes a lot of people crazy, out of their head. They don't even know they're out of their own head. When you're gettin' drunk you know you're gettin' drunk. When you smoke this stuff you don't know how far gone you are until you're totally gone. And then sometimes you go and never come back.

John
San Francisco, California

John and his family have been waiting for the money to buy bus tickets out of San Francisco. Together with his wife and children, he is a crack victim and survivor.

In his late thirties, John is an African American.

LET ME TELL YOU a little about my background. I'm a vet. I spent ten years in the military, including Vietnam. I came to California to start my life after the military because my mother and sister were here. Everything was good. We were doing all right, my wife and me, our kids ... and I got caught up in crack. I put us in this situation [homeless], and I can hardly stand myself for it.

I've been clean four and a half months now, no counselor or anything. My wife decided one day she was gonna leave me. We had already lost my job, the apartment, everything. That snapped me out of it. Now I'm gonna put it behind me and be the person that I was before I started on the drug.

Let me tell you how foolish I was. I worked for an insurance company. I was making six-fifty every other Thursday. Paydays I had my Citicorp card right there to pay the dope man. I ain't ashamed to admit it. Anybody try rubbin' it in my face, they can do it. I know I made a mistake. Big time. I never messed with drugs in the military. I just got hooked with the wrong people here. But I don't blame the people that turned me on. I blame myself for taking that first hit of crack.

I think about that. I mean I don't put myself on a pedestal so high and think, "Yeah, I'm so high and mighty that I've got this thing beat." I don't believe that I have it beat. I really don't. 'Cause crack is dangerous. And I'm scared of it, scared of it bad. There's still that possibility that if I get weak, then I can destroy everything that I have going for me.

Sometimes I feel like crying when I think about it. You know what? Let me tell you something. We was talkin' yesterday, me and my oldest son, Calvin. Calvin is very smart. I said, "Remember all the times that I used to tell you I was going to take you to the zoo and I didn't, ended up backing off all the time?" I said, "It was because your daddy was on cocaine." This is my six-year-old son I'm talkin' to. I said, "Your daddy was on cocaine." And he remembers every time I promised to take him on this payday and didn't. "Your daddy was on cocaine. I was blowin' the money. I was takin' it from you. I was stealin' it from your mom and your brothers!" [he weeps]. I said, "I was taking this from you."

I'm serious, I'm telling you straight from the heart [he continues to cry]. I need someone to talk to sometimes like this. 'Cause I made mistakes, man, and it hurts me. I'm not used to this, to what I did to my family. I hurt my family bad. I hurt myself even worse, knowing what I know now. I won't hurt them, I thought. But I did.

I didn't ... I can say I knew, but after I got that first hit I didn't care, you know. The most important thing to me then was getting that hit. Hey, get that hit off good! By the time half the day was over I was stone cold cryin' the rock man blues, as they say. I was stone cold cryin'. But it was too late. All the money'd be gone.

But now, you know, end of the week we'll be out of here. And this woman, my wife, she loves me. We got a family that's just like this! [he wraps his fingers together to indicate "close"]. But I blew it ... and man if I ever go back I think I'd commit suicide. I could not go back through the things I have gone through and hurt my family again.

What happened was my family got kicked out of the house where we were staying with my mother and we had to move into a place quick, and we moved to the wrong area. See my sister and my mother got arguin' with my wife one day.... Anyway, we were in this house of a friend's, where they got these housing projects. They had kicked their own son out for the same thing. For crack. Then one of his friends came by looking for him, didn't even know he was gone. I said, "No, he don't live here no more." We started talking about some things. Next thing I know I'm hitting the pipe:

"You tried the crack, man?"

"Oh no, I just smoke the weed."

"Try the crack."

"No, I heard it... "

"No really, it ain't like that."

I let them out-and-out talk me into it. I took that first hit ... they play it so smooth, give you one hit, give you another hit. Then when you start really hard tweakin', you ask for another. *I* asked for another. Then it's, "You got some money?" See, you start askin'!

Then, you know, you can't think of anything else. You get a hit, the very first hit is what gets you. It takes your brain so high, but it doesn't last very long. It may only last two or three minutes. So then you go for another one, to try to reach that high or higher, but you never get there. So you keep goin' and goin'. It will rush your brain so high so quick, it give you such a feeling....

Sometimes I wouldn't go to work 'cause I'd been up all night. Sometimes I'd call in sick. Sometimes I'd go on a break, sit in the bathroom and sleep. Or my work wouldn't be as proficient because I was sittin' there nodding all the time in front of the computer.

I quit, I didn't get fired.

It's terrible to live with. It is terrible. I'm gonna tell you.... One of the guys [he weeps] ... This is hard. One of the guys that used to smoke with me raped my wife. And she didn't want to tell the police because she thought they would take me in for being on the drug. You understand?!

My wife talks to me sometimes and I'm in another world. I'm thinking about all this. She says, "What's wrong?" I say, "Nothing," but she knows better. She knows I'm still thinkin' about it all. See she stayed with me. And I be stupid enough to go back to that shit? No way! But man ... this drug is the devil. It's, it's just ... terrible. I don't know what word I could use ... some slithering, evil word.

I used to have eight, nine, ten year olds selling it to me. And I've got four children! Before ... before I'd had a hit that day I would never buy it from them. But after it hit my head and I was going back for my second one it didn't hurt, 'cause I was gonna get that good stuff.

When I get home I want to tell some people this. And I think they should have more counseling programs. This shelter should have some kind of program so when people come in they can talk, have a counselor talk with them. They need someone to talk one on one with. I know they need that 'cause I know why 90 percent of the people are here—the same reason I am.

Myself, I feel fortunate that I didn't need counseling. I had my wife to step on my head and get me right. But I'm still sayin' that I need somebody to talk to, 'cause I've had the urge.

You read about the drug and they say you can go ten years without doing it, but the urge is still going to be there. A song or a person will bring it back to mind.

Sometimes I can't even talk about it without drifting into that feeling. And sometimes when we're waiting for money I'll dream about the drug. The next morning I'll say, "We'll get a check soon." She'll ask me about it. "How do you know?" I'll say, "Last night I dreamed I was smoking crack." Within two days we got money. The drug'll talk to you and tell you. It lives on money.

I can tell you stories.... Most of the people I did it with lost their children. A case worker would come to their house and take their kids. Or they'd be pregnant and get so high they'd end up in the hospital. They'd draw their blood, 'cause they'd be almost comatose, and find the coke. If they survived the doctors would tell 'em they'd lose the baby—when the baby come out they're gonna take it. San Francisco don't play with any of this stuff. They'll take it from you.

But it never stopped them. When you're high it just all seems a big joke. And I was too stupid to realize what was happening. But after my wife did what she did to me, after she said she was leavin', then I saw myself losing her and the children....

But that's where the drug is so dangerous, it blinds you! It blinds you.... It just ... nothing is important to you but that, nothing.... Like me, even after she got raped, it still wasn't enough for me to stop. It still wasn't enough for me to stop!

Carlo
Philadelphia, Pennsylvania

Seeking shelter from the rain, we sit huddled on a small stoop off an alley in Philadelphia, our feet wet where they protrude beyond the awning of the doorway. Carlo sips the coffee I've bought him, his strong shoulders hunched forward over the cup as if to catch the steam rising from it.

"I don't know what you wanted to hear," he begins. His voice is sure, measured. He straightens a leg—they are remarkably thin for his muscular arms and chest. Dark, sinewy muscles rise along the nape of his neck where his hair has been clipped short. Carlo is an African American in his early thirties.

WHEN I FIRST EVER STEPPED on the streets, slept on the streets, pride was the problem: didn't have a job; didn't want to live for free; didn't want to ask anybody for anything.

Now it's different. Now drugs is the problem. All people want to do now is get high. They would rather get high than pay the rent. You see? It's drugs. And it's the main thing that runs people out here.

You know what got me? Though I was livin' on the streets I'd never done anything more than smoke weed and drink beer. Okay? And I very seldom drank beer. Now we're talkin' two, three years ago.

I get this job with the city and everybody was messin' with drugs. Right? And everybody was like, "Hmm, you don't do this?" And I felt like, this job is my insurance I won't have to come back out here on the street again. I had to be accepted. Now how do you be accepted in an environment where everybody's taking drugs? You take drugs with 'em. And I did.

It's been about a year in my life that I've messed with drugs. My drug addiction was not so much physical ... they say I don't even have a drug addiction. I had a social problem, it was for acceptance. I couldn't knock it because it was part of the job and I wanted the job. It's the truth—I want you to know what's goin' on in this city. They got the biggest drug problem you ever seen.

So now I'm homeless again. I was messin' with like ... let me see, I was on the average doin' six or seven hundred dollars worth of drugs a week. And I wasn't really making that much money. I was extending myself. So when I went into this drug program I lost my apartment. But it wasn't that I didn't pay my rent; I was messin' with so many drugs there that the landlady didn't want me back in the house. I understood that. Subconsciously I really didn't want to go back there anyway because a lot of people I knew messed with drugs there.

So when she told me to leave it wasn't really a problem, you know. But that was in April and it's July now. See I got hit by a car on a holiday. I took my vacation time and I went to the drug program. I had just got back to work—I went back to work for two days—and got hit by the car. So I haven't worked in 35 days, haven't even received any workman's comp. yet.

So I'm stuck. I'm homeless and broke, but I have a job. I can't work yet, but I do have a job. No place to live, no food, no money. But I have a job I'll return to. You see, as long as I work there's no assistance for me. I told 'em, I said, "Well look. I just got out of a drug program, then I got hit by a car. I don't have any money yet. Put me somewhere and I'll start payin' rent first check I get."

But when I tell 'em they don't say, "Hey brother, this man went through some changes. He needs a little time to get on his feet." Instead it's, "We can't do that." Because I have a job I can't get into a shelter. But I don't got no money because I haven't been able to work. I can't win. I just can't win. My problem is I tell 'em the truth, I tell 'em I have a job. I shouldn't ever tell 'em that.

Right now I have two dollars in my pocket. I got to use a dollar and a quarter to go back to work, soon as I'm over my injuries from the car wreck. Then I might have to work for two weeks before I get a check, seeing how it doesn't look like I'll get my workman's comp. first. But I gotta eat, I gotta stay some place. And I gotta take care of myself so I can look presentable when I go back to work. Now how am I gonna do that?

CHAPTER 8

FAMILIES

Families are more likely to form during periods of economic expansion and more likely to dissolve during periods of economic decline.[1] This pattern, which can be traced back through the Depression, also correlates with the incidence of single-parent families and with some measures of child abuse and neglect.

There was a time when this was understood. Scholars regularly attributed family dissolution to unemployment in the 1960s, for instance, and historians have long described changes in family structure in terms of the economic contexts in which they occurred.

However, over the last twenty years the link between economic conditions and family stability has been overlooked. Instead, it has been argued that a family's structure and stability, even its finances, are driven by values and motivation—factors said to be undermined by state assistance.[2] Aid to Families with Dependent Children (AFDC), food stamps, and other programs for poor families have been particularly demonized in this climate. And the welfare system in general has had to stand the blame for marital discord, gang violence, drug abuse, low test scores, and, now, homelessness.

Fear of the effects of welfare payments on families gained particular momentum as the costs and size of public assistance programs grew through the 1960s and early 1970s. Since the number of poor and single-parent families also rose during this period, it seemed natural to assume that the two trends were linked.

Interestingly, when cutbacks in welfare programs yet more dramatically increased family poverty and dissolution in the 1980s, the correlation between those two trends went largely unnoticed. Similarly, it is rarely observed today that rates of homelessness among families break down along strict economic lines that tell of sharp declines in family income. Together with other situational factors, it is these declines—and not some deficiency in values or motivation—that has caused the great surge in recently homeless families.

Unfortunately, evidence to support such a purely economic view of family destitution is obscured by the nature of the debate over welfare. Data that would otherwise help us make sense of the details of the matter are as frequently abused as used in the course of the discussion, and the issue is unnecessarily complicated by fear, prejudice, and resentment. Finally, the facts we do have appear contradictory.

It should be admitted, for example, that there are neighborhoods throughout the country in which virtually every family is supported by AFDC, and in which the children tend to also become dependent on AFDC. However, it is also true that most families who rely on AFDC do so only temporarily, and that high welfare payments have been shown to reduce welfare dependency.[3]

While paradoxical from the perspective of "values and motivation," these facts are easily aligned in the earlier association between family status and economic well-being. Under this model, a parent who had no opportunities other than to remain on AFDC would be expected to do so—especially when faced with more frightening alternatives, like prostitution or homelessness. Conversely, a parent whose assistance provided the means to pursue better opportunities would naturally reach for them.

Moreover, part of the reactionary equation is true: work does bring stability—or at least "employment" does. And lack of adequate employment is the most salient factor in the decline in family income. There is little evidence that mere "work" (without remuneration) is redeeming, however. And there are no statistical grounds for claiming that receiving something simply because you need it is debilitating. College students do very well on need-based scholarships, and industries that receive tax waivers during recessionary periods benefit much more than they suffer from such arrangements.

Arguments to the contrary claim that family dissolution and state-dependency have increased through periods of recent prosperity—periods when an economic model of family stability would predict they should fall. But family income, while falling with downturns in the national economy, no longer swings upward on economic rebounds. Average family income for all but the richest 20 percent of American families fell from 1977 to 1988, for example, and the poorest fifth of American families saw their incomes decline by 11.4 percent.[4] Overall, the percentage of families below the poverty line grew rather steadily through the mid '70s and early '80s despite the much-heralded economic expansion, declining family size, and an increase in two-paycheck households.[5]

As has been mentioned before, the incidence of extreme poverty grew even more sharply during this period, and the effects of these trends were particularly felt by minority and working-class families whose men once held jobs the service economy no longer needs. Consequently, unemployment rates for black men skyrocketed from less than 10 percent in 1969 to highs that currently top 50 percent in some areas.[6] This trend swept the foundation out from underneath thousands of households and is the single most important factor in the increased number of black, single-parent families.[7]

Such families now account for 40 percent of those who receive AFDC, the largest federal welfare program. Roughly another 40 percent are white, while Latino recipients make up almost 20 percent.[8] And most use welfare just as it was meant to be used—as short-term assistance to help families stay together through hard times. In California, for example, the median period for first-time recipients is nine months, and more than half of all families that get on the dole get off by the end of their second year.[9]

But economic stability entails more than mere income. Rising housing costs have lowered standards of living for people in most income brackets, and the very poor have felt the brunt of these changes more than anyone. Of this group, families, whose living and shelter expenses are higher than those of individuals, are by far the hardest hit—a pattern that continues to gain momentum over the period of the current recession. Ultimately, families can fall to such abject levels of destitution that self-sufficiency becomes nearly impossible to attain.

This is particularly apparent in the narratives that follow. Each of the families that appears in this chapter had a home; each now has lost it. And the type of housing they could once afford they can no longer find. Government support for low-income housing fell 76 percent by the time they became homeless, and the kinds of employment many of them depended on disappeared nearly as quickly.[10] Together with demographic changes, inner-city gentrification, and mismanagement of Department of Housing and Urban Development funds,[11] such cuts and changes foretold a housing market destined to run out of room for them.

Moreover—and contrary to current views—willingness to work did not solve their problems. Two of the families are virtual models of the work ethic, and all sought to one day support themselves. Indeed, the fact that many of them fell into homelessness despite strong values and motivation remains a source of disappointment and confusion for these families. "We had jobs, we worked hard," I was told. "It's not supposed to be like this for people like us."

And whereas assistance programs once kept such families afloat, the families that appear here found little help from government agencies.[12] In fact, no other group has experienced as sharp a decline in income as have AFDC mothers and their children over the last twenty years.[13] While intended as punitive—a means of motivating such people to find work—these cuts have had rather the opposite effect. Karla, whose story follows, is a prime example. While she had hoped to use her benefits as a stopgap measure while she returned to school and looked for work, rising housing costs eroded her assistance to the point where she was literally pushed into the street.[14] Belle, whose story concludes the chapter, ironically found herself too poor to even qualify for help.

Nor could these families have predicted the emergencies and health costs that played such an important role in their difficulties, or the changes in the industries that had employed them. And child-care costs eroded what these families could earn, a fact nonetheless crippling for its obviousness.[15]

Another thread common to these stories is "family" itself. Each of these families lacked familial connections—either with friends, relatives, a neighbor, or any other community—to sustain them through their difficulties. At other times families did receive family help, but not to the extent they needed. The lack of such a support network, arguably the most salient characteristic of homeless people, is particularly devastating for homeless families.[16]

Finally, each family was impacted by a variety of factors. Most families can endure unemployment, a housing adjustment, or medical emergency, but few can weather all three, especially if they are poor to begin with and lack a support network. Drug addiction, alcoholism, and child and spousal abuse—common at all levels of our society—also prove devastating for poor families. Belle, for instance, saw the dysfunctional nature of her parents' lives sadly re-created in her own.

Together with shrinking incomes and the spiraling costs of housing, these factors contributed to the more than fourfold increase of homeless families that occurred from 1984 to 1988—the period that put all of these families out of their home.[17] Unfortunately, we are yet to enter the era in which they can afford another.[18]

Don and Terri
Roanoke, Virginia

Don leads me through a shelter door to introduce me to his children. "This is Sarah; she's ten. Here is Jason; he's nine. And this little rascal is Anthony; he's eight."

The children politely shake hands with me, confidently asserting their "Hellos." Sarah says, "Glad to meet you." It is not me they want to see, however, but their father. The introductions concluded, they leap into his great arms, his wide grasp engulfing them all.

Don is an African American and Terri is white; they are in their thirties.

Terri:

WE BOTH HAD full-time jobs. He was a plumber; I worked in shipping and receiving in a warehouse for a mail-order company. But even working—even working overtime—trying to make ends meet was ridiculous.

We've been at the situation where you work sixty-, seventy-hour weeks, and when you bring the paycheck back, it's gone. And then you don't have time to be with your kids. We saw the kids on Sundays, and at that time it was washing clothes, cleaning house, trying to rest. It is rough. We've had more times than not when the paychecks come in and you have to wonder, "What bill do we skip this time so we can buy the kids shoes?" Or "Wintertime comin', what bills can we let slide until we can get 'em winter coats?" And when you're workin' out there it shouldn't be that way. If you're willin' to work, and do for yourself, you should be given some kind of a break. You should at least make it.

It makes you feel like you're going out there and breakin' your back and not accomplishing anything.

Don:

We got behind in our rent several times and had to catch up to keep from being evicted. We'd patch our work pants, put off buyin' another pair for a month, and put that forty extra dollars on the back rent. Or I'll give you a better example, our kids looked at us one day and said, "You all sure love cheese." Because me and her lived on cheese for a solid week, 'cause we didn't have nothin' else. We made sure the kids had other food, but for us it was nothin' but cheese.

Terri:

See it really got worse in the last few years. The economy ... things are a lot more expensive, children's clothing and things. Utility rates go up, rent goes up.

Like I had insurance for me and the kids at work, but there was a $600 deductible. So you still couldn't go to the doctor. One time I walked around for a solid week, sick but not missing work, until I fell down and they called the life-savin' crew and took me to the hospital. I had double pneumonia. I was hopin' it was just a flu and was takin' Alka-Seltzer Plus to try and knock it out of me so I wouldn't have to pay for a doctor and miss work. And I ended up even worse.

Then Donnie, he was in a car wreck. He was hurt real bad, and so they had a lawsuit going and all this. I had to miss work to appear before our lawyer, the insurance company, that type of thing.

The employer was a bigot. He liked me up until the first day that Donnie came in to pick me up and he saw that he was black. After that he gave me a hard time, constantly. I had the paper work, I had approved permission to miss those days. But when I come back to clock in, my time card wasn't there. He says, "Well, I need someone dependable." Fired me because I had "missed work."

I had worked there three years. In fact, I had more seniority than he did. And it wasn't even whole days—it was three afternoons that I missed.

And the job that Donnie was on, by the time he was medically released to go back to work, they had layed him off. So we were living on my unemployment there for a while.

Don:

It was a drunk driver. Ran into us, knocked us around this corner, sort of snapped my neck. I had muscle damage in my neck to where I couldn't do no liftin', no nothin'. It hurt to even lift your head up in the morning, you know. I walked around with my neck about that big [holds his hands in a wide circle]. I mean it was huge.

I didn't get a penny from it—even got layed off in the process. Hadn't been long enough there to draw unemployment off of 'em. The company I'd worked for before, they protested against giving me unemployment since they didn't like it that I had gone to work for someone else. So no unemployment and no compensation.

I tried to go out there and work, neck hurtin' and all. Do little odds and ends jobs to try to make a little money. All we had then was her unemployment—$482 a month, plus whatever we could get together.

Altogether, I've worked as a plumber now for about five years. I mean if you would of told me five months ago this was gonna happen, I'd have told you you were crazy. Then all of a sudden I can't work, we lose our jobs, and we have no home. And I have three kids and a wife. No money to go somewhere else.

It's a rough situation. Wake up one day and say, "Hey, we're not going to be in this house anymore and we've got nowhere to go." I didn't know what to do and she cried, she cried many a night, sayin' "What are we gonna do?" And I'd say, "We'll just keep tryin', we'll just keep our heads up and something good will come by eventually."

I have three children. Sarah, Jason, and Anthony. They were worried; they didn't know what to expect. And you know, if the government agencies, child protection, heard we had three children on the street we would of lost 'em. And that's a scary feeling. We could've lost 'em very easily. That's something we prayed about every night.

[Don pauses for a moment, then turns to Terri.] It's been rough, hasn't it? [She nods in agreement, thinking.] But with the Good Lord's will we're gonna make it. We're gonna make it.

The Smiths, Gerald and Connie
Des Moines, Iowa

The Smiths have lived throughout the Midwest, seen a variety of hard times, and held a number of jobs. White, they speak in an easy drawl. They are affable and middle-aged, though they appear much older. An entourage of their four children answers the door as I approach the church-sponsored home they've lived in for the past month.

WE'VE FOUR KIDS, ages nine to six. From Arkansas, but we moved from the Marshalltown [Iowa] area. Got ripped up there for $275 by a landlord who said he'd have this apartment ready and up to welfare standards. We paid him; but when they went out to check on it, he didn't have the lavatory hooked up, didn't have hot running water. The outside walls were rotten for two feet. The fire marshal just looked at it and ordered us out.

We couldn't move in, and 'cause he had our $275 we didn't have enough money left to do anything else. So there you sit. Some of our stuff's still out there in a building behind the apartment.

We stayed with my mother a while, and it kind of worked a hardship on her with her landlord. We stayed with some friends and it didn't work out. So then we got hold of the Salvation Army and the DHS sent us to Des Moines, 'cause there's no shelters or emergency housing for homeless families in Marshalltown.

There was work in Marshalltown, but it was in meat processing plants. I've been involved in two different truck accidents, and I've got back injuries. That puts an awful, awful damper on what I can do 'cause I cannot do a lot of heavy lifting, or anything like that. It also causes me to have some trouble with my insides, where if I'm on my feet for any length of time I have some trouble standing and stuff. My leg gets crappy and just goes out from under me.

The first accident was in '80. I was drivin' for Atlas Van Lines. We had to drop a load in Oklahoma and pick up two in Texas comin' back. The driver that was with me, well he hit the back end of this truck's trailer. I was up in the bunk and it threw me clear through the windshield. Pinned me between our tractor and the back of the trailer we hit.

'Come to find out this driver had no chauffeur license, no DOT physical card, no DOT papers of no kind. He was a friend of one of the office personnel, and he went and hired him without doing a driver's check on him. And I went through an awful battle to get anything out of the insurance company because of the fact that they had an unlicensed driver on that truck with me.

Company paid the doctor bills and the hospital bills but I didn't get nothin' for the damages. I did get an attorney and go to court against 'em, but all I got was $500 for the six months' work I lost.

Wasn't enough. Didn't have much savings either. And pain like you never know, layin' up in bed all the time. Thing of it was, different family members on both sides helped us along, and that's how we made it.

Then I went to work for another company and in '84 I was out in Cleveland, Ohio. I was supposed to load a load of freight but the trailer had all kinds of holes in the top and the floor and stuff. I called the company and told 'em it wasn't safe to be loaded. They said, "Well you get it loaded, bring it home, get it emptied out and we'll fix it."

So I went back there to load it, but 'cause of the holes in the trailer the boxes had got wet. I moved a couple and the whole thing came down on me—400 boxes that weighed 50 pounds apiece. The dock man there helped me out and called my dispatcher, said, "We're not loadin' the rest of the freight on this man's truck." He said, "That trailer's unsafe; he just got injured."

Dispatcher got me on the phone, cussed me out, and told me when I got home I could go to the doctor. So I had to drive all the way from Ohio home, back to Arkansas with a second back injury.

I never did get compensated for that, no way, shape and form. They paid the doctor bills and that was it. And I was off work eighteen months that time. It was a small company. Right before that happened they took and sold out to this company out of Denver. Because they sold out prior to my accident I wasn't hardly covered. But I didn't know that they had sold out until I came home.

They did it dirty to me, 'cause by the time I got to the doctor back in Arkansas they took the load of freight that was on my trailer, put it on another trailer, and sent it on. And they took the trailer that I was pullin' to a trailer company, had a new floor, siding, and top put in it.

So by the time that my attorney and I went down there to take pictures, the freight was gone and the trailer was fixed.

Then, when it came time to settle up on the last payroll they charged me for all this damage that was the fault of their equipment. The judge said to me, "Can you show evidence of the shape the trailer was in?" I had a written affidavit from the man that was loadin' it in Cleveland. I had a written affidavit from the man where we was loadin' it in New York and Pennsylvania, but that still wasn't substantial evidence to the judge. He said, "I've got to see pictures of it." We even requested the right to bring these guys in from Pennsylvania and Ohio, but the judge wouldn't give us the subpoenas. The one in Ohio had even dropped his forklift through the floor of the trailer trying to load his pallets.

It was hard. We was still in Arkansas then. And in Arkansas things is a little worse, as far as aid for families and that goes. The homelessness I've seen there is mainly rural. People living in tents, shacks made of tree limbs, cardboard, and things. We were in unsuitable housing at the time ourselves. The landlords didn't want to fix the plumbing and the wiring and stuff. You could get shocked just turning the light switches on.

But between my family and her family, they helped us with rent and food and our utilities. Then, after that eighteen months, I went to work at a meat processing plant, a chicken processing plant. Connie was on the cut-up line, she can tell you more about what that was like than I can. The wages wasn't bad, but it just didn't work out and we got layed off.

Going back to the first accident, in '80, the thing of it was, on April the 12th, our oldest girl was born very premature and she spent 89 days under an intensive care unit. The doctors gave her no hope for life. And me bein' on the road then, that made it worse. But when she rallied out and she made it, that really was a blessing in itself.

And then our other girl, she was born three months premature. And she was flown from Joplin, Missouri, to Kansas City. And she had to spend some time in the hospital.

We had help with the hospital bills, but the last girl, her hospital and ambulance bill was $14,000. The oldest girl, when they released her from the hospital I went down and signed her bill out and almost died. They didn't have her last two days' charges on there yet but it was already $299,000. We got help through some of these different children's organizations. St. Jude and them, the Kiwanis and stuff, bless their souls. But I had some money saved up and had to pay all we could plus some. It took me five and a half years. On the second girl at Mercy they had me fill out an application about the accidents and everything. They only had me pay $2,200 of that one.

It's just been kind of a rough road to go. There's lots of jobs I can't do. And my injuries aren't bad enough where I can pull any kind of permanent disability. They just make it difficult working. But never you mind, I plan on overcoming it before I'm through with it. I'm willing to take anything I can get to get started again. Connie's figurin' on working again too, soon as the kids go back to school. She's done lots of things: meat-packing, nurses-aid, maid work, and cleanin' houses. We've been through this three, four times now.

Marsha
Arlington, Virginia

> *Marsha and I meet in the conference room of a church shelter*
> *where she and her two youngest daughters now live. Playing*
> *with my cassettes, they dance about us as we talk. She has other*
> *children, now grown, and had lived in an upper middle-class*
> *suburb of Washington, D.C.*
>
> *In many ways Marsha's narrative is a success story: the*
> *testimony of a woman who escaped an abusive marriage, who*
> *did find shelter, and who does have skills.*
>
> *Marsha is an African American in her thirties.*

WE SPENT THE FIRST NIGHTS in the battered women's shelter. I had tried
to do that when I was still living with him, but I couldn't get myself in.
I guess I didn't explain it right. So when the problems arose again I was
out on a limb. I had to either try to live with him under the
circumstances—which was unbearable—or try to make it on my own.
I tried to find a job and a place to stay, but I just couldn't do it in time.

And then I was robbed. I was waiting for the bus when this guy
came up and threatened me, then robbed me. So I found myself
without money or a place to live. And I had to take the girls with me.
I would have been frightened to leave them with him at home.

But this time they checked us into the battered women's shelter.
From there we went to emergency housing, where Social Services gives
you a five-day stay. After that I got into a more long-term women's
shelter.

I just need a little more time. I do have skills—I'm in
accounting—but I've been working for my husband for the last eight
years so I can't get a reference, my resumé's old ... but now I've got

applications out and I'm taking the Civil Services test. Based on that I should be able to survive.

But it's hard. To get a two-bedroom you have to make between 16 and 19 thousand a year and we're talking about low-income, rent-supplemented housing. And the average job does not pay that. The majority of jobs—of what I do—are paying 15, some even 14 thousand. And with children you can't begin to look for a job until you find child care. Then my credit is messed up, because of my husband.

I don't know why abuse happens. I think a lot of men feel vulnerable, they feel ... I don't know ... he doesn't help with the kids—not at least with these two. I've seen him and all. He won't help with the finances or let me have a car. He doesn't ask about the children, living arrangements. I'm not saying that he doesn't care....

But when I left that morning I knew I could never go back. I said, "I have to find a job, I have got to find a place to stay today!" I ... I don't care to describe it, the things he did to me ... and I shudder to think what would have happened if there wasn't a place to go. It was desperate. I can just see myself now, jumping off from five floors up. I'm serious.

Karla
St. Louis, Missouri

> *"We'll start with what happened," Karla begins. Young,*
> *bright, a mother of two children, she is part of a growing*
> *phenomenon: single-parent mothers on assistance who cannot*
> *afford a place to live.*
>
> *Cities handle such families differently. New York City*
> *houses many women like Karla in so-called welfare hotels, while*
> *other cities place them in barracks-style emergency shelters or*
> *housing projects. Karla could find nowhere to go.*
>
> *Karla is an African American in her twenties. We met at a*
> *Salvation Army shelter for homeless families.*

I WAS WORKING up until the time I had my second baby. I lived with
my mom but we weren't getting along. She took care of the first child
but the second, that was too much. Then she felt that once I had the
children ... well, her words were, "Two grown ladies can never
manage in the same house." So I got on AFDC and went to stay with
my littlest girl's aunt.

Well, three weeks ago now, her landlord called and said the
building didn't pass inspection. See, the building was infested with
bugs and mice.

I didn't have any money saved 'cause I was spending all the AFDC
and food stamps on us. I do have qualifications for a lot of jobs, but
they're all $3.35. And it's not worth getting a job where you have no
medical or dental insurance, not if you have kids. It's not worth giving
up welfare. I would work at $3.35 if they let me keep Medicaid and the
food stamps, but they don't.[19] They'll cut you off.

But AFDC's not enough to live on either. I started looking for another place but all the apartments I could afford were just like the one we were living in. It wasn't worth leaving one condemnation to go to another.

Then my daughter's aunt, she moved in with her sister. There was no way I could afford an apartment on my own, not and eat too—and like I said, they were all as bad as the first place. So me and the kids—I have a 3-year-old and a 9-month-old—we just stayed in the building. They boarded it up but we got in through the back window.

There was this older lady that lived next door. We were friends and if she could have helped me she would have. But she already had her four grown kids, plus their kids, livin' with her in a two-bedroom apartment. There's a lot of that these days.

She gave us blankets, though, and I wrapped us up in them. We'd stay outside all day, do something—go to the library or I'd take 'em to the museum. Something. Nights we'd go back into the apartment, light candles, and sleep.

Then it rained real bad. And it was cold. The electrical was off, the gas was off, we were going by candlelight. Mice and rats came out really bad. I woke up one morning and there was a mouse on my 9-month-old's head … we couldn't stay in there.

So we went outside, walked around all day. Night came and we slept in a car I found. We were wet and both my kids caught a cold real bad. I took 'em to the emergency room and we slept at the hospital.

The next night we were in this laundromat … it was so awful. I was crying, the kids were still sick. And my oldest, Robert, he asked a lot of questions: "Momma, why did we sleep in the car? Why are we outside? It's raining, Momma, I'm cold. I don't feel good."

I couldn't explain. And we had been out for the last three days, never being able to rest. He hadn't eaten anything that night 'cause I didn't have any more money.

Then the man at the laundromat, he gave me $4 to get Robert something to eat. And I stole my baby a can of milk.

The Armstrongs, Mark and Linda
Seattle, Washington

The Armstrongs lived in Bellevue, a young, largely affluent city east of Seattle, until a medical emergency and the sudden loss of Mark's job forced the family to seek emergency housing.

Since Bellevue has little emergency housing, the Armstrongs were advised to seek shelter in nearby Seattle. Eventually, the family was moved to a large public housing project in the city's Central District. Each morning they awake at 5:00 for the long bus ride back to Bellevue for work and school.

Mark and Linda both work, as do their teenage children. Speaking to them, I am struck that they are the quintessential American family: hard-working, supportive, patriotic, loving. And now homeless. The Armstrongs' difficulties— underemployment, housing, grocery bills, health costs, insurance problems—mirror those of other homeless families driven from affluent communities.

They are African Americans in their early thirties.

Mark:

I DESIGNED AND BUILT conveyor belts, and was good at it. I was making over $15 an hour. And I can go back there right now and get you a letter of recommendation from the company and let you read what they wrote about me. That in itself tells you what kind of worker I am.

The company went out of business. Bang! Didn't even know it was coming. I was between jobs three or four months. I could have found work right away if I wanted to make minimum wage, but I got pretty high standards for myself. I don't even want to make what I'm making now. We could barely afford rent then, how can we now? But when you got kids to feed and bills to pay, you have to do the best you can.

But minimum wage—that's insulting. I don't knock it for high school students. They're getting training, learning about working, making their pocket money. That's fine. But you take a person ... I got six kids. $3.35, $4 an hour, I spend more than that wage in a day's time on a grocery bill. I mean you can accept some setbacks, but you can't tell a person, "I don't care if you've been making $15 something an hour, the minimum is what you've got to make now." If I hand you this letter, give you my resumé, my military record, show you the kind of worker I am, talk about my family, how can you degrade me by offering me the minimum wage?

Then we had trouble with the house we were renting. And, well, the biggest part of it was hospital bills. My son had to have emergency surgery. Since the company was going out of business it let the insurance lapse, so I got stuck with the bill. Spent every penny we had saved and there's still fourteen hundred dollars on it. You would think by being medical that it wouldn't affect the credit, but it does.

Now I'm working with Safeway's warehouse. I work in the milk plant. Swing shift. Sometimes I'm off at 12:30, 1:00 at night, and then turn right around and go back at 8:30 the next morning. Yeah, it's hard sometimes. I'm not making half of what I used to. I'm a helper—I used to have people working for me. I'd worked my way up through the ranks. But like I was saying, you adjust, you do what you have to do. I'm the kind of person, I get with a company I want to stay, be a part of it. I like to get along with people and work, get my hands dirty. See something accomplished. I'm low man on the totem pole but I'll stay and work my way up.

The warehouse, it's refrigerated on one end and kind of hot on the other. They make their own milk cartons out of plastic so you have to deal with heat and cold. You have to know how to dress 'cause you're dealing with both extremes.

Linda:

I've been a custodian, nurse's aid; now I work at K-Mart. I still have to bus back to the East side [Bellevue] every day. It's okay but I'm looking for something else. You know, it's $4 an hour, and there's no benefits, no discounts at the store, nothing like that.

And I'm in school now, too. I'm going for business training, probably computers or administration. When school starts I'll either bring the little ones there with me or have one of the older ones bring them home.

Working full-time and going to school. Six kids, seventeen on down to twelve. Three in high school, three in grade school. Two of them work at Jack in the Box. They've been working the same shift but my oldest, he's on the football team, so he might be working at a different time than my daughter. And then there's the church, and those football games. Yes we're busy! Just an all-American family. One that's hit a string of bad luck, that's all.

The hardest thing is getting up early enough to bus back over there. As soon as school gets started that's really going to be a problem. It might be a couple of hours, both ways. And if they find out our kids are living here they'll want them in school in Seattle. But they like the schools there and I like them. They're better. And that's where we've lived, that's where we work.

But we get by. The kids, they cook, they clean, they wash and iron their own clothes. And the older ones, they all work. We're so proud of them. Oh, we have the same problems everybody else has, with teenagers and so forth. But we get through 'em. Just thank God they're not on drugs. That's the biggest problem here.

Mark:

When we had to move and lost the house, when I lost my job, we told the kids the truth, the flat out truth. With no misconception; none whatsoever. Kids are not dumb. If you lie to kids, why should they be honest with you? They know exactly what we're going through and they know why.

Same thing when we moved here—six kids, three rooms, writing all over the walls, the drugs and crime. We tried to avoid the move but we didn't have any choice. They knew exactly where we were moving to, as best as I could explain it. We told them we didn't want to come, but if it came down to it we were coming. And we did.

Now my worst fear ... there's so much drugs in this area. And people think every apartment in the projects is a drug house. They knock on the doors, knock on the windows—they stop me out there and ask where it is. It's here, so close to us all the times. And all the shooting and fighting ... you can look out the window any given night and see the police stopping people and searching everyone.

If I can't look out my door and see my kids, I send for 'em. And I'm afraid when I can't see 'em. 'Cause when they get to shootin' and fightin' and carryin'-on a bullet don't got no names on it. Sometimes when I come in from work, three, four o'clock in the morning, I wonder just when they're going to get me. But my worst fear, my worst fear is the kids.

Linda:

Over in Bellevue they think if you can't afford it then you shouldn't be there. You know, who cares if you work there.

The first house that we had, we were the first blacks in the neighborhood. When I moved over there I said, "Where the black people?" [laughs, then moves her head from side to side as if searching] ... no black people? Then the neighbors, they got to looking, came out, they were surprised, too. "Oooh, we got black people over here now" [laughs]. The kids were the only black kids around.

Mark:

People don't want to rent to a family. And you know the kind of rent they're asking over there in Bellevue, that's not easy to come up with. And you need first, last month's rent, security.... And then people automatically assess, they stereotype you. Maybe sometimes it's 'cause we're black—I'm not saying this is true, I'm saying that sometimes I *felt* that the reason we didn't get a place was because we were black. But most of the time it's the family. People would rather you have pets than kids these days.

One guy, he had six bedrooms in this house. But he didn't want a family. Why would you have six bedrooms if you didn't want to rent to a family? May not be legal, but they do that all the time.

Now there is some validity in what they say about children tearing up things. But the child is only as bad as you let him be. You're the parent, he's going to do exactly what you let him do and get away with. If my kids tear something up I'll pay for it. But me, I tell my kids that if I have to replace something they've destroyed, then one of their sisters or brothers isn't going to get something they need. And when they do something they answer to me.

I'm not bitter ... I mean I'm somewhat so. I'm not angry bitter. It's just that I don't like dragging my kids from one place to the next, and I don't think we've been treated right. We had to take places sight-unseen, just to get 'em. We paid $950 a month, and during the wintertime $300, $400 a month for electric and gas bills. Then bought food, kept my kids in clothes. How you supposed to save to get ahead with all that?

And the house, when we moved in the landlords said they'd do this and that, fix this and that. Said we would have an option to buy it. We said, "Okay, and we'll do these things." We had an agreement.

We never got that chance to buy, and they never fixed those things. But we kept paying that $950 a month. They had a barrel over us: we needed some place to go. And they made a small fortune those years. A month after we moved out we went by: all those things they wouldn't do were done.

Before that the guy decided to sell his house, just like that, and we had to move. It was December, wintertime. For a while we were staying with her mother in a two-bedroom. Nine people. We had to be somewhere so we took that second place before we had even seen it.

Everybody has to have a place to live. And people will do what they have to do to survive. A lot of things that you see going on around here are for survival [he sweeps his hand, indicating the housing projects]. I'm not taking up for them, there's a lot of things happening here that I oppose. But where there's a will there's a way, you know.

Belle
Bremerton, Washington

Belle had always hoped to be a housewife and mother, one who "took care of everyone." But the poverty and dysfunctional behavior that characterized her parents' lives also characterized her own. And her attempt to be what a woman "should be" left her with neither skills nor resources. Now, homeless and alone, she has no one to take care of, no one to take care of her.

Belle is white and 27. We met at a small shelter for homeless women sponsored by Help-line, a community-service organization.

WE WERE IN GEORGIA. I took care of my brothers and sisters, and my dad ... it was just, "Take my word for it or go to hell." And my mom, everytime he would say something, my mom would say something else.

I always tried to make sure everybody kept out of trouble and did things so my dad wouldn't get mad at 'em. 'Cause he'd smack ya, just haul off and smack ya.

I didn't know who to trust. My mom? My dad? And they were always fighting. So if I had a problem of my own, I'd keep it to myself. I didn't want to ask because I didn't know what I'd get for askin'. We were way out in the country so there wasn't anybody else. And I wanted to ask my mom ... you know, about things a daughter asks her mother.

So I walked out of there into my own life and got pregnant. I had my own child, she's ten now. And we left Georgia, me and this guy, and tried to make it on our own. He was handicapped—without kneecaps—and was 23 years old. He had been walking without kneecaps since he was 12.

It was ... it was really hard. He was imprisoned for most of his life. After I met him he had to go down to Phoenix, to serve more time. We wanted to start a life together, as a family. So I went down there.

I was pregnant again, and I was trying to get assistance. But on welfare you have to be in a home before you can get any money. But to get in a home you have to have money. I didn't have no money—I was flat broke. He was in prison and I had to take care of the children, only there wasn't any way to.

I went back to his home but everybody there was broke because his mom had married someone else and it caused problems. I became a total house person. I cleaned the house, took care of everything, made sure every child had clothes on that were washed and ironed.

And then he stepped out of prison into my life and I didn't have nothing. His mom put us into a house so we could get onto assistance, but it takes time to get onto assistance, time to get on a program. And then not being married ... they said either he had to leave for me to collect a check, or I had to leave for him to collect one.

It was so bad. They took our child from us because we couldn't support it. I had barely had it. They had already taken the other one for all the problems there in his mom's house. They said we didn't care for the child.

Actually the problems with the first child came from a long time ago. When he was in prison I would take our daughter and go visit him. The prison system was so slack that ... that you could see any kind of sexual activity whatsoever when you walked into that visiting room. It was just ... so bad, so crowded with so many people. Sometimes you even stood to do it because it was so crowded. You'd, you know, hide behind other people and do whatever you wanted.

My child saw this from the ages of two to five, and she took it upon herself to believe that's the way it's supposed to be. I didn't realize it was happening at the time, I didn't realize what I was putting her through. I had this head trip that I had to do what this guy said, else he'd be gone as soon as he got out.

So later, once when we got home, she told this kid, this seventeen year old, what she'd seen and asked him ... [she breaks off, in tears]. And I didn't know, I didn't know, and when I found out it was too late, after the investigation started.

See, I heard that this guy messed with my daughter and I was going, "Oh my God! I've got to get out of here." So I went to the welfare office and told them I've got to get out of his mom's house because this guy's messing with my daughter there. You see he lived there, he was a child of the man married to my husband's mother.

They send a worker out to the house and the worker takes my child. She takes her back and they go into this room … it's all on video tape, what she said. She told about it, and then she said my man, her father, had messed with her too. I didn't understand that because when she said it was done, it couldn't of been done. But it made me realize, you know, I said, "Wow, what did I do to this child?"

He got out and tried to work, but the work that he knew how to do he couldn't do. He could weld, but he burned his eyes really bad in prison and couldn't do that anymore. He also plays guitar. Like I was tellin' these girls here, the fingers on the right hand are much longer than the fingers on the other, because all those years playing the strings. So he knows how to do that but there wasn't any work with that, you know. He knows construction, too, but he couldn't do that because of his knees.

See, his ligaments are gone. When he was a kid he got a little tiny cut under the bottom side of his knee. And it got infected in there. His mom didn't have the money to take him to the doctor, so she took him to the closest thing, which was the vet. And the vet stitched it up and his knee got bigger and bigger and pretty soon he was at the children's hospital with gangrene. And he lost it. Everything with gangrene had to come out, which was the kneecap.

So he couldn't get work and we went to the welfare and it was like I said—one of us had to leave. And all this was in the same time period when the baby was sick.

So they take the child and it's all up to us to do whatever we need to survive, right? So we come … home, home to where my parents are. That's the only way I can put it because my mom has never been in a permanent or stable place either. Always moving around. But we headed there. They gave us a ticket when we left, only they wouldn't give us a ticket all the way there and we had to hitchhike and then stop in this place and fanagle, sort of lie about why we needed another ticket. That really hurt and … I mean, I was just so caught up in what had happened and how things had gone down … and here we were stuck halfway home, hitchin' and begging these social service people for another ticket … and my children … in fact, I signed adoption papers, me and the guy, and it was like … we really didn't know what we were doing.

Each of us regretted what we did. But at the same time we didn't know what to do. If I had took the children I could have been on AFDC, or he could of. But we didn't want to split up[20] … and I didn't have no place to go there … I mean, it was too much for one, but two, we might have been able to … we were pulling together but the state was tearing us apart. We thought we were doing good by staying together but that's what got the children taken from us.

CHAPTER 9

SOLUTIONS

Homeless people seek solutions that account for their own experience. Persons homeless through loss of work see employment as their greatest need; others stress a safe and affordable home as the foundation upon which they can base other progress. Most recognize that effective drug and alcohol treatment must accompany job assistance and housing programs for people who need it.

Assumptions about such solutions vary widely among homeless people, depending—again—upon their experience. People recently homeless through accident or mishap tend to want "another chance," a little help in getting back on their feet. "I've always worked, always gotten by," one recently homeless man told me. "Now I just need that chance to show what kind of a worker I am."

Homeless people with little experience of middle-class success have less faith in the viability of hard work and perseverance to lift them out of destitution. As previous chapters have shown, many of these people remained poor while working hard and fell into homelessness despite their determination to do otherwise. They argue that the conditions of life, employment, and housing they face make middle-class notions of "boot-strap" success nearly impossible to achieve. Their feelings range from despair to anger, buttressing their view that only drastic measures can bring the changes they need to solve the problems they face. Disillusioned, they see homelessness as an urgent crisis of immense proportions few understand or care about. As a friend of mine puts it, "No one hears our cries."

These people cry for help beyond housing—for child care, medical attention, substance-abuse programs, and jobs. Surveys that cite high rates of personal problems among the homeless come as no surprise to homeless people themselves, many of whom freely admit personal difficulties that complicate their situations. "I need some help," "I'm still weak for it," "It was my fault I dropped out," are statements common to their stories. Those without debilitating problems see them in their family and friends, in the people who share their soup lines, and in the other homeless people they meet on the street.

But the idea that people should be punished for behavior they already suffer under makes no sense to homeless people. They view so-called austerity programs, designed to make emergency housing purposefully uncomfortable, as ludicrously cruel and counterproductive—measures akin to feeding starving children sour milk as punishment for missing breakfast. And that thousands of street addicts and alcoholics want rehabilitation they cannot get, strikes them as beyond comprehension.

Most homeless people I've interviewed also want to cut defense spending, the charitable assistance we send abroad, and tax breaks for the rich. They are nearly unanimous in wanting to substantially raise the minimum wage, increase support for dependent families, veterans, and the disabled, and in their desire for housing programs that integrate poor families into middle-class neighborhoods. Most see universal health care as an essential human right. They want schools that give a ghetto child a chance, streets that permit safe passage, a war on drugs that cares for the wounded, and job assistance programs that provide jobs, not assistance.

Most homeless people also mistrust the social service system. This is not to say they disagree with the idea of such services; rather, they fault the system for its failure to deliver them. They say that government and charitable funds earmarked for the poor and homeless rarely reach them, that caseworkers become adversaries, not advocates, and that job-training programs too often provide jobs for the trainers, not the trainees. It would be more effective, they argue, to receive assistance directly—either as employment, housing, or cash—rather than through service agencies where much of it is siphoned into salaries and operating expenses.[1] Interestingly, it was a conservative administration—Nixon's—that actually proposed such a plan, the "Family Assistance Program."[2] Of course, the plan met stiff opposition from Democrats and Republicans alike and was soundly defeated.

But one should resist the temptation to paint the suggestions raised by homeless people in the terms of party politics. Less concerned with affixing blame than finding solutions, most homeless people have little patience for the ideological battles that characterize public discussion of the crisis. As one man explained it to me, "Don't tell me I ain't got a job, I know that. And don't tell me why I ain't got one either. Tell me where I can get one."

Consequently, the solutions that homeless people suggest not only lack the political homogeneity common to those who speak for them, they point to new ways of thinking about the problem and the nation.

This is particularly evident in the frequent references homeless people make to communities. Whether speaking of family, neighbors, neighborhoods, or "the homeless," homeless people commonly speak of themselves in relation to a body of people who share their situation and who live where they do, and they frame their ideas in terms that are at once personal and community-based.

This sense of community is particularly evident in what may be the most salient characteristic of the solutions homeless people seek for themselves: the desire to help each other. I have heard versions of the following scenario, for example, from homeless men and women on both coasts, and in the North, South, and Midwest:

> I think maybe if I could get some money I'd get a house and put some people up. Because, well, I can't say for you or for anybody else, but now that I've been homeless I'd see it as a waste of money to spend much on an apartment. You know, one of these bi-level apartments, six, seven hundred dollars a month. I'd rather get a place where I can put some people up, give 'em a place to stay where they can actually live—not permanent, but some place where a man or a woman can be long enough to get themselves together and get back on their feet. Where they can live. Have some rules, you know, but a place. Give 'em a door key and kind of work together.

Wishful thinking? Perhaps. But homeless assistance programs that succeed—even those that attract mainstream attention—speak to the viability of such ideas. "Study after study" has shown that "the homeless are different from other people," notes one essay on programs that work for homeless people: "They are profoundly alone."[3] Accordingly, building support networks and community alliances is a key to their success.

It should be noted that this sense of alliances is much more than a vague wish for togetherness or cooperation: it is a strategic response to perilous conditions. Like survivors of a devastating earthquake or other natural disaster, homeless people have little choice but to take shelter together. Similarly, it is a mistake to assume these communities to be racially bound. Homeless people frequently say they have much more in common with other homeless people, regardless of race, than with any larger, housed community. And many of the communities homeless people form for themselves—whether a precarious "squat" in an abandoned building, or a cooperative household—are virtual models of integration.

The programs described in the testimonies that follow reaffirm these concerns. Whether the target population is homeless youth or homeless men, the programs that homeless people themselves advocate provide stability, opportunity, and the kind of community-building that fosters self-reliance *and* long-term structures of peer-support.

Community-based, long-term approaches of this nature are especially prevalent among shelters and programs established for women.[4] One of many such organizations is the Elizabeth Stone House, which operates a residential mental health alternative, a battered women's program, and a transitional housing program in the Boston area. Stressing a "therapeutic community" and individual goal-setting to foster self-empowerment, the Elizabeth Stone House provides a broad range of programs and assistance options through which the women it serves work to meet their own needs.[5] Furthermore, because the organization serves a broad population and sets no financial restrictions for admission to its programs, the communities and networks it fosters are themselves rich with opportunities for mutual assistance. Women combine households, make friends, and share support and encouragement across class and racial boundaries.

Elsewhere, informal communities of poor women have led cooperative, neighborhood campaigns to rescue buildings that threatened whole communities with homelessness. Many such efforts have generated new "community households" on the model of large, extended families. In them groups of precariously housed people combine resources, skills, and housing in small networks of mutual support.[6]

Other communities combine peer support with opportunities for homeless people to work for their own betterment on a political level. Justice House, a radical Christian community of homeless people in Roanoke, Virginia, fosters rehabilitation and personal growth among its members, while encouraging lobbying, marches, and other direct action campaigns on behalf of homeless people.[7] In this way organizations like Justice House build solidarity among homeless people while empowering their own participants through meaningful work and peer suppport.

But the communities to which homeless people refer are not merely those they have formed among themselves. While people with homes may not accept the homeless people in their streets as neighbors, the reverse is rarely true. Homeless people usually have a much more inclusive definition of community, which includes those with homes and those without.

This recognition is painful. It affirms the alienation and abandonment that homeless people feel. Similarly, reintegrating homeless people into other communities is no easy task. In many ways it is like welcoming veterans back from war: they return changed and scarred, sometimes disillusioned and bitter. Reintegration, moreover, means building housing instead of hotels, bringing jobs to poor communities, and accepting the poor as our neighbors. It means placing comparable schools in disparate neighborhoods, and considering new paradigms of cooperation, interdependence, and of the maintenance and distribution of resources.

Yet, while homelessness exposes the fragility of our lives and the vast inequalities of our society, it also points up the great resilience of people and their ability to create networks of support and connection under the most harrowing of circumstances. Solutions that work for homeless people draw strength and momentum from this resilience and ability.

Finally, allowing homeless people to work together for their own betterment is self-perpetuating. Solutions that build communities give meaning to people who suffer in isolation, creating contexts in which other difficulties can be overcome.

The testimonies that follow give witness to this. Each addresses a disability—drug addiction, unemployment, or destitution—and in each case rehabilitation occurs in the context of a community. This fact points up the initial absence of community in the inception of the problem, and the responsibility of the larger, societal "community" in the breakdown of its smaller, communal units.

Similarly, the testimonies often reframe the notion of a "solution." "Some people want to get back up into the mainstream where they can get that apartment, that washer and dryer, and keep them to themselves," explains Stewart Guernsey, a Boston-area lawyer who left Harvard's divinity school to form a cooperative household and advocacy center with a group of formerly homeless people. "But others have come to see that vision of independence as part of their problem."[8]

This perspective generates what might be called New Movement solutions—cooperative, grass-root, self-help programs that place responsibility upon homeless people while entrusting them with the tools, services, and resources they need to better themselves. Although disparate, such programs share certain features: they tend to be formed through trial and error, to depend on peer support, to be long term, to be "tight ships" with strict, consistent rules, to be small, and to employ few "experts"—though this is not universally true. Such programs have been shown to benefit both those who seek to (re)enter the mainstream and those who fit Mr. Guernsey's latter description and seek other alternatives.

The programs described in some of the testimonies that follow are not necessarily the best or most proven. But each is a program that speaks to the concerns of homeless people and one that homeless people eagerly speak for. There are not many such programs, though the "movement" is clearly growing. Those described here were chosen for the alternatives they suggest and the stories through which they are told.

However, it must be remembered that, with the proper context of support, homelessness need not have occurred for any of these people. To this end, efforts that strengthen family connections and community ties among people before they become homeless are implicitly advocated in each narrative. Homeless people, perhaps more fully than anyone else, recognize the value of a home and know that keeping one can mean the strength and support people need to maintain everything else.

Interestingly, there is evidence that the "new movement" of programs described here may become just such an effort. ACE, which began by organizing women in the so-called welfare hotels of New York City, has already changed its focus to the neighborhoods of Central Harlem, where many of the hotel residents come from.[9] And Second Home, which initially sought to provide a refuge from the streets of Boston, has now begun a neighborhood boxing program as an alternative to the attractions of the local gangs who make those streets so violent.

It is said that some people are stronger where they've been broken. Perhaps, ultimately, this will be true of these immediate communities, and, by extension, of the larger communities of which they are a part.

Doug Castle

SHARE
Seattle, Washington

In the fall of 1990 Doug Castle walked from his encampment under Seattle's I-90 freeway to a "tent city" he had heard of near the Kingdome. Helping set up tents and distribute materials donated to the city, he became swept up in the current of a movement among Seattle-area homeless people to create their own alternative to the shelter system. That alternative continues today in one of the most closely watched and controversial programs in the country—closely watched because of the strength of its model; controversial because it stands as a direct challenge to the shelter and social service system which, it claims, unnecessarily wastes millions of dollars paying social workers, sociologists, and other experts for programs the homeless are better able to run themselves. Mr. Castle is white and in his late thirties.

SHARE MEANS Seattle Housing And Resource Effort. There is no agency that is SHARE. Any person who believes that there is a homeless crisis, and that the solution must come from the efforts of homeless people rather than the government, can be a member of SHARE. There is no president, no dues, no board of directors.

I wasn't involved until tent city. This was late November, right after Thanksgiving. All the shelters were full and it got around on the streets that that's where everybody was going, so I walked on down. There were 39 people living in 5 tents. I'm a big camping enthusiast and know a lot about tents, so I started helping out. And, you know, it was either that or go back under the I-90 bridge. So I stayed.

Less than three weeks later we had 45 tents, 148 people—we were the third largest shelter in the state of Washington, and we were doing it in a mud field with tents.

I expected the community to be up in arms about it. But where I was just shocked is that we had all this community support. The community was feeding us, bringing us blankets, bringing us clothes.... We passed out five thousand sleeping bags and seven thousand coats, to homeless and low-income people down there. I mean people brought donations down by the truck load.

See people liked the idea that homeless people were looking for a helping hand, not a handout. I mean we were willing to get up and do something about our own future and were not going to be dependent upon social agencies to decide that future. That was the start, the key. Everything else just followed from that.

Because of our community support the city became forced to find an equitable solution and ... well, the Metro bus barn was sitting vacant, so we got that as a transitional building. The deal was, if we could run things for ourselves, the city would find us a permanent location.

Realistically, I don't believe the city expected us to succeed. That way once we'd failed they could come in, say "Oh this place is too whatever." You know, too many fights, too many drunks, too much neighborhood impact. Then they'd say, "Hey we tried, but the homeless people can't do it."

We surprised everybody. We got the panhandlers to go somewhere else. Every other Saturday we'd average fifty big black trash bags full of trash, cleaning up the area. It wasn't even our trash, but it proved a point: we were saying, "We're solving our own problem. Now unless you can come up with a better solution, just let us do our thing."

Not that there wasn't problems. The third day we were in the bus barn we had a fight between six people, four of them men, two of them women. In the process of getting this fight broke up, I got my nose broken, I got five stitches in my eyes, a detached retina, and a concussion. Spent the night in the hospital. And like I said this was the third night the bus barn was open.

It was chaos, and everybody in the place knew it. Everybody knew we weren't going to make the month of December if we didn't do something. But that's what I think is so remarkable, what we did: we voted ourselves the toughest set of rules of any shelter anywhere. And we chose it for ourselves. No sociologist making sixty-thousand a year crammed it down our throats. And that's why it worked. And because it worked the city was forced to come through on their word. That's how we got this place, the Aloha Hotel.

Back in tent city, the bus barn, even here today, we have had 24-hour security—all done internally, by homeless people. Everyone works: we man our own telephones, we prepare our own meals, wash our own clothes. Only three of us are paid. Myself, I make $150 a week for the 96 hours I spend on the job, but it's worth it for me because we put people into jobs and homes. I know how important that is because I know what it means to be homeless.

Our target population are single men, 25 to 40 years old. We're not exclusionary, but that's our target population, the group that has no other place to turn. And if you divide the homeless into the 30 percent drug or alcohol addicted, 30 percent mentally ill, and 30 percent down and out for situational reasons, the last 30 percent is the one we're after: people we believe can function in society if they're given some transitional help in getting reestablished.

But if someone's action plan includes drug or alcohol rehabilitation we'll accept that. As long as it's part of their success plan we're more than cooperative. See we give you 90 days. If we give you those 90 days we want to know what you can do with it. What will be your action steps financially, employmentwise, housingwise, and your other personal goals?

You have to line out a personal success plan and you're required to show that you're working on it. You're required to save $75 a week, you're required to put in 15 hours a week of work around here, and you're required to pay $5 a week for room and board. If you can't find the work yourself, we'll find it for you. Lots of our residents find each other jobs. They find a job, come back the next day and say, "Hey, they need two more people!" But you have to save that money, and you have to follow the rules.

It takes dedication to make this work. But it works. Already we're running a 50 percent success rate. Our first 90 days isn't even up—it won't be up until this weekend. But of the original 30 we moved in with, 15 have already moved on to some form of permanent housing. Another 6 or 7 have been thrown out for rules infractions. The idea there is not to waste time on people we can't help—or who won't help themselves. 'Cause this is not a flophouse. We need flophouses, I mean people deserve a bed, but there are other places for that. But if someone's willing to work to help himself, he deserves more. That's what we're here for.

This way we can free up bed spaces in shelters and help that 30 percent we're shooting at. And this kind of concept can work anywhere in America because there are homeless people who want out everywhere. We've even had Canadians come down and do interviews here; they're interested in starting this kind of program there.

Our success goes back to our stringent rules, the 90 days we offer, and the people we work with. By and large, these people just want a chance, and they're willing to scratch and claw every inch. They make that inch and they go for another. You give 'em that break and they'll work for it.

It's a way of getting back in control of your life. Little things, like running our desk or being security around here, it gives you a sense that you're doing a job well done. That helps your self-worth. A lot of these people come in with a poor outlook on things and it just turns them around.

We had this woman, Crissy, who came to us pregnant. Shy, quiet, and timid. I mean all she had was a garbage bag with some clothes in it and the baby she was carrying. She had been a dispatcher for one of the cab companies. Then her husband skipped town, and that cost her where she was living. Eventually she lost everything: house, family, job, then her kids were taken away from her becuase she was homeless.

At the bus barn she helped run our desk. Then when we moved over here, she was on the executive committee, the screening committee, head of the desk, and probably the only person that got less sleep than me. She was here two months and when she left she was a fireball. Nothing was going to stop her. At that point she had a car, two vanloads of stuff, $700 in the bank, and an apartment.

Then this couple we had, they just moved out. He's disabled, and they had been living on the street for I don't know how long. But we helped him receive Social Security, she got a job, and they saved up the money until they could get an apartment over in Freemont. It's not public housing or anything. And she was able to get a son back that she had lost. Just one big happy family.

See, it doesn't take paying somebody $60,000 a year to run a transitional house like this. A man making $60,000 a year, that has never been homeless, what does he know? There are people among the homeless who can do it. And it's more cost-effective if they do.

Most homeless people are intelligent. Many have some college education. I have two years of training in audio-engineering; I used to be the sound man and assistant manager for one of the largest nightclubs in NYC. But when people saw me living under a bridge, they just assumed that I'd always been living under that bridge.

Once you get that far down, where you're worrying about your absolute day-to-day survival ... believe me I could take you around and let you stand in some of the food lines, let you stand in some of the clothing lines, and you will see that it will take up all of your day. You don't have time to go job hunting, you don't have time to worry about staying clean. You're worrying about putting a roof over your head that night and putting a meal in your belly. And due to the bureaucracy and red tape it takes to get those things, that's all you have time for.

See, to be an ally to a homeless person is very simple: approach him with an open mind and listen to his story. Don't listen with the idea that he's a typical Terry the Tramp—listen to him as a person.

And don't go to a bureaucrat for answers; ask a homeless person what he needs, and what he can do with your help. And let us in your neighborhoods. You know, if we can put a good program together, accept us in your neighborhood.

I mean, to start, people are gonna need clean clothes, a hot shower, and a place to sleep. Now some people who are homeless—lots of society—if you covered those needs that's all they want. But others, all that's going to do is jump start 'em enough to want more. And that's where we come in.

Anne
Banana Kelly Community Improvement Association
South Bronx, New York City

In 1978 a handful of South Bronx residents stopped demolition of three abandoned buildings on the crescent-shaped section of Kelly Street where they lived. Working with brooms, buckets, and their bare hands, the residents began the long process of cleaning and repair that eventually transformed the buildings into a housing cooperative for twenty-one families.

Out of that self-help success emerged the Banana Kelly Community Improvement Association, a grass-root housing rehabilitation organization.

Banana Kelly (BK) stresses a multidimensional approach that provides job training, employment, substance-abuse prevention, and education in the process of restoring and upgrading housing. In this way precariously housed people become permanently housed participants in BK's building-by-building South Bronx crusade.

Broadening their work to include homeless families, Banana Kelly set aside whole buildings for their use. When housing alone did not prove sufficient for the myriad needs of these families, BK set out to try something different. Under the guidance of the National Center for Housing Management, a Washington, D.C., consulting firm, they established a trial project that tied a work preparation and community improvement program to the leases signed by 18 previously homeless families who received apartments in a recently rehabilitated building. BK then placed staff members in the building to better foster a sense of community-based support for the families and their plans.

Results have been startling. After 20 months in the program, five of the families have found work and four have returned to school. Others volunteer at a day care and Red Cross shelter. Banana Kelly is now working to expand the program to all the buildings they manage.

Anne, whose story follows, is a resident-participant in the test program. She is an African American in her thirties.

I WAS IN THE PRINCE GEORGE. I don't know if you've heard about it, but it's a New York City welfare hotel, and it's hell. The murder, the rape, the corruption ... crack vials and garbage. Hundreds of people in that hotel and it's like that everywhere.

I couldn't exist in that environment. I had to separate myself from it—stay away as much as possible. I enrolled in college; I had my kids in school. And when the bus dropped them off I was there to take them to a youth center, keep them out of that hotel. Because if you don't you lose them, you lose yourself.

I remember I was there 16 days when my social worker gave me a check for $1,600 to give to the hotel. I said "Damn, you pay this much for me to stay in that filth and you won't let me get an apartment?" I think they want families to get in and stay in that system, 'cause there's no way they're helping them to get out of it. And the hotels will suck you in, keep you in the system even more.

I wasn't always homeless. I had an apartment for three years. But then the landlord decided to sell the building 'cause there were so many problems. The new landlord came along and wanted more money for my apartment, a lot more. I fought it. I went to court with him for six months. The judge gave me a section 8 certificate and told me to find another place. But nobody would take a section 8 certificate. I couldn't find a place anywhere. So I became homeless and they placed me in the hotel.

But I refuse to waste my brains and life. I prayed and worked every day to get out of there. To stay there would have been to give up and I couldn't. I know what I want for my life and my kids, and it wasn't that.

Other people get weak and give up. They say everybody has a backbone, but it depends on you and what you got for a backbone. People give up, use drugs to hide from reality, 'cause that reality is so bad. I saw it happen. The kids stand there hungry and they use the foodstamps to shoot up. Then they come to my door and beg for bread for their children. 'Cause it will get to you....

I got out because of Banana Kelly. I realized what was on the other side and they were there to help me work for it. I got my interview and

I was approved for an apartment. The work-prep rider came in then. That helped a lot because I looked at it like, there are people out there who still care, who believe I can do it for myself. And that was a shock, because when you're homeless you find the people you meet don't care, and you have to stay out of their way. But with Banana Kelly it was different.

We learn how to care for our building. We meet in a tenants' association, meet together when we have a problem. And if we have a problem with a tenant *we* decide what to do. Banana Kelly helps us learn how to handle the problem but we handle it ourselves.

Like if a tenant is involved in drugs, we say to them, "Hey, do you want to stay here? Then treat this place like it's yours." We send warning letters. Then we see what happens and decide what to do.

We also take charge to help select the families that come into our buildings. We take charge of our problems. When we hired a super and the super didn't live up to our standards, we fired him and got another.

There was another situation where one tenant was robbed in the building. I put out a memo for an emergency meeting and we got together to decide what to do. We were doing tenant patrols in the nighttime but we boosted it up to the daytime too. Those who work or go to school participate in the evening and the others help out in the day.

And we share childcare, baby-sit for each other. Me for instance, my neighbor helps out. And Banana Kelly helps out. They've got after-school programs: people meet your child to help them with their school work.

Right now I'm working as a VISTA volunteer for my work-prep. I work with Banana Kelly to help set up more programs like this. I'm in contact with new tenants, working to help screen tenants and to expand this model to other buildings. But mainly I'm in school. I enrolled in Laguardia College in Queens. Right now I go to school at night 'cause I'm working with Banana Kelly during the day.

It's what I want, not what I need. See you can't just look at what you need 'cause then you'll backtrack. You have to look for what you want, and to keep looking only at that.

That's why Banana Kelly works. They don't do it for you. But they make it so you can do it. They give you the confidence by helping you see what you can do. It's what you can do for yourself with Banana Kelly as your backbone.

Carol Quarles
Action for Community Empowerment
Central Harlem, New York City

Of the many organizations that have attempted to assist residents of New York City's infamous welfare hotels, the efforts of the Hotel Tenants' Rights Project (HTRP) stand out. That, according to Ruth Young, who once directed a tenants' organization at the Brooklyn Arms Hotel, is because HTRP gave the women of the hotels the tools to help themselves.

For the past three years those tools have included leadership training and the legal documentation to defend their freedom of assembly and right to humane and affordable housing. Brandishing court injunctions in the face of belligerent security guards, residents learned to stop illegal evictions and to empower themselves through direct action and tenant solidarity.

Those successes led to other tenant campaigns. As for the Hotel Tenants' Rights Project, work in the hotels convinced them of the long-term need to assist families from becoming homeless. Going to the site of much of the problem, the debilitated row housing of Central Harlem where many of the hotel families come from, HTRP transformed itself into ACE—Action for Community Empowerment—an association of tenants fighting to maintain and upgrade their housing. Because the lack of affordable and decent housing is a key cause of homelessness in Central Harlem, ACE campaigns target the area's largest slumlord—the City of New York. Their goal: to hold the city accountable for the affordability and quality of the housing it owns.

Carol Quarles, now a member of the board of directors that governs ACE, began working with the organization while a resident of the Harriet Tubman shelter. She is white and 45.

I BECAME HOMELESS in October of 1987. I was living in a bungalow in Rockaway, Queens, when the manager rented an apartment to a drug dealer. Everything went to waste. The building became so dirty, broken, rat- and roach-infested that it was unliveable. We went to court and the landowner condemned it himself, said he wasn't going to bother with it.

Six families got evicted. I had six children, and my 15 year old daughter was pregnant. I had nowhere to go so I scattered my children among relatives and went, myself, to live with a friend.

Then in December I brought my family back together at my niece's apartment. There were 15 of us in one bedroom. We stayed that way until February, but it just got to be too much.

I went to an EAU, a welfare assistance place where they put you in hotels or shelters. First they put me up in a motel in the Bronx, only it was a long way away and I had to travel back and forth to the EAU each day. Then my daughter had her baby, and a woman there, she felt sorry for us and got us a 14-day stay in the Martinique Hotel. That stay lasted until the city closed the hotel, seven months later.

The city payed the hotel $3,000 a month to house us in two rooms. I was fortunate enough to have a bathroom—some rooms didn't have one at all—but the conditions of the hotel were so bad it was ridiculous. Drug dealers set a woman's room on fire because she didn't pay her drug bill. They threw a baby out a window. There was a murder. People came to our room at all hours of the night, knocking, trying to sell drugs.

When they closed the hotel they sent me to the Harriet Tubman Living Center on 143rd, between Lennox and 7th, one of the city's tier-two shelters. It's three buildings together, six floors each, and it's almost as bad as the hotel.

The security guards openly sold drugs and harassed the women. They opened my mail. The maintenance men took the things they were supposed to give the tenants—blankets, sheets, things like that—and sold them. There were no phones—once we tried to call an ambulance and my son had to go three blocks to find a phone. I wanted to complain but everyone said that if you did, they would put you out in the street.

Finally I went to a meeting HTRP had. They convinced me that I could not be legally evicted for asserting my rights. I went to more meetings and I spoke at a demonstration. Then we got an appointment with a city official and I told him of all that happened at the Harriet Tubman. Two weeks later I had my own apartment. After living there all that time I got nothing. But after opening up my mouth and demonstrating, I got out.

And I'll tell you how bad I wanted out. When we saw the apartment the manager said, "Ms. Quarles, there's something I want to tell you about that apartment: four people were executed there by drug dealers." And I said, "Oh my God! Will they be back?" "No," she said, "No, they got who they were looking for."

I was scared but I told the kids about it and they said to take it anyway, that anything was better than a shelter. And I've been here now for several months and there hasn't been a problem. It's nice; I'm active in the tenant association and I'm on a tenant's patrol to keep it safe. And it's better for the city. I mean it don't cost no $3,000 a month.

But if ACE hadn't convinced me of my rights, I would still be in a shelter. They gave me the self-confidence inside and showed me how to speak out and protect myself and my family. Because I spoke about the guards they changed them; and because I stood up for myself I got my family out.

I'm on SSI because of health problems—asthma and diabetes mainly. But working with ACE made me want to do more. I went back and got my GED so I would be better educated and able to help. Now I'm a board member for ACE, and a volunteer at the office. I speak with people who are in the same situation I was in. It gives me a good feeling inside to know that I can help someone like they helped me.

Because people here need better places to live. I mean the city-owned buildings, they're incredible. There are people with no water, no windows, rats and roaches ... and there is no excuse for it.

That's why ACE is so important. It's not ACE, it's tenants doing it themselves with ACE helping them to become empowered, and to rely on themselves.

I work now as a teacher in our leadership training retreats. We teach tenants their rights and show them that they can have power if they learn how to use those rights and if they work together. That's what it is mainly. There are so many homeless people in the shelters, but if people knew their rights and how powerful they can be when they get together, it wouldn't be so bad. And that's what ACE shows them.

Jeff Tedder
Catholic Worker House
Des Moines, Iowa

Dorothy Day, founder of the Catholic Worker movement, believed international struggles to be inherently linked to local concerns. Out of her effort to blend the two arose Catholic Worker houses, small cooperative communities committed to working for peace and justice at home and abroad.

For the Des Moines Catholic Worker house, "home" is a cooperative household on 8th Street, the heart of one of the city's most debilitated and crime-infested neighborhoods. An "intentional" community, it is there on purpose, just as it is small on purpose and poor on purpose.

In this sense the Catholic Worker model is something of an antithesis to the shelter / social-services paradigm. Because community members and "guests" live and eat together, and because incomes go into the community, distinctions between the two are diminished.

Like other Worker houses (and many of the programs mentioned here), the Des Moines home fosters an inclusive yet strict environment. Alcohol and drugs are forbidden, as are all manifestations of violence. One need not be Catholic, or even a Christian, to stay, but members describe their philosophy and concerns in Christian terms and organize the house in a cooperative manner that stresses mutual support and nonviolent strategies for resolving both in-house and international conflicts.

Jeff Tedder, whose testimony follows, lives with his three children in the Des Moines community. He is white, and middle-aged.

MY WIFE LEFT ME with three very small babies. It was very hard. I worked construction, but even working as much as I could it barely covered the cost of day-care. Then someone broke into our house and sabotaged it—broke the pipes and furnace. It was unlivable. With no place to go we left and came here.

By that time I had more or less closed myself off to people. I didn't like to talk to people, to go to the grocery store—I plain didn't like them, not after all that had happened to me. But when I saw the community's love and care for people ... well, it changed me. It taught me to resolve my own problems by helping others. Now I'm on staff and live as part of the community in one of our guest houses. I feel adopted. And my kids have become part of the community.

We work on two fronts: we care for these people individually, and we work to change the larger, societal causes of homlessness. Most homelessness arises out of socioeconomic difficulties such as the closing of factories, or the loss of housing. When people who have gone through this get to us we are their last resort. Like me, they usually have no other family or anything, no one to care for them. And the various government agencies you have to deal with when you're homeless—they take what's left of your humanity away. You become a case file, not a person.

But everyone needs to be recognized as a person. We need someone to care about us. Christ says if you see someone who is hungry to take them in and feed them; if they're homeless, to provide a place to stay. The way Dorothy Day, our founder, put it is that we're not just giving our homes, we're giving our hearts. We do that personally, one on one. And for us it is a reaching out, not a reaching down.

We live in voluntary, abject poverty. Because we live on so little ourselves we are more open to the problems of the people who come to us. We run our homes on what is considered an absurdly small amount of money. But we can do it. We live on what we can, sharing our food, growing what we can, and getting by on less.

Our freedom to help comes from this poverty. I was homeless when I came here, so I understand where the people we work with are coming from. The way we live now helps me to be able to continue to do that. We live in what is considered the heart of the city's violence, drug abuse, and prostitution. But we are free to live here because we are poor, we have nothing to steal, little to fear.

When our guests see our sharing, when they see how this place works, they begin to help. They see that by collecting cans for a day they can help out, purchase food for dinner. When that happens they're not helpless anymore, they're not dependent on us. It's not as if we're giving them something anymore, it's as if what they have to give is as important as what we have to give. That's why this is not charity; it's caring.

There's other things too. By helping us make meals our guests learn to live on less. They learn you don't need pre-prepared food, that you don't need expensive cuts of meat to eat well.

We believe that the more we can be self-sufficient the better we can use that which is given us. That way people have more and need less. It's another way, not only of helping ourselves and our guests, but of making the societal changes we need to prevent homelessness and poverty.

We grow a garden on a vacant lot owned by the county. The soil isn't good. When they destroy an abandoned house they pretty much push it in on its own basement, then they bulldoze, burying it by scraping off the surrounding topsoil to cover the hole. That destroys the soil, leaving clay. So we have to compost and use manure, we had to bring the soil back to life. But we were able to do it. We stored away some fifty quarts of tomatoes and peppers this summer. We even grew a watermelon for the kids.

We don't require our guests to think the way we do. And we don't believe we're here to teach them a way of life. But we do have a way of life and while they're here they share it. They follow our rules. We forbid alcohol and drugs and all violence. We practice pacifism. This creates an alternative model. If a fight starts across the street we go and stop the process with nonviolent action. Guests see this and are shocked. But they also see that this place is safe, and that there are alternative measures for dealing with conflict and difficulty. I've seen children learn nonviolent strategies and become radically changed. They learn to use them with each other, with their siblings.

I like to think of this place as a family. The first problem many people face, the one that leads to others, is their families have broken down, fallen apart, or become lost. Our society doesn't encourage extended families, and the problems we suffer destroy them. Because of that people are losing the care that used to be associated with family. That was true in my own life.

The Catholic Worker house is a way of extending the notion of families to others, of recognizing our homeless neighbors as our brothers and sisters. If these people were my family I would do everything to take them in and care for them. The Catholic Worker house did that for me and my children, caring about us as if we were their own. That's what we needed—myself and my children. Even with all the love I could give them it wasn't enough. They needed an extended family, a community. And they have that here. That's what I try to provide for others.

Niki
YouthCare: Orion Multi-Service Center
Seattle, Washington

The Orion Multi-Service Center opened in 1983 as a collaborate effort by YouthCare, a private, nonprofit agency founded to assist the city's many runaway, homeless, and abandoned youth. Designed to offer and coordinate a broad range of services, the center's many programs include drug, job, and casework counseling, health care, meals, recreation, a drop-in center, a school, and an outreach team that's on the streets of the city every night.

YouthCare services—including family reconciliation, gang intervention, in-home counseling, and emergency and transitional housing—are available by referral through the Orion Center. A program of intensive mental health services will be added this year. Like all Orion services, its approach will be custom-tailored to the needs of the youth the center serves.

According to Phil Sullivan, development director for YouthCare, these needs include respect, individual self-help plans, and as much distance as the youth want.

As one teen put it, "I want a place that doesn't want to make me a son, but that gives me my own space and helps me to make it through." Many of the homeless and runaway teenagers in the Seattle area I've spoken to believe the Orion Center is that place. The story of Niki, who now works for YouthCare, demonstrates the effectiveness of such an approach. Niki is white and 20 years old.

I WAS AT HOME with my parents and I was on drugs. Heavily. I didn't want to go back to school because I needed drugs to be there, but to be there meant I couldn't be out getting drugs. I told my mom I wouldn't go and she told me I'd have to move out if I didn't. So I left.

I'd live off people who would support me, or we'd find an empty house and just stay there with sleeping bags or blankets. And then I lived off of my dealer. He gave me drugs and money and I did runs for him.

And there was one time—lots of people at the center still don't know this—but I was downtown with a "boyfriend" quote pimp and two of the outreach workers from the Orion Center came up and offered me condoms. I refused them, like to pretend I wasn't out there doing that. But I was. Only they didn't come up and say it, you know, they didn't call me anything. And though they knew what I was doing they never brought it up at the center. Even to this day.

I mean that was important, that earned my trust. They offered me something and left it at that. Never judging me or bringing it up.

Everyone at the Orion Center is like that. They give you the support you need but they don't tell you what to do with your life. And when you do something good they let you know it. They stand behind you in everything. And that's what helped me.

At home it was all negative. Don't do this, don't do that. Like I would do one good thing and they would say, "But look you're still bad over here." That brought me down because nothing I did was good. But at the Orion Center they focused on where I was improving and gave me the support to keep on going. They never brought up negative aspects of my life and that was what I needed. I mean look how far I've come with my life now.

I got started there when a friend introduced me and I began to see Tom, who's a drug counselor there. Because like my nose was bleeding real bad ... even the dealer I was with wanted me to get off. Tom wanted to get me to this program where you go away for a month or two to get drug help, but I didn't want to be away that long. People move around quickly on the street and I didn't want to come back and not know where everyone was.

And he was cool with that, because that was what I wanted. I mean he'd been there before himself, so he knew what it was like. He was there on my side and because of that I started to quit on my own. I even started school there 'cause they have the best teachers that help you one-on-one and work with you from where you're at.

I moved out from the dealer and into an apartment with a friend who was an alcoholic and started drinking. I went from drugs to alcohol. And I was still trying to go to school—drinking, going out all night, running around, trying to get the money to pay for all that alcohol. 'Cause remember, where I was before the drugs were free.

And then I got a job working for YouthCare and they gave me ... I mean even working there I got support. Because they knew I was still living out there and having difficulties. But I finally got sick of it because I had to get up early and go to work and that's no fun if you're out all night and hung over. I moved in with a friend's uncle, who said I could stay there to get away from the alcohol. I wanted to concentrate on the job, get on with my life because I could see the opportunity they were offering.

I stayed there until I could get into the YAIT—that's Young Adults in Transition—at the YMCA, and I stayed there for a month. You have to have a job, open up a savings account—things like that so you can get an apartment when you leave.

I found an apartment, cheap, and stayed there and saved up some more money. And then my job went to full-time and I moved into a better place, got medical and dental insurance, and passed my GED. I took my GED book to work every day and during slow times they let me bring it out and study. And like if I had a question about something all I had to do was ask.

My plans now are to start college as soon as I get a little bit more stable, then go on to become a counselor to work with youth. I still speak to lots of the youth out on the street and they know I'm there to listen to them and that I know what it's like. And I've helped other friends, people who've followed in my footsteps and who now have apartments and jobs. I feel good about that.

It's not like everyone I talk to listens. I can think of lots of people who came into some money, like they inherited it or something, and who decided to go out and blow it. And I have other friends who tried to get off the streets but fell back down and who are now working again to get into an apartment and a job. And like ... well, my boyfriend right now—he's a supporter for me and I'm a supporter for him. He says if it wasn't for me he'd be back in the CD [Central District] doing what he used to be doing.

See the thing the Orion Center understands and that other places don't is that when you're out on the street you do what you want when you want it. You're very responsible. You have to be to take care of yourself because out there anything can happen. It's pretty scary. This is especially true if you're female. I mean I got into some rough spots, but I was always pretty sly and able to take care of myself.

But when you enter a program or a foster home you've suddenly got all these constraints. And if you've been out on you're own you don't want that. And you learn to have a hard time trusting people because so many people have turned on you.

That's why you have to deal with youth the way the Orion Center does. It's not like going into some office to get help and they tell you to do this and that. A lot of places, they'll say "Hey are you living on the

street! Well gosh, tell me about it!" The Orion Center doesn't demand
that kind of information. They treat you like a friend. If you don't want
advice they won't give it to you.

People on the street don't like nosy people. I think that's why lots of
them open up to me. 'Cause I come out being their friend. I don't care
about where they're living or what they're doing. But I know how to
deal with them, based on my own experience, and that makes me a
good person for them. That's why I'm getting involved in it from this
end now.

Tim Dunn
Philadelphia, Pennsylvania

Tim Dunn is a lithe, thin man with closely cropped brown hair. He walks lightly in easy, gentle strides and speaks in the comforting voice of one who spends much of his time assisting others.

As I spoke with Tim he was approached by a homeless woman, ragged and apparently mentally ill, whom he called Joe. Rummaging through some bags he was sorting, he came up with a pair of women's shoes and walked over to give them to her. I saw that she was barefoot and wondered that I hadn't noticed.

Joe kept her distance and watched me as Tim helped her with the shoes. My presence seemed to frighten her and I turned away so as not to intrude. Tim asked if she needed anything else but Joe didn't respond. She left a few minutes later and Tim returned to where we had been speaking on the street.

"That's what I do," he said. "That's what I'm here for."

Though homeless, Tim is generally able to find some kind of alternative living situation for himself, and as many other homeless people as he can accommodate. In this way he has provided shelter and, at times, a home, for hundreds of homeless people at absolutely no cost to anybody. Tim is white and in his thirties.

I WAS INVOLVED in the new music scene, sort of the punk-rock subculture. The Ethiopian famine started making news and we began to do rock-against-hunger benefits for Amnesty International and the local shelter programs around here. I got more and more involved and people started calling me Rock Hunger, which became something of a nickname.

Then I read about St. Mary's soup kitchen and said, "Wow, that's only a few blocks from our concert spot." So I brought the food we collected down there. They were so happy about it and, well, I started to help cook and pretty soon I got involved in the whole homeless scene.

It was around this time that my life began to change. I fell into debt and lost my apartment, began to have troubles. Everything was bad except the soup kitchen, which was this positive element in my life. It made me think.

That's when I began to squat. At first it was a secret thing actually, not public at all. I had a part-time job as superintendent of an apartment building and there was a secret room in the attic you could get to by climbing up a ladder in the fire tower. I stashed a bed up there and so, even though I was homeless, I had a place to sleep and one of the most beautiful views of the city you'd ever want to see.

Then the owner began to cheat me and I lost that job. I found myself walking one day and I noticed this house on Chestnut Street. It was abandoned, it had been abandoned for years. But now I was looking at it from the perspective of a homeless person and I said, "Wow, what a charming house."

Anyway, I squatted this house ... it's like a role in my life where I become curator of a building and take care of things. I worked nine hours a day on this house just hauling garbage out of it. Junk. The room I picked for myself was three feet full of trash and I hauled out bags and bags of garbage, spent days cleaning it up, working on the garden out back.

It had a secret entrance in the back that I used for a while. But eventually the fear fades about squatting. You take pride in what you're doing. You're making a home. You put your trash out on the side just like anyone else. The neighbors would see me doing this and they'd say, "You're doing a damn good job on this house, I hope you get to keep it."

I'd run into people at the soup kitchen and if they needed a place to stay I'd bring them home. I had a big bed, an extra bed, sleeping bags, and blankets. I made the place cozy. Winter came and we winterized. Quite a few people found shelter there.

Because of that I see squatting as a viable alternative for homeless people, a way of caring for neighborhoods and people. If you want to change things that's the only way to do it: from the neighborhood up. Business and landowners are abandoning the slum areas, why not let people squat them? If it's done responsibly, if it's done with some contact with the neighbors—you know, get to know them, let them get to know you—it can work. It depends on the quality of the action.

When it works it provides shelter; it gives people responsibility, a way of helping themselves; and it refurbishes deteriorating neighborhoods.

Squatting can also be an act of survival, of desperation. It can mean a person climbing into a place that's too dangerous to live in, just to keep from freezing to death. But our house, we beautified that place. And there's tons of abandoned houses in this area.

Other people say squatters come in, they bring their beer and their drugs, and they just want a place to shoot up. There's some truth to that, it depends on the people. It depends on what you want out of the place. But basic housing, people deserve that. And if they're homeless and willing to do the work to fix a place up, why not?

I felt strongly about this. As I became more aware of homelessness I instigated the first shanty demonstration on the university campus. This was in December, just before the students left for Christmas. We built shanties out of milk crates, tarps, and table tops in this field, next to the high-rise dormitories, and hung a banner that said "There's no place like Home for the holidays." The purpose was to raise community consciousness about the fact that there were no overnight facilities in the university area for homeless people. We passed a petition and had thousands of signatures.

That was when Charlie froze to death. Charlie was an older, homeless man who had been living in this shacklike thing, a university tool shed maybe. Anyway, Charlie was discovered by some workers in that shed and they tore it down. Charlie left the area because he had nowhere to go and wandered into Center City. It was bitter cold, I remember it was zero the day he died. They found him dead on the sidewalk outside a hospital.

I haven't really dealt with his death yet. I have to kind of put it in terms.... Charlie could be so funny. He would help out at meals and be fine. Then he could be out of his mind and wrap himself up in a piece of carpet and lie there moaning.... His death changed me. It made me more dedicated than ever to what I'm doing now.

I think everyone is potentially homeless. And if it's not our home that's threatened it's our planet, which is home to all of us. The whole planet has to become more survival oriented, we have to start that kind of a system. Our lives are too much about struggling to get ahead of each other. There's no reason to freeze to death outside of a hospital. We need to form communities to better meet our needs of food and shelter. The dominance of capital in our world destroys a lot of people through greed because capital lends itself to greed. But food doesn't. It's much easier to share food than money. Shelter too—that's why squatting works.

If we can learn to take care of the ecology of the earth we'll be working for our own survival. And if you help to provide food and shelter for the survival of others you're helping your community at the same time as you're living a good life. In that way people are happier, better cared for. There's less crime, more dignity. Less homelessness.

Now I spend my days working for the community, working to create food and shelter for myself and those around me who need it. Right now I'm packing away winter and fall sweaters and stuff like that, giving clothes to people who need them. Like Joe.

Joe is very unhappy. She's a bit like Charlie—constantly talking about people murdering her on some days, and happy and laughing on others. She likes to draw when it's a good day, but she's manic-depressive on some level and she doesn't take medication at all. She can be like an animal, roaming through the street, sleeping in allies, pissing herself. I do what I can. I give her food and clothes, take her to the soup kitchen. But it's only occasionally that I see her, and I don't think she gets any other help.

She's got wraggly hair and she wears all kinds of things in it, like pens and bands. Sometimes her last dollar will be in some knotty nest in her hair. And sometimes things are wound so tight she gets headaches and I have to cut them out to calm her down.

She needs more than I can give her. I can only help by being nice to her—and I do like her. She's the kind of person you get to love. But no one gets to know her because she's physically repulsive and smells so horrible. She comes into soup kitchens and they tell her to get out. That's why I try to take her, and why I'm glad she can find me.

Tara
Second Home Inc.
Boston, Massachusetts

Second Home Incorporated is an association of homeless persons and advocates that rose out of a large, tent city demonstration on the Boston Commons in 1984. The community, which regularly participates in fasts and other direct-action campaigns to call attention to the societal causes of homelessness, aggressively pursues innovative, grass-root alternatives for homeless people. Current projects of the community include the development of cooperative households of homeless people, and plans to purchase a farm to provide a respite from the city and an opportunity for the community to become yet more self-reliant.

Second Home Inc. currently operates three innovative residence programs for homeless people in the Boston area: Second Home, "for people who buy into society's notion of independence," and two group homes—Family House and Cornerstone Community—"for those who don't."

Second Home is an 18-month transitional housing residence for homeless people who have completed a detoxification program. It stresses peer support, strict rules, and a highly structured program of stages that combines self-help planning with job-placement and a savings plan. Many of its graduates form households of their own to maintain the cooperative, drug- and alcohol-free atmosphere of support which characterizes Second Home.

Tara, whose story follows, is a graduate of the program. She is an African American in her mid thirties.

WHEN I FIRST CAME to Second Home I had to sit down in front of the other residents and listen as they told me the kind of place it was and what they could offer me. Then I had to tell them why I wanted to be there and what I could offer *them*. That told me right away that this would be a different kind of place, because it was up to the residents whether I would be accepted.

I knew right then that it would work. We had a two-week trial to see if I would fit in, but I knew I would. I'm a very shy person but for some reason it was like I already knew these people. You know what I'm saying? I thought my shyness was going to be a problem, but it wasn't.

Now I have an apartment, my own place. And I'm working. If it wasn't for Second Home I wouldn't have any of that. Because apart from the programs you have to work. You come into the program at a certain phase and then you start working, start saving. The program's eighteen months long so when you leave you have a good amount saved up.

Rules like that make it work. We have certain things we had to do, to learn to be responsible again. Because that was what it was about, being responsible. I followed the rules because I wanted to get to where I am today. I wanted that more than anything. And without the rules I couldn't have done it.

And with Second Home I could see that improvement could happen, I could see that once you're down you don't always have to be there. Seeing that, I could bring myself up. And the group helped—you know, being there with other homeless people who were on their way up. We came a long way. By the time I left I was Senior Resident. I was the one who told people about the program and sat down to talk with them and help them out.

Before this I was an addict. It was getting high, getting high all the time. I wasn't responsible. I had five children and I wasn't responsible to them. I lost my place, lost my kids.

That was the worst time, when I lost my children. I used to get high so much I thought I would die that way. That seemed the way it was going to be. But that wasn't how it ended—it ended when they took my kids. I say now that God did the right thing to me then. 'Cause that's the only thing that would have stopped me.

I went through detox and that helped to break the addiction, but I needed more. I needed support to save money, to stay responsible, to stay clean. Just getting clean wasn't enough to get it all back together. That's why I went to Second Home, they gave me the support I needed.

I had female friends at Second Home. See that was one of my problems before, I didn't have female friends. I could never socialize with females, even before I started getting high. I didn't know how to socialize. But the program helped me learn to communicate, to deal with people, to talk to them if I have problems. And I got along with people there, I made friends.

They'd talk about their problems to me and I'd talk about mine to them. And they'd help. You know, instead of holding things in all day, if you talk about them it helps.

There are two counselors, a female and a male counselor. The female counselor there, she was important to me. There were quite a few times I talked to her. And I was able to talk to her about my children, or what I was doing to get them back, and she'd be there to help.

At first I thought the rules were too strict. We had to go to three meetings a week—you could go to AA, NA, whatever you needed to stay clean; you had to do chores; you had to attend a weekly house meeting; you had to work at the house one day a month; and you had to do other things, according to what stage you were in. People would say "Wow, I have to work then come home and do my chores?" But I looked at it like, well, this is what I'll have to do when I get my own place, and this is gonna help me get that place, so I'll do it.

And I still do. I still go to meetings. I go to counseling, I go to group. Some people go to AA, others to NA. NA helps me so I go there.

I didn't relapse because I knew how it was for me when I was using. My life was unmanageable out there and I didn't want to go back. I didn't want to lose what I had. I wanted to stay clean, for me and my children.

And by the time I left there I was everybody's mother. People looked up to me; I helped them, socialized with them. And like I said, I used to have problems with that. But at Second Home they called me "Mother Tara." They used to say, "Mother Tara, I have a problem ... " and I'd talk to them. They knew I'd always help them out.

You see you have stages. In the first stage it's just to see if you can stay clean and make it work there. That's two weeks. You're getting acquainted with the house. You can't leave except with a buddy, which is another way of getting acquainted with people.

In the second phase it's like, if you don't have a job you have to start looking for one, start paying your program fees, start saving money. You're supposed to save $30 a week in Phase 2. In Phase 3 it's $90, and in Phase 4 it's $120. If you don't have a job during Phase 2 you look for one three days a week and do temporary work for two. They give you a key in Phase 2 and after a month you come back in front of the house to see if you'll work out for the rest of the eighteen months.

At the third phase you design a program for yourself, like to go to school or keep working, find a better job. At stage four you work towards getting a place of your own. 'Cause in the third stage, when you're making the plan for yourself, you start talking about where you want to live, what kind of place. They have a staff member that helps to find the aparment, and a contact man and a contact woman to help.

Like my goals ... well, at the time my goals were to get my kids back, to save, and to get to where I am today.

Now I'm in my own place. I got my five children here. I've been going through my little ups and downs, but that's the financial problem of dealing with five children. But like I keep saying, if it wasn't for Second Home I wouldn't be here at all.

I work at Family House, which is another part of the organization. Basically I'm a contact person. I answer phones, I cook. I help with the mentally ill—Second Home is mostly addicts, but this place is for long-term people.

One guy, I help him get up in the morning, get to his day program. I love it. And the people here, they like me. I always had this thing—even when I was out on the street—I had this thing about helping people and here I can do that.

I feel beautiful because my kids are proud of me. My kids have seen me change, and I feel good about that. Don't get me wrong, they drive me crazy. I've got five of them, you know. But I feel good that I have a place, that I can put food in the house, cook for them. I can't always give them what they want, but I can say, "Well, this is what we've got left so let's wait for the next paycheck."

My oldest is 15, he's a boy. I have a 13-year-old daughter, a 6-year-old daughter, and a five- and a 4-year-old boy. And with my oldest two, I'm able to talk to them about drugs and alcohol. They don't want me around people that use, and that goes for their lives. They're really against it. Like my son, all he does after school is stay home, even if he's with his girlfriend. He doesn't go out, and my daughter doesn't either.

And even though I did what I did I'm very overprotective. I ask him what he does when he's out and he says, "Momma, if I see a gang of people—even if it's just a small group—I cross the street or go the other way."

And that's another thing too: I have a lot of fear of the streets. I was shot twice. Once in my apartment before I was homeless. And that was gang-related. So I'm protective of my children. 'Cause even though we've got our own place, it's still around us. The addiction, the streets, and the gangs. ... So we stay home and we stay together.

Sue
PATH
Birmingham, Alabama

Partnership Assistance to the Homeless (PATH) is an innovative assistance program for homeless women and their children in the Birmingham area. While recognizing the importance of emergency housing, PATH has always emphasized long-term solutions that enable women to become self-sufficient. To this end, they have initiated a remarkable program wherein homeless women receive assistance in purchasing their own homes.

Apart from the homeowners' assistance program, PATH provides emergency shelter, food, clothing, transitional housing, job training, counseling, and a broad array of other services. Like other programs that have proven effective for homeless women, PATH encourages a self-help orientation that places responsibility and resources in the hands of the women it serves.

Like all PATH programs, the homeowners' program relies on the support and effort of a large cadre of volunteers. Volunteers help locate abandoned or run-down homes, donate labor and supplies for refurbishing, and provide legal and financial services.

Sue, whose story follows, hopes to purchase the home she now lives in through PATH. She is in her mid thirties and describes herself as being of "mixed" descent.

I CAME TO PATH in May of '90. Prior to that, like just before Christmas, things just ... it's like a powder keg exploded in our house.

My husband had been abusive before, but it had mainly been mental cruelty. When it turned physical I wanted out.

My children are resilient, but there's always inner turmoil when children see violence between people they love. There's an inner scar then and I couldn't, I couldn't keep them there and know that would happen to them. And, you know, he had started to threaten them too. So I just left.

I was teaching at the time. I know it's hard when a teacher resigns, but I didn't have any choice. It's not the way I wanted it to be. I wanted to leave under my own circumstances, so I could plan things. But there wasn't time for that, so I just walked into the principal's office, turned in my resignation, and left—not knowing where I was going or what I was going to do.

I met a lady I had taught with earlier and she said I could stay in her place until I could get situated. She had a young child and I took care of her baby. Then my husband found out where I was and started threatening the family, like he was going to blow their brains out—all kinds of stupid stuff—so I had to run from there.

The children, they suffered the most. They were uprooted from all their friends, their grandparents, everyone. And trying to explain it to them ... that's what really hurt me. We were living in a car then and they were having nightmares. First it was about the things that had happened at home. My husband is big, six-four, and he used to box. I am very fearful of him and the children are too. One night he put his fist through a solid door, just put his fist right through it to show how mad he was. So you know what he could do if he struck you.

They had nightmares about that, and about all the fighting. Then they had nightmares about the way we were living—living in a car, not having any money. I remember they kept asking for juice and I kept having to explain to them that we didn't have any.

But I didn't give up. 'Cause I think as long as you're alive you have hope. And I said, "Lord, I just need someone to help me make this line."

We had to hide because my husband, he has friends in the police. That's how they found us the first time. So we left Tennessee and went to Birmingham and I looked in the phone book.

I saw the name PATH and I just called it. I don't know why: all it said was PATH. But I tried it and got through. I explained my situation and they accepted me. They know you need shelter first, and someone you can trust and depend on, and that's what they gave me. I don't even like calling them an organization because they're more of a family. I didn't have friends here and I kept a lot of things private when I first showed up. They taught me how to share my feeling ... now everything doesn't have to be shared, but things that you need to get worked out, it helps to talk about those things. And PATH helped me do that.

But one thing I want to say is they keep you from that baby bird syndrome, where everything you want they go get for you. It's not a place like that. You start by setting goals, and by breaking them down into small steps. You have weekly meetings and you discuss what you're doing to attain that goal. And they make you see that it is attainable, as long as your aspirations are in sight. Because you can't go overboard, you know. You have to start small. But they help there too. They help you attain what you can, to focus on that goal. Like you tell them what you want to do and they say, "Hey, I know somebody that can help." It's like networking, 'cause they have so many people helping out there and donating their time that it seems like there's always somebody to connect you to.

Like everyday things, or emergencies. They network to handle those things. Let's say your car breaks down. They know who will charge a nominal fee or who will let you pay in payments. So you call them and set it up. It gives you this group of people you can work with and helps you do for yourself. Or say they come and fix your car—you make sure to make those payments, even if it's just a little bit you can send each month, because they went out of their way for you. You build up confidence that way and learn to trust yourself. Little things like that, they provide order in your life. You plan and trust yourself, believe in yourself again. That's what I needed.

Another thing, they use active listening. A lot of people just listen to words and phrases, they don't connect. But at PATH they empathized with what I was saying. They cared and understood what I was going through. And that's what always kept me smiling.

I entered directly into transitional housing. It's a building divided into four apartments, all of them associated with PATH. It's a community-type setting because everybody supports everybody. We had apartment meetings where we would all get together and talk about what we were feeling—a rap session. And we'd all fix dinner for everybody and, like if one of us didn't have food the others would. There was real comradery. You squabble, like all humans. But there the squabble was different. We were careful when we squabbled. And then we'd hug and say we were sorry.

You really don't have to do a lot of encouragement for that because when you're down you just want to find somebody. We're social creatures, we want to be listened to. We want to be loved. So we gave each other those things. And we weren't threatened by it, not like people who are established and have everything get threatened by things like that. They don't like to show they care because they think that makes them seem vulnerable and weak. But we didn't have anything more to lose so we didn't worry about it.

And we learned to help others. Because we'd been homeless ourselves we'd go and visit the shelter, talk to the women who had just come off the street.

Alabama's teaching requirements are different, so I couldn't teach here without going back to school. Well, that's a long-term goal I have but there wasn't time for it then. So I took the civil service test and looked for other jobs. At PATH I had gotten by without ever applying for AFDC or any type of welfare. Those things are good for people who need them, but I'm a college graduate and I wanted to depend on myself. For me it would have been the baby bird syndrome, and I didn't want that. So I took temporary jobs while I looked for other work and in the meantime PATH helped me learn to save and budget.

Then I was called in for an interview at the Department of Human Resources. The person who interviewed me said she was impressed, but there were twenty more people applying for the job. Then lo and behold they called me the next day and offered it to me.

I called PATH to tell them and they said, "Hey, let's come in for your session, talk about the goals you set six months ago, see where you are, and set new ones." Because there were all sorts of things I needed: I needed attire for the job, day-care, transportation, all of that.

So with my new job I moved into a regular apartment. Then I became part of their new program, where they help you purchase a house. See they prepurchase a house, like a HUD home, and then they help a single mother save the money to make the payments. What you do is you stay in the house a year or two and make payments as if you were purchasing the house. At the end of that time you make an application to actually buy it.

Lots of the houses they refurbish themselves. Like for this house they had to redo everything: painting, carpentry, masonry work—I mean everything to get it livable. Then people donated furniture. Now I have a porch, a yard—front and back—a dining room I use as a den, a large kitchen, a bathroom, and two bedrooms for my three children.

I'm still afraid. I mean my husband doesn't know where I am but he's looking and he's intimated what he'll do when he finds me. He tells everyone that I just up and left for no reason. And he's very persuasive. That's why I can't contact people I once knew, even my own sister.

And I don't understand it, I don't understand what makes men violent. It's like, if they're not dominating they go haywire. They feel out of control in their life and they say, "This woman has made me mad and I'm going to knock her block off." You know, take it out on her and watch her squirm.

And a lot of them act out what they saw as children between their own parents. They become products of their own environment, even if they've been educated. It's easier to fall into that mold than to change.

Then when the children grow up and begin to exercise their independence, when he can't control them anymore, he begins to take it out on them. The children, they're not being defiant, it's just that they're growing up. I remember he drew back to hit our 4 year old, right before I left. Two hundred and twenty pounds, an expert boxer, and he's about to lay it to a 4 year old. I said no way, it's not going to happen again. And since that day my daughter, she's never been the same, she never quite got over it.

What I do now is I look at relationships. Let's say a woman and a man are friends. I watch them then and I can always tell when their relationship becomes sexual. The friendship changes, they get mad at each other ... and let's say the woman moves in with him. Well, I know the man is going to get angry somewhere down the line. Then she's either got to take it or get out of there. And if she has no other place she'll just take it, which only makes it worse.

I hate to say it but with men, it's like their nature. They have this domineering syndrome. It can sound like, "I'm going to take care of you," but it means "I'm going to dominate you." And women, we play our part. We like to please. So we become submissive, lose our identity to assume what he wants us to be. You become just a shell of a person. Men and women you know, if they just had the ability to switch places and see....

And since at PATH they're all women, they help you to get a better understanding of yourself and how to deal effectively with a man. Because how you start out with a relationship is how the relationship will go and end up. So if you start out being submissive and six months down the road you start speaking up for yourself....

So you need to start out not letting people dominate you, I've learned that. And I've learned to look out for the kind of man I was drawn to the first time so I don't go out and make the same mistake again.

But it's hard here. Some days I feel like I'm working for nothing because every dime I make goes to somebody. There are days when I have seven dollars and I have to buy groceries and gas. But I don't let myself get depressed. Because when I was homeless I realized depression just makes you see the negative side of things and I was seeing too much of that anyway.

What I do now is I think back on times at PATH. Crazy times when we did something nutty or joked around. And it helps, it helps me to remember where I've been and where I'm going.

Now I work with DSH. I assist people with AFDC, child support, food stamps. I understand because I've been homeless myself. I don't tell them what to do, but I listen and encourage them. And people come back to me later and thank me. I just say, "Hey, it's all about helping each other." Because that's what PATH did for me. And as far as I'm concerned, it's impossible to go through all they did for me and not pass it along. They're laying the groundwork for the organization to grow on because there will always be someone they helped to carry on the work they've begun.

Right now I'm trying to get an alumni organization started to help do this. Because I really think we should stay in contact with each other. I mean I've seen homeless women as young as 18 and I've seen them in their 50s. And I know that it can happen to anybody. So I want to keep this thing PATH started going. It's a good thing, and it needs some more folks in it.

Cyrell
Philadelphia, Pennsylvania

I frequently dream of the homeless people I've met, traveled with, and listened to. Where are they, I wonder? What has happened to them? Cyrell haunts my thoughts more than anyone, though I think—rather than worry—about him.

Cyrell is a young African American living in the inner city. He wears a stocking cap, athletic sweats in maroon and blue, and numerous bracelets made of discarded chains and wire wrapped around his wrists and arms. He is remarkably calm, gentle, and kind, the most disarming individual I've ever met, a man remarkably present to both the hard realities of the ghetto and to the interior world of his own thoughts and vision.

Like Thoreau, Cyrell learned that to be simple is to be free. But whereas Thoreau learned to forgo luxuries, Cyrell had his taken from him. Indeed, he has learned to live with much less: no cabin, no pond, no axe. Yet, like Thoreau, he has turned his poverty to his own benefit in thought and articulateness.

"Situations on the street force you to express yourself," Cyrell explains. "To keep from being disrecognized, isolated, alienated, you learn to make contact with others and to communicate. Your body and mind seek to release tension and pain, and self-expression is a release. The more you exercise it, the better you are able to put into words what you feel and think."

I'M TRYING TO ESTABLISH a survival center that deals with homelessness through a root-cause perspective. A place that sees that people need hospitality to the level of food, shelter, and their minds. A place where a person can become self-rehabilitated through working with other people, and where they can have a cooperative base from which to regain stability, dignity, and personal direction and success.

Because the poor are in a very unstable, fluctuating situation. You're dependent. Whether it's welfare, SSI, food stamps, or an uncertain job, you're dependent and in trouble because you don't know when these things are going to ... when that carpet's going to be pulled from under you. That happened to me many times.

But when you fall and climb back up again and then fall again, you start to see what you gained for what it is. You see that most of the things people do are not done for meaning, they're done for self-absorbed self-interest and personal survival. Even if you're rich.

By knowing that, I have seen more convenience in not following the mainstream. See the mainstream turns us against one another. And when you're homeless you have no one to turn to, you feel like everyone's against you, and they are—because the system makes it that way. That's the problem. The solution is to work together. I've found a lot to live for because I've realized that; it's given me a reason to move forward, to survive.

It's similar to the situation where people leave whole buildings where they work empty at night, even with the lights, heaters, and everything on in the wintertime. Yet people sleep in front of these buildings—homeless. Nowhere to go. Or people hold services in churches on Sunday; the rest of the week they're just empty buildings. This happens because the trends of society are becoming more impersonal, destroying the virtues of mutual cooperation—working together and sharing. The ends of life are material gain, self-status, everything except community, which should be the ultimate goal.

No one living without community is living the ultimate reality. They're missing freedom, the freedom to face life in its most basic sense: facing the hardships of life upfront, together; working and living together.

There's other ways—beyond the dollar, beyond hustling—where people can live and work for a cause, doing something about it. Fighting homelessness is one of these. It keeps me self-motivated towards embetterment. And I know I can pull other people in that, too.

See, community isn't just the streets, lights, houses, stores, and all that. Your church, your business, your group or whatever. Community is people working together for their own mutual survival. People are mutual beings, but we live in a society that is destroying our mutuality, alienating us from each other. That must be changed.

We must all live together, in a true sense. If we do that, this trend of the impersonal society will start to reverse. People may even go back to the old virtues of mutual help, caring, and sharing, and see less need in material pursuits. Because the material struggle is what people think life is all about: struggling to gain material satisfaction and wealth. There's a means but no end. Money is only a means, cars are only a means, houses are only a means. Everything, really, is only a means. People don't realize that. So the means never get them there.

What we're doing here as individuals is what we're doing internationally. War is indifference, lack of commonality and sharing. People think peace is simply when you put down the guns or halt the nuclear mechanism. No. If you don't have mutual caring and sharing, people working together in cooperation, you'll have war—which is what homeless people have here on a day-to-day basis. We're just as much at war with each other as two countries can be.

That's why the idea of a survival center, a community of mutual support, is so important.

We'll be both raising money and getting other people aware of this idea of mutual lifestyle as a way of overcoming homelessness. Many people suffer because they're trying to live on their own. That's another part of the mainstream lifestyle—to "make it" as an individual.

But the only way they can make it is through mutual cooperation and self-help, through community. When a person becomes homeless, or abused, or whatever the situation, he is on his own. First of all, he was on his own when he was working and laboring from day to day for his own personal survival. Then he's really on his own when he loses his job, loses his home. It's just different degrees of becoming more and more alone. Even in a job. But if you're not alone—if you're living in commonality—there's not just that one rug beneath you.

See, we live in a false ideology, what I call "domestic vanity." People think they can live comfortably in a complacent lifestyle, with nothing ever happening, while actually the circumstances of life itself are gnawing at the doorstep. It's gnawing at their feet. But they become complacent, caught up in comfort and technology rather than life itself.

The point is, if people stop being greedy—providing that they are resourceful—there would be prosperity. In other words, if I have this [he picks up a gallon plastic container] and it's full of water, and if someone asks me for some and I say, "No, you can't have none," I cause poverty for this person.

I could create prosperity simply by giving this person a cup of water. It works the same with a person in poverty. Or say you give someone a glass of water. He drinks it, and then he hands the cup back for more and keeps handing the cup back until all I have left is a cup. Now he's created poverty for me, he reversed it. So if we stop being greedy, in poverty or in wealth, homelessness will end.

A Note On Methodology

There was a time when oral historians had only their ears to trust. Skilled listeners, it was their job to note the details, tone, and feel of a narrative, and to re-create it on paper in the "voice" of the speaker.

Today we have the tape recorder to rely on. We know exactly what was said and can transcribe in the confidence that we have it right—word for word.

The benefits of this change are immense, and I have done my best to exploit them here. On many occasions this meant playing and replaying a sentence to hear exactly what was said over the car horn I had also recorded, or the sound of the bus that passed as the speaker spoke. On other moments it meant corroborating pronunciation with the help of a friend or acquaintance so that I could be confident I had heard "talkin'" and not "talking."

But people don't speak in print. Language lilts and shifts, swoons and falls. In transcribing a narrative we lose its orality, the rich texture of its sounds and the nuances of meaning they carry. Punctuation helps. In fact the question mark may be derived from musical notation indicating a rise in pitch. But punctuation connotes boundaries of convention that rarely coincide with real speech. And many characteristics of voice have no print equivalent whatsoever. Try transcribing the semantic weight of a pause, or shifts in the rhythm of an anecdote, and you'll see what I mean.

To overcome these limitations I've tried to bring back some of the old craft of oral history and to listen with my ears as well as my machines, to re-create as well as record. Apart from the editing necessary to shrink many pages into a few, this takes the form of additions and changes. Where an utterance rose to signify an episodic statement, for example, I added "and" or otherwise tried to capture in print the conjunction implied by voice. On other occasions I added nouns that had been implicit in speech or restated a phrase whose meaning, while clear on tape, was lost in direct transcription.

On a few occasions I rephrased a statement altogether. This occurred only in instances of grave difficulty—moments when an essential comment was lost or adversely changed in transcription. The decision to do so was never easy, but when faced with a choice between fealty to narrative or transcript, I chose the narrative. Should readers find such rephrasing objectionable they might—as Alessandro Portelli has suggested—compare it to the translation of a novel or poem from one language to another.[1] In such cases, Portelli notes, "the most literal translation is hardly ever the best, and a truly faithful translation always implies a certain amount of invention. The same may be true for transcription of oral sources."

Inconsistencies in pronunciation, however, were maintained as accurately as possible. In this sense it is not by any oversight in proofreading that a narrator may speak in dialect in one sentence and not in another. As is customary of most people, many of the narrators moved in and out of dialects and shifted registers with respect to topic, emphasis, other listeners, and my own speech. These changes carry meaning and I've tried to maintain them as best I can.

The use of contractions to represent pronunciation and dialect is a compromise. While aware that the best of writers can capture varieties of speech without such machinations (Ralph Ellison—who learned to do this through his own work in oral history—comes to mind), my own efforts to do so proved futile. Short of linguistic notation, punctuation was simply the best mechanism I had for communicating these features without sacrificing meaning. In no way should it imply that a term or speaker was at all incomplete or deficient.

Nevertheless, it should be noted that my own race, gender, and appearance most likely affected the stories I heard and the voices with which I was told them. In one instance I was explicitly told that my race precluded me from being taken to a particular site. On other occasions (always after several hours of conversation with a person) I was told, "You know, I can't believe I'm tellin' ya all this," as if to suggest that my race (or gender) had not affected the story as much as the speaker might have thought it would.

It is also likely that my background affected the "shape" of the testimonies as I've presented them. It has been amply documented, for instance, that the stories many African Americans tell are more characteristically episodic (moving from topic to topic in the development of a theme) than those told by Anglo-Americans, which tend to be more restricted in focus and directed toward a single "point."

Being aware of this phenomenon, I've worked to maintain the structural integrity of each narrative. As is evident, however, the book is arranged topically. Each narrative was shortened and a few were broken up for inclusion in separate chapters. While facilitating the book's purpose, these changes nonetheless altered the shape of the narratives.

Content has not been changed. Indeed, it should be noted that the opinions expressed by the narrators are not necessarily my own. The purpose of the book was to create an alternative perspective on homelessness by giving voice to homeless people themselves. This sometimes meant printing statements I disagreed with and, in the case of my introductions, working backwards from the testimonies to create contexts in which they might be more fully understood. The only statements I out-and-out censored on the basis of content were misogynist or racist diatribes.

Persons interviewed for *Street Lives* spoke of their own volition and with full knowledge of the project and of the uses I would make of their narratives. Typically, I spent a good deal of time establishing rapport with people after broaching the project and in no case did I ever record a person without receiving explicit permission to do so. Many of my best interviews occurred in situations where I had the chance to become part of a community, shelter, or soup kitchen for an extended period of time. This happened in Philadelphia, in Roanoke, and to a lesser extent in Washington, D.C., and Seattle.

After securing permission to record a person, I placed my tape recorder in full view of the interviewee, turned it on, restated the goals and purpose of the project, and asked once again for consent. Each recording begins with my description of the project and the subject's authorization to be recorded. The process of transcribing the narratives, and of editing them for publication, was also described. Subjects were told that any profit I might realize through their narratives would be shared among homeless shelters, soup kitchens, and advocacy groups.

The only exceptions to this process were my interviews with Anne, Carol, John, Niki, Tara, and Sue (all in "Solutions"), which occurred over the telephone. In these cases I did not record the interview but transcribed directly via keyboard. The same process of requiring consent was followed, however, and copies of the transcripts were sent to the narrators through their organizations for verification. In the case of Nancy ("The Homeless Mentally Ill") I did my best to explain who I was, kept the tape recorder in open view, and made sure I had permission to speak with her from the women who provided her care.

As might be imagined, the question of whether to compensate interviewees for their time was one of the most difficult I faced in this work. Many speakers spent several hours with me—time they would otherwise have spent looking for work, collecting cans, or getting a meal. Virtually everyone I spoke with was hungry, and many were abjectly destitute. The idea of recording their stories without compensation seemed steeped in exploitation, while paying them for their narratives undercut the very purpose of the book.

Ultimately, the issue was decided by my own relative poverty: I simply had nothing to pay these people with. While fed and housed by friends, soup kitchens, and shelters in the course of recording the testimonies, it was all I could do to cover the cost of driving from city to city. Nevertheless—and as happens with almost everyone who works with homeless people—I shared what I had. I did my best to help people find places to stay, and when conversations lapsed into the evening, I sometimes bought dinner. I bought a lot of coffee, and some cigarettes. And there may be people wearing my clothes in any number of cities across the country.

Homeless families were the only exception to this policy. One shelter requested that I compensate families for their time and, in another instance, I was given money by a friend to distribute to homeless families I met. But most families I spoke with were not compensated, and money was never used to initiate a conversation. On more than one occasion I offered assistance and it was declined.

Finally, except where otherwise noted in the text, I made no attempt to verify the facts and events described in the narratives. Oral history is much more concerned with the meaning and significance of events than the events themselves, and I accepted as "true" the meaning of events as described to me by those I spoke with. Next I perused the research and data on homelessness, poverty, housing, etc., from the perspective of what I had been told, and presented that information in my introductions to the chapters.

Does such a perspective render the book biased? Well, of course. But no more so than a text written from a psychiatric, sociological, or religious point of view. And who, ultimately, is to say which "history" is the more accurate: that which attempts an objective description of events as we have observed and recorded them, or that which sounds the psychological depths and significance of those events in the experience of the people who have lived them? The literature on homelessness is replete with reports written from the points of view of various professionals. May it be the strength of this book to have considered another way of knowing, and those who know it so well.

NOTES

Preface

1. Most names are pseudonyms.

Chapter 1

1. For the sake of convenience, I accept Peter H. Rossi's understanding that a person is homeless if he or she does not have "customary and regular access to a conventional dwelling," such as a room, apartment, or house. "An unconventional dwelling is any structure that is not intended to be used as a (permanent) sleeping place," including shelters, cars, and shanties (*Down and Out in America: The Origins of Homelessness*, Chicago: University of Chicago Press, 1989, p. 11.) The Department of Housing and Urban Development (HUD) defines "homeless" in a similar manner (*Safety Network* 10.9 (1991). It must be noted, however, that "homeless" is a relative term. While useful, it suggests false distinctions between similar levels of poverty and inadequately describes certain "in between" situations, such as permanent housing in so-called "welfare hotels," or "doubling up" in overcrowded apartments.

2. Numerous reports and studies confirm this statement. See, especially, The U.S. Conference of Mayors (COM), *Status Report on Hunger and Homelessness in America's Cities: 1991*. The COM study cited a 17 percent increase in requests for family shelter. See also Gregg Barak, *Gimme Shelter: A Social History of Homelessness in Contemporary America* (New York: Praeger, 1991), p. 4. In some areas this phenomenon is true for middle-class families (*Memphis Business Journal*, June 19, 1991).

3. See Osha Gray Davidson, *Broken Heartland: The Rise of America's Rural Ghetto* (New York: Free Press, 1990), pp. 80-84.

4. *New York Times*, June 22, 1986, reported that as many as 235,000 families may be doubling up in city projects and private apartments in New York City alone.

In a subsequent article, the *Times* reported 100,000 such families (*New York Times*, June 17, 1987). More significantly, a separate study found 52 percent of families in New York City's shelter system lived doubled up before becoming "officially" homeless. Similar findings have been found elsewhere, even among the rural poor. See, for example, Richard Towber, *Characteristics of Homeless Families* (New York: City of New York, 1986), and *Rural Homeless in America: Appalachia and the South* (New York: National Coalition for the Homeless, November 1987), pp. 46-48. Nationwide, as many as 14 million people are now doubled up, precariously housed, or otherwise on the verge of homelessness (*USA Today*, August 9, 1989).

5. New York City's infamous Fort Washington Shelter, for example, is a "sprawl of 700 bodies" where rape and other forms of violence have come to be accepted as facts of homeless life" (*Los Angeles Times*, May 6, 1991).

6. By 1987 more than half of all children in female-headed families lived beneath the poverty line, while fewer than one-third of all poor households received federal housing assistance (Center on Budget and Policy Priorities, 1989). It should also be noted that, while the number of families on assistance is now soaring to record levels (the *Los Angeles Times* (June 6, 1991) notes that nationally, 12.5 million Americans now get cash benefits from the Aid to Families with Dependent Children (AFDC) program. That number surpasses a previous record set in 1981.) the number of families beneath the poverty line, which receive no assistance, is also rising. Michigan, for example, recently ceased welfare payments to more than 100,000 people—a move that was opposed by social service agencies and the police (*Detroit Free Press*, May 22, 1991).

7. According to a 1989 report by the U.S. House Ways and Means Committee. These findings are confirmed by a U.S. Census Bureau report ranking Alabama as 50th, and Texas as 49th, in per capita spending for public welfare, a general grouping of aid to the poor.

8. A report on the "poverty gap" received by the Massachusetts State Welfare Department, for example, cited Boston-area families on state aid as receiving less than 80 cents for every dollar required to make ends meet. Notwithstanding this crisis, the National Housing Task Force (1988) reported that more than one million families are on waiting lists for public housing nationwide. In response to the current recession, state-funded rent vouchers in Massachusetts and other states have been drastically cut back while applications for vouchers and public housing have soared (*Boston Globe*, August 3, 1991).

9. This is particularly true of healthy, single men, for whom it is virtually impossible to get assistance or housing after unemployment benefits have run out (Peter Marin, "Why are the Homeless Mainly Single Men?" *The Nation*, July 8, 1991), pp. 46-51.

10. Rossi (note 1), whose work considers more than 40 separate reports and studies, finds "the street homeless are at least equal in number to the shelter homeless and likely closer to double" (p. 70).

Chapter 2

1. The U.S. Congress of Mayors, *The Continuing Growth of Hunger, Homelessness and Poverty in America's Cities: 1987*, p.23.

2. *Star-Ledger* (Newark), March 12, 1989.

3. *Washington Post*, December 4, 1987.
4. See Charles Hoch and Diane Spicer, "SROs, an endangered species: Single-room occupancy hotels in Chicago" (Chicago: Community Shelter Organization and Jewish Council on Urban Affairs, 1985), as cited in Rossi (note 1, chap 1), p. 134.
5. U.S. Conference of Mayors, *Status Report on Hunger and Homelessness in America's Cities: 1989.* Consequently, more working poor are entering food lines throughout the country (*San Francisco Examiner*, May 29, 1991).
6. Southern Regional Council, Inc., *Hard Labor: A Report on Day Labor Pools and Temporary Employment* (Atlanta: Southern Regional Council,1988).
7. *Wall Street Journal*, June 22, 1983.
8. Peter T. Kilborn, "Drugs and Debt: Shackles of Migrant Worker," *New York Times*, October 31, 1989.
9. Conversation with Shelley Davis.

Chapter 3

1. Reviewing his own research and that of more than forty other studies, Rossi writes, "the more I looked into homelessness the more it appeared to be misstated as merely a problem of being without shelter: homelessness is more properly viewed as the most aggravated state of a more prevalent problem, extreme poverty" (note 1, chap. 1, p. 8). While one of many researchers who make similar statements, Rossi's conclusions are particularly noteworthy given the breadth of research his work considers.
2. A study by the Survey Research Center of the University of Michigan found just over one-half of those people living in poverty remain poor the following year. According to the study, only 2.6% of all people living below the poverty line could be considered "persistently poor" (Greg J. Duncan, *Years of Poverty, Years of Plenty: The Changing Economic Fortunes of American Workers and Families*, Ann Arbor: Institute for Social Research, University of Michigan, 1983, p. 34). A more recent California survey found similar results (see "Families").
3. "Money Income and Poverty Status in the United States: 1988," *Current Population Reports: Consumer Income*, series P-60, no. 166, and "Poverty in the United States: 1988 and 1989," *Current Population Reports: Consumer Income*, series P-60, no. 171.
4. Rossi (note 1, chap. 1), p. 78. Interestingly, Rossi shows that the 224 percent figure remains accurate when the "extreme poverty" cutoff is lowered to $2,000 or less (figures expressed in 1987 dollar equivalents and based on Current Population Survey Data, 1970 to 1987).
5. Ibid., p. 79.
6. William Julius Wilson, *The Truly Disadvantaged: The Inner City , the Underclass, and Public Policy* , Chicago: University of Chicago Press, 1987), pp. 46-55.
7. Ibid., pp. 39-46.
8. Ibid., p. 41.
9. Ibid., pp. 60-62.
10. Ibid., p. 38. See also Alex Kotlowitz, *There Are No Children Here: The Story of Two Boys Growing Up in the Other America* (New York: Doubleday, 1991).
11. The most striking difference between homeless people and people who are extremely poor is assistance, either through government programs or friends and family. This pattern is evident in the 1987 Current Population Survey. See Rossi (note 1, chap. 1), p. 116.

12. See Edward B. Lazere et al., *The Other Housing Crisis: Sheltering the Poor in Rural America* (Washington, D.C.: Center on Budget and Policy Priorities and the Housing Assistance Council, 1989), p. xx. See also Davidson (note 3, chap. 1).

13. See Jeffrey Shotland and Deanne Loonin, *Patterns of Risk: The Nutritional Status of the Rural Poor* (Washington, D.C.: Public Voice for Food and Health Policy, 1988), p. 9.

14. Interestingly, most studies show the opposite effect. In fact, after reviewing over a hundred studies and conducting one itself, the General Accounting Office determined that welfare encourages neither out-of-wedlock births, family disintegration, nor unemployment (*"Welfare Reform: Projected Effects of Requiring AFDC for Unemployed Parents Nationwide,"* General Accounting Office, March 22, 1987). See also Francis Fox Piven and Richard A. Cloward, "Sources of the Contemporary Relief Debate," in *The Mean Season: The Attack on the Welfare State*, by Fred Block et al. (New York: Pantheon Books, 1987).

15. See Jonathon Kozol, "The New Untouchables," *Newsweek*, special edition, The 21st Century Family, Winter/Spring 1990, p. 52. According to the Center on Budget and Policy Priorities, the percentage of total federal outlays spent for all human resources fell from 28 to 23 percent from 1980 to 1987. The percentage spent on defense rose from 23 to 28 percent for the same period. See Kevin Phillips, *The Politics of Rich and Poor: Wealth and the American Electorate in the Reagan Aftermath* (New York: Random House, 1990), p. 87.

16. Marc Leepson, "The Homeless: Growing National Problem," *Editorial Research Reports* (Washington, D.C.: Congressional Quarterly Inc., 1982), p. 800.

17. A high percentage of the testimonies for this, and the following chapter, includes examples of such "accidents, injuries, and other unforeseen circumstances."

18. See Kozol (note 15), p. 48. Overall, average family income for the poorest 17 percent of the population fell by 6.1 percent in the period from 1979 to 1987. Conversely, wealthy Americans saw family income rise 11.1% in the same period (*New York Times*, March 23, 1989). Citing slightly different figures from the Congressional Budget Office, Kevin Phillips notes that the poorest 10 percent of American families saw their incomes slashed by almost 15 percent over the period 1977-1988, while incomes for families in the tenth income decile grew by almost 17 percent for the same period. Incomes for families in the top one percent expanded by nearly 50 percent (Phillips, note 15, p. 17).

19. This is especially the case in the SRO hotel and cheap lodging-home sectors, where government-sponsored gentrification and urban-renewal schemes have removed much housing suitable for the service-dependent. In Chicago, for example, 300 SRO units were lost to gentrification in 1981-2, and a total of 18,000 units have been demolished or converted since 1973" (Fustero, 1984, p. 59; City of Chicago, 1985, p. 23). In New York, government-sponsored urban-renewal legislation encouraged the demolition of SROs and their replacement by luxury apartments; between 1975 and 1981, over 31,000 units were lost (Kasinitz, 1984). References as cited in Michael J. Dear and Jennifer R. Wolch, *Landscapes of Despair: From Deinstitutionalization to Homelessness* (Princeton: Princeton University Press, 1987), p. 198. Sadly, this trend is apt to continue. Contracts are now expiring for upwards of 250,000 low- and moderate-rent units constructed as parts of privately owned developments that received federal mortgage subsidies. Under the terms of the original agreement, owners can rent and convert these units as they please once contracts reach expiration (20 years in most cases). Slightly less than a million

housing voucher contracts will also be soon expiring—all at a time when budget deficits make refunding such programs unlikely. One congressionally-funded study estimated that, altogether, 523,000 units, or 80 percent of all low-income housing, may disappear over the next 15 years ("Preventing the Disappearance of Low Income Housing: The Report of the National Low Income Housing Preservation Commission to the House Subcommittee on Housing and Community Development and the Senate Subcommittee on Housing and Urban Affairs, United States Congress," (1988). See also Teresa Riordan, "Housekeeping at HUD: Why the homeless problem could get much, much worse," *Common Cause Magazine* 13-2. March/April 1987, pp. 26-31. For a description of how the loss of low-income housing has affected one city (Minneapolis), see Dan Nicolai, "Eviction Notice: How City Hall helps Washington push people into the streets," *The Progressive*, December 1988, p. 22.

20. *Washington Post*, June 3, 1987.
21. See Robertson et al., 1985, p. 20, as cited in Dear and Wolch (note 19), p. 197.
22. Rossi (note 1, chap. 1), pp. 143-44.
23. Not surprisingly, the growing gulf between rich and poor is also a multinational phenomenon (Phillips, note 15, p. 25).
24. U.S. Conference of Mayors, *Status Report on Hunger and Homelessness in America's Cities: 1989*, p. 92.

Chapter 4

1. Statistics on the poverty of children are from "Money Income and Poverty Status in the United States, 1987" (Washington, D.C.: Bureau of the Census, Current Population Reports, *Consumer Income* (Series P-60, no. 161).
2. Conversations with youth counselors and staff members at the Orion Center, Seattle; the Bridge, Minneapolis; Diamond Youth Shelter, San Francisco; and United Action for Youth, Iowa City, Iowa.
3. *Miami Herald*, November 16, 1988. Robertson (1989) reports lower rates of prostitution among homeless and runaway youth ("Homeless Youth: An Overview of Recent Literature," a paper presented at the National Conference on Homeless Children and Youth convened by the Institute for Policy Studies, 1989). I asked Niki, who describes her own life as a teenage prostitute in "Solutions," about the 90 percent figure. She said it was "about right" for Seattle, where she lives.
4. See Paul G. Shane, "Changing Patterns among Homeless and Runaway Youth," *American Journal of Orthopsychiatry* 59.2, April 1989.
5. *Miami Herald* , January 2, 1989.
6. According to the *Miami Herald* (November 16, 1988), a Covenant House and New York Department of Health study concluded that 7 percent of New York City's estimated 20,000 homeless and runaway youth are infected with the AIDS virus. Covenant House, moreover, already provides hospice care for street kids suffering from AIDS.
7. The National Network of Runaway and Youth Services, *To Whom Do They Belong? Runaway, Homeless, and Other Youth in High Risk Situations in the 1990s* (Washington, D.C.: 1991). Robertson (note 3) cites lower figures while noting, "neglect and abuse are often underreported."
8. Figures on neglect reviewed in Robertson (note 3).
9. See Robertson (note 3).

10. In a number of significant studies, Ellen L. Bassuk has shown homeless children to have roughly a 50 percent chance of demonstrating a significant development lag. It is my assumption that street youth—homeless and unaccompanied—would demonstrate yet greater lags. See Bassuk, E.L. and Rubin, L., "Homeless Children: A Neglected Population," *American Journal of Orthopsychiatry*. 57.2, 1987, pp. 279-286; Bassuk, E.L., Rubin, L., and Lauriat, A., "Characteristics of sheltered homeless families." *American Journal of Public Health*. 76.9, 1986, pp. 1097-1101; and Bassuk, E.L. (Ed.) *The Mental Health Needs of Homeless Persons: New Directions for Mental Health Services*. San Francisco: Jossey-Bass, 1986.

11. See Robertson (note 3).

Chapter 5

1. Quotations from Howard Zinn, *A People's History of the United States* (New York: Harper Colophon Books, 1980), p. 80.

2. See Marjorie J. Robertson, "Homeless Veterans: An Emerging Problem?" in *The Homeless in Contemporary Society*, ed. Richard D. Bingham, Roy E. Green, Sammis B. White (Newbury Park, CA: Sage Publications, 1987), p. 68.

3. *New York Times*, April 27, 1989. See also *New York Times*, November 12, 1987; April 27, 1988; May 15, 1988; November 11, 1988; November 20, 1988; *New York Post*, November 12, 1988; *Newsday*, November 25, 1987; and *Times Union* (Albany), May 2, 1988.

4. *Christian Science Monitor*, February 23, 1987. A separate Outreach and Rehabilitation Center for Homeless Veterans was opened in Brooklyn in 1988 (*New York Times*, May 15, 1988).

5. Noting that "the literature on homeless veterans is limited," Robertson (note 2) cites three studies, one of Los Angeles County and two of Boston, which found homeless veterans to comprise 47 percent, 37 percent, and 31 percent, respectively, of the larger population of homeless men. More recently, a study by the National Coalition for the Homeless estimated that 30 percent of all homeless men are veterans (Heroes Today Homeless Tomorrow?: Homelessness among Veterans in the United States. The National Coalition for the Homeless, 1991, [monograph]). "Officials at the VA, meanwhile, say the problem is being blown out of proportion. ... The VA figures that 31 percent of all civilian males are veterans. Assuming that one-third of homeless adult men are veterans—a conservative estimate many experts say—the number of homeless veterans almost mirrors their mix in the general population" (*Christian Science Monitor*, February 23, 1987).

6. Robertson (note 2), p. 72.

7. Harrison J. Goldin, *Soldiers of Misfortune* (New York: Office of the Comptroller, 1982), pp. 3-4.

8. Ibid.

9. The House Veterans Affairs Committee later charged the Veterans Administration with removing more than thirteen thousand beds from VA hospitals while reporting that federal budget cuts had not hurt their services. Rep. G.V. Montgomery, then a member of the ommittee, commented that "the dramatic contrast between what we are learning from the field and what we are told officially" was "amazing" (*Washington Times*, August 30, 1988).

10. "Evidence suggests that more homeless veterans appear entitled to services than receive them. ... Homeless veterans add that VA services are often

inaccessible or inadequate. Interview field notes include stories of many veterans who reported repeated frustrated attempts to make use of various VA services. ... Many veterans who had found access to VA services also found them to be inadequate. Homeless veterans suggested that they choose other health care providers such as free clinics or elected to seek no treatment at all rather than approach the VA because of their perception of inferior care. Many described the staff as slow and unprofessional" (Robertson, note 2, pp. 76-77). Separately, a Louis Harris study (1980) found that veterans with a college degree "are 25 percent more likely to have contact with the V.A. than those who did not finish high school" (Harrison J. Goldin, New York City Comptroller, in a letter to the *New York Times*, April 1983).

11. See Robertson, and Everett A. Chasen, "VA's War on Homelessness," in "Letters," *Newsday*, October 21, 1988. Chasen was regional director of the New York Office of Public Affairs, Veterans Administration.

12. See also Marilyn Rauber, "Homeless Texan, 77, who haunts Capitol Hill," *New York Post*, November 14, 1988.

13. Neither I nor the history professors I have contacted have been able to confirm or deny that any such conversation ever occurred between Roosevelt and Stalin.

Chapter 6

1. See E. Fuller Torrey, *Nowhere to Go: The Tragic Odyssey of the Homeless Mentally Ill* (New York: Harper and Row, 1988), p. 35.

2. See Torrey (note 1); also Michael J. Dear and Jennifer R. Wolch, *Landscapes of Despair: From Deinstitutionalization to Homelessness* (Princeton: Princeton University Press, 1987); and Rael Jean Isaac and Virginia C. Armat, *Madness in the Streets: How Psychiatry and the Law Abandoned the Mentally Ill* (New York: The Free Press, 1990)

3. Documenting the preference of psychiatrists for the suburban "worried well," and their general reluctance to treat the seriously mentally ill, Torrey (note 1) implicates the psychiatric community in this situation.

4. Jonathan Kozol, "Distancing the Homeless," *Yale Review*, Winter 1988, p. 153.

5. Johnson (1990), p. 118.

6. Jonathon O. Cole, George Gardos, and Michael Nelson, "Alternatives to Chronic Hospitalization—The Boston State Hospital Experience," in Leonard I. Stein and Mary Ann Test, eds., *Alternatives to Mental Hospital Treatment* (New York: Plenum, 1978), p. 221. See also Carol A. B. Warren, "New Forms of Social Control: The Myth of Deinstitutionalization," *American Behavioral Scientist* 24 (1981), p. 727.

7. U.S. General Accounting Office, *Returning the Mentally Disabled to the Community: Government Needs to Do More* (Washington, D.C.: U.S. Government Printing Office, 1977), pp. 10-11, as cited in Johnson (note 5), p. 275.

8. See Kozol (note 4), p. 158.

9. Rossi (note 1, chap. 1), p. 121.

10. Rossi (note 1, chap. 1), combining twenty-five studies, finds 26.8 percent of homeless people have had "mental hospital experience." This compares with a less than 5 percent rate for the general population (pp. 146-47). A larger discussion of mental illness rates among homeless people appears below.

11. One study found fewer than 5 percent of homeless people treated in a 19-city health-care demonstration project were deinstitutionalized patients (*U.S. News and World Report* 106, March 20, 1989), p. 28.

12. Data regarding mental illness among homeless people remain contradictory and inconclusive. Nevertheless, there is value in an estimate. To my view, the most persuasive figures are those presented by Torrey (note 1) and the National Conference of Mayors, both of whom estimate that the homeless mentally ill represent 30 percent of the larger population. Assuming that a small percentage of the homeless mentally ill have never received "mental hospital experience," this figure would corroborate Rossi's estimate. For its part, the Department of Health and Human Services has said 33 to 66 percent of all shelter residents are severely mentally ill, while the National Institute of Mental Health has estimated the figure to be as high as 50 percent (*Washington Post*, April 20, 1985). Other studies have found yet greater rates of mental illness among the homeless. One psychiatric study of homeless people staying at an emergency shelter in Boston found that 46 percent suffered "major mental illness," with an additional 21 percent suffering "severe personality or character disorders" (Ellen L. Bassuk et al., "Is Homelessness a Mental Health Problem?" *American Journal of Psychiatry* 141, 12 Dec. 1984, pp. 1546-50). Greater rates of mental illness have also been found among runaway and homeless youth (Paul G. Shane, "Changing Patterns among Homeless and Runaway Youth," *American Journal of Orthopsychiatry* 59.2, April 1989, p. 208). In contrast, a study by the University of Chicago's School of Social Service Administration concluded that homelessness among their subjects stemmed largely from poverty, rather than from preexisting illnesses or disabilities. The study, which surveyed participants of free-meal programs (rather than those staying in shelters), found the homeless largely similar to other very poor people (Rossi, note 1, chap. 1 p. 288). The differences in the conclusions reached by the Chicago study most likely lie in the populations studied. By surveying meal participants, the Chicago study broadened its survey beyond shelter inhabitants who, after all, represent but a small percentage of the larger population of homeless people. Homeless people who are neither mentally ill nor substance abusers tend to avoid inner-city shelters due to poor conditions and the same high concentration of mentally ill and substance-abusing patrons.

13. Johnson (note 6), p. 150.

14. M. Harvey Brenner, *Mental Illness and the Economy* (Cambridge: Harvard University Press, 1973), p. ix.

15. M. Harvey Brenner, "Estimating the Effects of Economic Changes on National Health and Social Well-Being," a study prepared for the use of the subcommittee on Economic Goals and Intergovernmental Policy of the Joint Economic Committee (Washington, D.C.: U.S. Government Printing Office, 1984), as cited in Ruth Sidel, *Women and Children Last: The Plight of Poor Women in Affluent America* (New York: Viking, 1986).

16. Ramsay Liem and Paula Raymen, "Health and Social Costs of Unemployment," *American Psychologist* 37 October 1982, pp. 1116-23. More recent research supports such conclusions. See, for example, J.L. Hagen and A.M. Ivanoff, "Homeless Women: A High-risk Population," *Affilia: Journal of Women and Social Work* Vol.3, number 1. 1988. pp. 19-33.

17. As determined by the CES-D scale developed by the Center for Epidemiologic Studies at the National Institute of Mental Health (Rossi, note 1, chap. 1, pp. 147-149).

18. Brenner, note 14.

19. Conversation with Reggie Goldman, manager of the Alfred Benjamin Counseling Service, Jewish Family and Children Services, overland Park, Kansas.
20. See Alan R. Sutherland, "Health Care for the Homeless," *Issues in Science and Technology* 5 Fall 1988, p. 79.
21. E. Fuller Torrey "Forced Medication is Part of the Cure," *The New Physician* 35. 9, December 1986, pp. 34-37 (reprinted from *Washington Monthly*).
22. Susan Stefan, "The Psychiatric Cure for Homelessness: Wrong Diagnosis, Wrong Treatment," *The New Physician* 35.9, December 1986, pp. 44-45.
23. Stories abound of homeless people who commit atrocious acts to get themselves admitted for psychiatric treatment. Alice K. Johnson and Larry W. Krueger tell the story of a woman who reportedly "drew a razor from her pocket and slashed it across the eyes of a small child" reasoning, "maybe if I hurt someone else I will get the help I need" ("Toward a Better Understanding of Homeless Women," *Social Work* 34.6, November 1989, p. 537).
24. It should be noted that epilepsy is a disorder of the central nervous system, not a mental illness.

Chapter 7

1. This situation is changing. Together with other advocates, Robert M. Hayes, who helped found the National Coalition for the Homeless, now acknowledges that treatment for homeless people who are substance-dependent may be as important as housing (*New York Times*, May 22, 1989).
2. Just as there are no precise data on the percentage of the general population dependent upon drugs and alcohol, there are none on what percentage of homeless people suffer those addictions. Surveys and studies of people who frequent inner-city shelters have found rates as high as 90 percent (*New York Times*, September 10, 1989). But it is characteristic of homeless addicts to frequent such shelters and common for homeless people who are not addicts to avoid them. Broader surveys, such as one of soup kitchen patrons, have found rates of addiction slightly higher than those of very poor people in general (*Economist*, September 10, 1988). Most homeless people, however, remain effectively hidden. They are all but impossible to count or survey.
3. Research on addiction to crack cocaine remains inconclusive. Some research indicates that there may be physiological determinants of cocaine addiction (A.M. Washton, *Cocaine Addiction*, New York: Norton, 1989), and that family histories of addiction are significant (N.S. Miller, et al. "Family history of alcohol dependence in cocaine addicts," *Substance Abuse* 10:3, 1989, pp. 154-61). Significantly, much of the research points to similarities between alcohol and cocaine dependence, and to the role of alcoholism in becoming addicted to crack cocaine (N.S. Miller, et al. "The diagnosis of alcohol, cocaine, and other drug dependence in an inpatient treatment population," *Journal of Substance Abuse Treatment* 6, 1989, pp. 37-40; and N.S. Miller et al. "The diagnosis of alcohol and cannabis dependence in cocaine dependents and alcohol dependence in their families," *British Journal of Addiction* 84, 1989, pp. 1491-98).
4. Society also makes it hard to stop. Treatment for homeless people with dependencies is nearly nonexistent (*New York Times*, May 22, 1989).
5. Interestingly, one of the most significant consequences of poverty to be associated with crack addiction is stress. This seems to be particularly true for

African Americans. See, for example, Sabrina Ford, *Family History and Patterns of Addiction in African American Cocaine and Alcohol Dependent Individuals*, Iowa: The University of Iowa, 1990 (an unpublished doctoral dissertation).

Chapter 8

1. See Wilson (note 6, chap. 3), p. 82.
2. See Charles Murray, *Losing Ground: American Social Policy*, 1950-1980 (New York: Basic Books, 1984).
3. See Francis Fox Piven and Richard A. Cloward, "Sources of the Contemporary Relief Debate," in *The Mean Season: The Attack on the Welfare State*, by Fred Block et al. (New York: Pantheon, 1987). Also Wilson et al., "Joblessness versus Welfare Effects: A Further Reexamination," in Wilson (note 6, chap. 3), pp. 93-106.
4. Phillips (note 15, chap. 3) reports that over the period 1977-1988 the poorest 10 percent of families saw incomes fall by 14.8 percent, and families in the second income decile experienced a loss of 8.0 percent (op cit., p. 17). Together, the figures indicate an 11.4 percent change in average family income (1987 dollars) for families in the lowest two income deciles.
5. "Money Income and Poverty Status in the United States: 1988," *Current Population Reports: Consumer Income*, series P-60, no. 166, and "Poverty in the United States: 1988 and 1989," *Current Population Reports: Consumer Income*, series P-60, no. 171.
6. Citing the research of John D. Kasarda (1989), Kay Young McChesney explains: "as the manufacturing jobs typically held by blacks were (partially) replaced by white-collar information processing jobs typically held by whites, the result was massive unemployment among blacks. While the unemployment rate for white men in the central cities declined, the unemployment rate for black men skyrocketed, for example, from 7.6 percent in 1969 to 30.4 percent in 1985 in the Northeast, and from 8.3 percent in 1969 to 32.8 percent in 1985 in the Midwest. Combining unemployment rates with the rates of men not in school and not in the labor force ... by 1985 central city black men aged 25-64 had a real unemployment rate of 51.2 percent. In the Midwest and Northeast, these figures were as high as 45.6 percent for mature men and 68.0 percent for young black men" (Kay Young McChesney, "Macroeconomic Issues in Poverty: Implications for Child and Youth Homelessness," a paper presented at the National Conference on Homeless Children and Youth, convened by the Institute for Policy Studies, 1989, pp. 15-16). See also "Falling Behind: A Report on How Blacks Have Fared under the Reagan Policies" (Washington, D.C.: Center on Budget and Policy Priorities, 1984). See also Wilson (note 6, chap. 3).
7. See Wilson (note 6, chap. 3), pp. 95-106.
8. *New York Times*, March 15, 1992. But such percentages depend on how "welfare" is defined. See, for example, Barbara Ehrenreich, "Welfare: A White Secret," *Time*, December 16, 1991, p. 84.
9. David Maxwell-Jolly, *California's Welfare Dynamic, May 1989*. Sacramento, CA: Senate Appropriation Committee and Joint Oversight Committee on GAIN, as cited by Casey McKeever, "Old Myths, New Packages: A Response to Governor Wilson's Assault on Aid to Families with Dependent Children." Sacramento, CA: Western Center on Law and Poverty. January, 1991.
10. F.G. Reamer, "The Affordable Housing Crisis and Social Work," *Social Work* 34, 1989, ppl. 5-9.
11. At this time the full extent of the "HUD Scandal," as it has been called, has not yet been determined.

12. It should be noted that housing assistance is quite different from other assistance programs. No one is legally entitled to it, however eligible a person—or family—might be. Funding levels are determined by Congress and the President, not need. ("Housing," in this sense, is distinct from "shelter," which a few cities do guarantee.)

13. R. Greenstein, "Losing Faith in Losing Ground," *New Republic* (March 25) 1985, p. 94.

14. Combining AFDC and food stamps a family of four, for example, would have experienced a decrease in assistance of over 20 percent (adjusting for inflation) in the period from 1972 to 1984. Deducting the cash value of food stamps, families on AFDC saw real benefits fall 30 to 50 percent between 1976 and 1986 (David T. Ellwood, *Poor Support: Poverty in the American Family* [New York: Basic Books, 1988], pp. 40-59).

15. This problem continues to hinder work and assistance programs for single mothers. The Family Support Act of 1988, for example, designed to enable single mothers to finish school and find work, was effectively tied to a separate bill to ensure the child-care these—and other women—would need to attend school and job-training programs. While the Family Support Act passed, the other (to date) has not (*New York Times*, December 12, 1989). See also Anne Meadows, ed., *Caring For America's Children* (Washington, D.C.: National Academy Press, 1991).

16. A survey commissioned by the California State Assembly concludes: "The dire economic plight of homeless families must be viewed in the context of their social isolation" (David Wood et al., *Over the Brink: Homeless Families in Los Angeles*, a publication in the California Children, California Families Series [Sacramento: Joint Publications Office / Assembly Office of Research, 1989], monograph). Elsewhere, Rossi (note 1, chap. 1) notes, "Over all, the strong impression left by the data ... is of persons who have extensive ties to neither relatives nor friends ... Whatever the process, the outcome is that many of the homeless are completely isolated, and most have only very superficial ties to others" (pp. 176-77). Similarly, Wilson (note 6, chap. 3) notes that "the key theoretical concept" in understanding inner-city poverty "is not 'culture of poverty' but 'social isolation'" (p. 61).

17. U.S. Department of Housing and Urban Development, "A Report on the 1988 survey of shelters for the homeless," as cited by Alice K. Johnson and Larry W. Krueger, "Toward a Better Understanding of Homeless Women, *Social Work* 34.6, November 1989, p. 537.

18. If not already apparent, it should be noted that almost all the adults whose stories appear in this book are parents. Most of the men admitted having children, though few remained in contact with them. Some men bemoaned this fact, others did not. Most of the women are also parents. Most, like Sherry ("Dependencies"), and Karla in this chapter, remain with their children. Some, like Hell ("Falling from Grace"), have placed their children with friends or relatives. Others have lost their children through substance-abuse, neglect, or homelessness itself. Women like these include Tonya, Nancy ("The Homeless Mentally Ill"), and Belle, whose story appears in this chapter. Her story is particularly tragic because it was in seeking assistance for her children that she lost them. While guidelines prepared for the National Association of Public Child Welfare Administrators (NAPCWA) warn against just such a series of events, this continues to occur.

19. While the Family Support Act of 1988 improved this situation, AFDC and food stamps remain "income-tested" programs that phase out relatively rapidly as family earnings increase. See "Background Material and Data on Programs within the Jurisdiction of the Committee on Ways and Means: 1989 Edition," *Committee on Ways and Means* (Washington, D.C.: U.S. Government Printing Office, 1989).

20. The Family Support Act of 1988 has also improved this situation. Under new guidelines, incentives for one parent to leave so that the other can receive AFDC should be reduced. These guidelines appear in the Unemployed Parent Program of AFDC (AFDC-UP).

Chapter 9

1. Ironically, a presidential Commission on Income Maintenance Programs reached the same conclusion twenty years ago. See Theresa Funiciello, "The Poverty Industry: Do Government and Charities Create the Poor?" *Ms. The World of Women* 1.3 (November/December) 1990, p. 35.

2. See Charles R. Morris, *A Time of Passion: America 1960-1980* (New York: Penguin Books, 1986 [orig. 1984]), pp. 132-43.

3. "Hope for the Homeless," *U.S. News & World Report* , February 29, 1988, pp. 24-35.

4. I have found such nonprofit programs for homeless women universally better than comparable programs for men. One explanation for this is that women's programs seem to be modeled on programs and shelters for battered women, while programs for men grow out of the mission or workhouse tradition. Another explanation lies in societal expectations for men. See Peter Marin, "Why are the Homeless Mainly Single Men?" *The Nation,* July 8, 1991, pp. 46-51.

5. Conversation with staff members of the Elizabeth Stone House.

6. See Jacqueline Leavitt and Susan Saegert, *Housing Abandonment in Harlem: The Making of Community-Households* (New York: Columbia University Press,1989).

7. See S. VanderStaay, "Justice House," *Christianity and Crisis* 49.2, February 20, 1989, pp. 36-38.

8. Conversation with Stewart Guernsey.

9. Conversation with Clair Yoo of ACE.

A Note on Methodology

1. Alessandro Portelli, *The Death of Luigi Trastulli and Other Stories: Form and Meaning in Oral History* (Albany: State University of New York Press, 1991).

PARTICIPATING ORGANIZATIONS

Action for Community Empowerment (formerly Hotel Tenants Rights Project), 126 West 119th Street, New York, New York 10026

Anawim Housing Inc., 1548 8th Street, Des Moines, IA 50314

Banana Kelly Community Improvement Association, Room 313, 965 Longwood Avenue, Bronx, New York 10459

The Bridge for Runaway Youth, Inc., 2200 Emerson Avenue So., Minneapolis, Minnesota 55405

Catholic Charities of the Archdiocese of San Francisco, San Francisco County, AIDS/ARC Division, 1049 Market Street, San Francisco, CA

Catholic Worker House, 1310 7th St., Des Moines, IA 50314

Committee for Fairness & Dignity

Community for Creative Nonviolence (CCNV), 425 2nd St. NW, Washington, DC 20001

Community in Partnership, St. Louis, MO

Second Home Inc, 30 Pearl Street, Cambridge, MA 02139

The Emergency Housing Project, Inc., 331 N. Gilbert, Iowa City, IA 52245

Hamilton Family Center, 1525 Waller St., San Francisco, CA 94117

The House of Ruth, 651 10th Street NE, Washington, D.C. 20002

The House of Ruth, 6505 N. Cummings St., Los Angeles, CA 90033

Justice House/Justice Church, 720 1st Street, S.W., Roanoke, VA 24016

The National Coalition for the Homeless, 1621 Connecticut Avenue, NW, Washington, D.C. 20009, (202) 265-2371

Partnership Assistance to the Homeless, 607 21st Street North, Birmingham, AL 35203

Saint Anthony Foundation, 121 Golden Gate Avenue, San Francisco CA 94102-3899

SHARE—CCS, The Aloha Inn, 1911 Aurora Ave. N., Seattle, WA 98109

South Kitsap Community Helpline, 1770 Village Lane SE, Port Orchard, WA 98366

St. John's Hospice for Men, 1221 Race Street, Philadelphia, PA 19107

United Action for Youth, P.O. Box 892, Iowa City, IA 52244

University City Hospitality Coalition, 3601 Locust Walk, Philadelphia, PA 19104

Women of Hope, 1210 Lombard St., Philadelphia, PA 19107

YOUTHCARE, 333 1st Ave. W., Seattle, WA 98199

PUBLISHER'S NOTE

The first time I read *Street Lives*, as a huge sheaf of paper held together only by a rubber band, I knew it was an exciting, powerful book.

I knew that almost every other book on homeless people approached them as merely a socio-economic phenomenon, more interested in statistics and categories than individual human beings. I also knew that this was a rare opportunity for homeless people to address their own situation to a wide audience. And I knew that many people wanted and needed to hear these stories, but were unable or unwilling to go out and hear them first hand.

I knew all this from the beginning, but I didn't know the people. The stories were familiar, the descriptions common, but the people were strangers to me. But as I reread the book one last time, I realized that I have come to know some of the people in this book, and many others who aren't in it, but just as easily could have been. They are my neighbors and friends. And as I collect discarded produce with Cyrell, eat vegan waffles with Tim Dunn, swap stories of high school with Sweat, and watch Vicki's stomach swell with pregnancy, I can't help but appreciate the change that this book sparked in my life. It was *Street Lives* that finally broke down the walls, and thrust me into this community within the community.

As a relative newcomer to this community, I often find myself wondering why so many people are doing so little about this desperate crisis. Why are people so unangered and seemingly complacent about this situation? Why are they so unwilling to make an effort? After gentle nudging from a new friend, I am reminded to look within myself for the answers. And the obstacles I find—ignorance, fear and greed—are hard realities to accept.

But obviously there is great deal of ignorance about homelessness, This is clearly illustrated by two popular images of homeless people. One which is stigmatized: dirty, crazy, stupid, drunk, pathetic, and lazy. And another which is romanticized: rebels, loners, eccentrics, wanderers, and street philosophers.

These distorted and conflicting images absolutely saturate our culture. From the old folk song "Hallelujah, I'm A Bum" which celebrates homelessness as something to aspire to, to the contemporary TV show "In Living Color" whose regular character Anton Jackson vilifies homeless men as lewd, dangerous, foul-mouthed drunks who carry their excrement around in a glass jar, it is little wonder that many people feel ambivalent, even hostile, toward homeless people.

Of the obstacles, however, ignorance is easiest to overcome. All that is needed is an open mind and accurate information, and the ignorance gives way to insight. But where to get this information? The traditional sources certainly can't be trusted. After all, that's where these distorted images came from in the first place. Even the most progressive sources are clouded by their own biases and assumptions. Clearly, the only reliable source for accurate information is homeless people themselves.

This brings up the second obstacle, fear. For various reasons, homeless people can and often do strike a very real fear in the hearts of people with homes and other resources. This is particularly clear in urban centers, where many of the people most energized and angered by the situation are working not against homelessness, but against "the homeless." They hotly advocate closing shelters, closing parks, slashing welfare, arresting homeless people, and other myopic strategies for making the problem disappear. And while this is an extreme example of the fear many people feel, in composition it is the same fear that keeps them from getting to know and allying themselves with homeless people.

Like most obstacles, however, this one can also be overcome from several angles. This book is one of them. Here are homeless people sharing their stories, their hardships, their dreams and their strategies. Here are the people one might meet on a park bench, on the bus, or in a night shelter. Yet there is no fear in reading these stories. One can approach without hesitation, listen without distraction. And as the stories unfold and are at last heard, the distorted, confused images give way to a clearer understanding of the individuality of each homeless person, and their shared humanity.

If *Street Lives* can break down the stereotypes, undercut the fear and allow the voices of homeless people to be heard, it will have done a tremendous job. But that, in itself, is not going to alleviate homelessness. That work remains for us to do. If we extend ourselves, if we share our resources, if we work together, if we build connections, we can build healthy communities that embrace and support all of their members.

Which brings us to the final obstacle—selfishness. Or, in Cyrell's more stark words, greed. It took me a while to accept this final obstacle. I certainly didn't want to find it in myself. But after thinking about it for a while, I have come to agree with Cyrell's final analysis that it is the largest obstacle to ending homelessness. The connection was not obvious at first because I was thinking of greed in the purely monetary sense of the word. It is clear that monetary greed creates poverty, but many societies live in poverty without having a large homeless population, so it's almost possible to dismiss greed as a factor.

But consider non-monetary greed, the reluctance to share our time, our energy, our creativity, our*selves* with the people around us—our community. The tendency to "not get involved" is often lamented as a growing societal problem, but rarely is it acknowledged as greed. Time and energy, however, are just as much a part of wealth as money, and if our communities suffer because that wealth is being spent elsewhere, then they suffer from greed.

If we accept the resounding conclusion arrived at throughout this book—that community is the key to ending homelessness—we must arrange our lives so that we can participate fully in our communities. This does not mean quitting our jobs, dropping our other issues, giving up our pleasures or even adding another brick to our already over-loaded burden. We can continue to work and struggle and relax and play, while finding ways to incorporate more of these activities, more of our lives, into our community. We must learn to open ourselves to the people around us and to share our wealth in whatever way we can, if we are going end the alienation, isolation and destitution that create homelessness.

There are many ways to do this. Here in West Philadelphia, the most recent attempt is a local Food Not Bombs group, which collects surplus produce and prepares and serves weekly meals on the street. I will leave the details of this project for another Publisher's Note (see our recently published *Food Not Bombs: How to Feed the Hungry and Build Community*), but I can't help but comment on the almost palpable sense of community which has sprung up from this simple but sustained action. Recently, a homeless man and Food Not Bombs regular summed it up beautifully for a newcomer by saying. "The food's good, but I come for the people. It's not a handout here, it's like family."

I hope that this book will inspire people to take the next step, to extend themselves, and to create a similar sense of family within their own neighborhood. This is absolutely essential, because to end homelessness, we must not only get people out of the street and into good homes, but out of good homes and into the street.

See you there!

todd peterson
for New Society Publishers